At Work in Penn's Woods

A KEYSTONE BOOK

A Keystone Book is so designated to distinguish it from the
typical scholarly monograph that a university press publishes.
It is a book intended to serve the citizens of Pennsylvania
by educating them and others, in an entertaining way, about
aspects of the history, culture, society, and environment of
the state as part of the Middle Atlantic region.

At Work in
PENN'S WOODS

The Civilian Conservation Corps in Pennsylvania

JOSEPH M. SPEAKMAN

The Pennsylvania State University Press
University Park, Pennsylvania

Library of Congress Cataloging-in-Publication Data

Speakman, Joseph M., 1940-
At work in Penn's Woods : the Civilian Conservation Corps in Pennsylvania /
Joseph M. Speakman.
p.   cm.
"A Keystone Book."
Includes bibliographical references and index.
ISBN 0-271-02876-9 (cloth : alk. paper)
1. Civilian Conservation Corps (U.S.)—Pennsylvania—History.
2. Conservation of natural resources—Pennsylvania—History.
3. Forest conservation—Pennsylvania—History.
I. Title.

S932.P4S64 20067
333.75'1609748—dc22
2005035700

In memory of my father,

*who served at Camp s-119, Wolf Rock, near Philipsburg,
as a CCC enrollee in Company #373 from
June 1933 to March 1934.*

Contents

Preface

My interest in the Civilian Conservation Corps was originally stimulated by stories told by my father, Joseph A. Speakman, who was one of the early enrollees in a Pennsylvania camp at Wolf Rock in Moshannon State Forest near Philipsburg in 1933 and 1934. At the time of his enlistment, he was an unemployed young man of twenty-five with an elementary school education and no specialized skills. He was still living at home in Philadelphia with his parents. At twenty-five (falsified to twenty-four on his application), he was among the older recruits, but in most ways he seems to have been a fairly typical member of "Roosevelt's Tree Army," as the CCC was often called. Even lying about his age was not so untypical, although most of the recruits who did so were teenagers adding a year or two to their real ages.

The earliest enrollees came in at different times between April and July 1933. My father signed up at an army recruiting station on North Broad Street in Philadelphia on June 20 and was taken to the army base at Fort George Meade in Maryland for five days of conditioning to camp life before being sent out to the CCC camp at Wolf Rock. After three months there, he re-enlisted for what was termed the "second enrollment period" in October and completed a full six-month tour before receiving his honorable discharge in March 1934. (As a relative of a CCC enrollee, I was able to obtain copies of my father's service record from the Civilian Personnel Records Center Facility at 111 Winnebago Street, St. Louis, MO 63118.)

My older cousins have told me that when my father returned home, he had been physically transformed into some kind of bodybuilder. He later boasted to me that he had put on twenty pounds of muscle, engaging in competitive bouts of wood chopping after work hours with other would-be Charles Atlases. Marring a good story, his discharge papers credit him with gaining only nine pounds, which was about the average weight gain for urban men who served in the Corps. Like most CCC alumni, he always spoke of his experience as a wonderful time in his life and held Franklin Roosevelt in reverence as the most decent president in American history. My father died in 1997 before I embarked on this project, and I am left with the universal lament of surviving children, "Why didn't I ask him about that?"

This book will focus on the CCC in Pennsylvania, at the time the second largest state in population and, as it turned out, the state with the second highest number of young men recruited to work in CCC camps and the state with the second highest number of such camps. My hope is that an examination of one of the largest and most successful state CCC programs will draw attention to the considerable achievements of FDR's pet project while also pointing out its limitations. There are periodic calls for re-enacting programs like the CCC. Looking back to the original model may show how some things were done right—but also may raise caution flags about what not to do. My criticism is meant to be friendly, even loving, and is intended, as all historical study must, more to sharpen thinking for the present and future than to offer either praise or indictment of the past.

The information for this book has been gleaned from primary sources in archives, supplemented by many published accounts. Peter Finley Dunne, "Mr. Dooley," the political humorist from Chicago around the turn of the twentieth century, once commented on the work of historians: "Th' further ye get away fr'm anny perryod th' betther ye can write about it. You are not subject to interruptions be people that were there." Although my father is no longer around to interrupt, correct, or improve this particular historical study, there are, fortunately, tens of thousands of former CCC men still alive at this writing, many of them active in the National Association of Civilian Conservation Corps Alumni (NACCCA) and other similar local groups. I have had the pleasure of meeting many of these men at various reunions they have held in Pennsylvania and have interviewed some of them for this book. I have used alumni recollections to illustrate various generalizations about the CCC or, in some cases, exceptions to the rules. I can only hope that this account does not disappoint them or strike them as false to their experiences.

Needless to say, I have tried to be as accurate as possible, accuracy being more of an obligation than a virtue for a historian. But the subject is an immense story involving hundreds of thousands of people and the sifting of endless compilations of statistics that CCC officials collected and recorded. I have tried not to burden this account with too many numbers but some are unavoidable. Appreciating the relative importance of the Pennsylvania program, for example, requires some statistical comparisons with other states. The problem with handling so many numbers is that mistakes can easily occur. Discrepancies frequently appear in the statistics collected and reported by busy CCC bureaucrats, who were certainly much too busy to concern themselves with easing the work of later generations of historians. Clerical mistakes occasionally dot the records of the time and others show up in publications or online accounts about the CCC. I fear that I may have made my own mistakes in handling some of the data and can only trust that, if any mistakes are present in this book, they are not crucial to the large and important story I have tried to tell.

A word on terminology is appropriate here. The young men in CCC camps were often referred to as "boys." Clearly this is inappropriate language for men in their mid-twenties. But an increasing number of CCC workers were seventeen or eighteen, or even younger, and were, indeed, "boys." I have used both "men" and "boys," employing whichever term seemed more appropriate in the context but admittedly with no clear or distinct rationale. I have also used the official CCC terms "enrollees" and "Juniors" and, for variety, the word "recruit" shows up as well, even though that term was distinctly frowned upon by CCC administrators as too military in connotation.

Another sensitive issue of terminology involves African-Americans. They led segregated existences in the CCC and were officially referred to as "Colored." I have used that designation when it seemed suitable to the context but have more frequently used the terms more appropriate to today's sensibilities— black or African-American.

I hope this study of the CCC in Pennsylvania will help illuminate the administrative history of a New Deal program as it was implemented in a particular state and enrich our understanding of both American history as well as Pennsylvania history. I also hope it will contribute to an understanding of some of the political contrasts between then and now, the fundamental purpose of any history being to show the course of change over time. I hope it is true to the experiences of the men from Pennsylvania who served in the CCC and that it may help them and their families place their individual stories in a larger context. One of those men, Tom Frantz, who served both as an enrollee and later as a forestry foreman at Promised Land State Park, spoke at the CCC reunion held there on August 16, 2003. As he looked around the beautiful grounds, he spoke movingly about how the men in the audience and the trees they planted there have aged together. Tom and all the other CCC men did important work for the nation in their youth, and it deserves to be remembered and understood.

Acknowledgments

Although the writing of history is an individual activity, the research that makes it credible would not be possible without extensive social support services. The writing of history is also a private process, but the research requires frequent forays out of the study to meet and talk with people who are better informed than the writer on various subjects. Much of the satisfaction in researching this particular study has come from the kindness of both strangers and friends, and I would like to thank some of them here.

The time allowed me for travel and research was made possible by a sabbatical leave granted by the board of trustees of Montgomery County Community College. My colleagues in the Social Science Division of the college were always interested in what I was working on and helpful with encouragement and advice.

Most of the archival research underlying this study was done at the pleasant facilities of the National Archives in College Park, Maryland. The staff there is ever cheerful and efficient, and Gene Morris is well known to researchers as the "go-to guy" who can provide the surest paths through the labyrinth of the voluminous CCC files. While the CCC materials at the Pennsylvania State Archives in Harrisburg are not as rich, the archivists there are no less helpful and pleasant to work with. Another part of the required pleasure in researching New Deal history comes from excursions to the Franklin D. Roosevelt Library at Hyde Park, New York, whose courteous staff helped me find my way through their vast holdings.

Historians have a love affair with librarians, perhaps unrequited because of the one-sided benefits to the relationship. My first valentines must be sent to the librarians at my college's Brendlinger Library. They were all interested and helpful on this project, but I particularly would like to single out Janet Perry and Barbara Howard, who speedily obtained every single one of my numberless interlibrary loan requests. Staffs previously unknown to me at the Pennsylvania State Library in Harrisburg, the Canaday Library at Bryn Mawr College, and the Free Library of Philadelphia all provided me invaluable assistance. Nancy Flanagan at the National Park Service's Harper's Ferry Library guided me through some important source material there. Lawren Dunn and Carney Riggs of the Fort Necessity National Battlefield Site opened their ccc collections of photographs and documents to me. Rebecca Keenan and Anna Mae Moore at Washington and Jefferson College in Washington, Pennsylvania, provided guidance and assistance in researching the Papers of Senator Joseph Guffey in their archives.

Aside from archives and libraries, there is some important source material for the history of the ccc in Pennsylvania at some of the state park and state forestry offices. Jen Naugle helped me with materials at Promised Land State Park, and Carol Jones allowed me access to both the records at Pine Grove Furnace State Park as well as her own private collection. Gary Zimmerman at Michaux State Forest informed me of the materials on Camp s-107 and provided an introduction to Henry Sykes, who showed me around the largely intact s-70 Camp. Beth Garner of Cowan's Gap State Park took time to organize the park's extensive collection of ccc materials for me and also gave me a tour of the ccc projects still extant there. Bruce McFate of Caledonia State Park also provided me with useful documents and information. Paul Fagle at Greenwood Furnace State Park took time to share with me his extensive knowledge of Huntingdon County ccc sites. Paul also shared with me the park's extensive collection of photographs and some documentary material, including two audiotapes of men associated with Camp s-62. Kurt Muston interrupted a busy morning to provide me helpful orientation around the ccc sites in Black Moshannon State Park. Patrick Adams at Raccoon Creek State Park stayed late one afternoon to give me information about the two camps that worked in that park and also sent me copies of some useful materials relating to those camps. Sue Bittner at Laurel Hill State Park provided me invaluable information on the extensive remains of the two ccc camps at her park. Mary Hirst of Ole Bull State Park allowed me access to the documents dealing with Camp s-87, and Tom Chalmers drove me around some of the ccc sites there. Dale Luthringer, Deborah Steele, and Robin Hecei made available the ccc records of Cook Forest and Clear Creek. Jane Swift took time out of her preparations for an environmental class at World's End to allow me to examine the ccc materials in her office. Mary Lemerise at Colonel Denning State Park briefed me on the ccc work done there. Carly Hitzfeld gave me a grand tour of ccc work at French

Creek, and Frank Hebblethwaite aided me with his expertise on the adjacent Hopewell Furnace site.

The number of people with an interest in the CCC in Pennsylvania and with expertise on the subject has been a wonder and a joy to me, and I have benefited immeasurably from conversations and communications with Betty Frazier, Mary Sneshkoff, and Mr. and Mrs. Dale Dutcher about camps in the Wellsboro area, and with Michael Schultz about the Allegheny National Forest camps. Tony Shively took time one rainy Saturday morning to show me around the remains of the camps of Union County about which he has written a model study and shared with me some of his expertise on that area. I wish to extend special thanks to Lou Adams for his work in maintaining the CCC Interpretative Center at Parker Dam State Park and organizing the reunions held there each year and to Dolores Buchsen and Tricia Berberich for their assistance at the Pennsylvania Lumber Museum.

I would also like to thank the CCC alums who took the time to fill out my tedious questionnaires or informed me in conversations about what "it was really like."

When I thought all my work was done, Peter Potter and the staff at Penn State Press skillfully guided me through the process of making a book out of an author's raw materials, and I am deeply appreciative of their astute suggestions.

My sister, Dorothy Kadel, has supplemented my own memories of my father's CCC experiences in important ways, and at one point or other Colette and Pete, Natasha and Leo, and April and Joe helped me overcome the various crises that would arise in my use of the computer. A final thanks to Karen—for everything else.

Introduction

The Civilian Conservation Corps was one of the earliest and one of the most popular programs of President Franklin D. Roosevelt's New Deal. It was created in March 1933 as part of the "Hundred Days" package of programs intended to combat the myriad causes and effects of the Great Depression. Before it was shut down in the summer of 1942, the Corps recruited more than two and one-half million unemployed young men and placed them in army-run residential camps in mostly rural locations to work on natural resources conservation. We might think of it as an early "green" project. A Gallup poll in 1936 found 82 percent of the American people supporting the program, and another poll in 1939 found 11 percent picking it out of the extensive alphabet soup of programs in existence by then as "the greatest accomplishment" of the entire New Deal.[1]

The numerous agencies of the New Deal have often been sorted into the categories of relief, recovery, or reform, but the CCC was one of several programs that actually embraced all three categories. Intended primarily as a work relief project for needy youth, it was also designed to promote economic recovery by sending most of the men's pay back home to their families, thus increasing the purchasing power of consumers. But, in the minds of Roosevelt and many of the CCC administrators, the program was also going to reform the moral health of the nation's youth while it promoted more rational conservation policies. As Sherwood Anderson put it after visiting a CCC camp: "They are making a new kind of American man out of the city boy in the woods, and they are planning at least to begin to make a new land with the help of such boys."[2]

The CCC had a complicated administrative structure—a direct result of the enormous logistical challenges associated with mobilizing large numbers of men from around the country and transporting them to designated work sites. The Departments of Labor, Agriculture, and Interior worked closely with the War Department in recruiting and supervising the men. The army, with its nine domestic Corps, provided the organizational framework for bringing the CCC to the states.

Pennsylvania, part of the army's Third Corps area, proved to be one of the most successful state programs, uniquely characterized by an abundance of unemployed young men and plenty of conservation work to occupy them. The CCC was meant to alleviate the dual stresses of unemployment—the economic and the psychic—and Pennsylvanians were suffering these stresses to an appalling degree. But the Corps was also designed to relieve some of the stress on the land; here, too, Pennsylvania was in sore need.

The Depression that began in 1929 hit Pennsylvania particularly hard, creating a large number of potential recruits for CCC camps. In this regard Pennsylvania resembled other eastern states. It was also typical of eastern states in that many of its young recruits, particularly in the later years of the program, were sent out to western states where there was always more conservation work to be done than locally available men could handle. But Pennsylvania was also a bit like those western states in that it was able to employ the vast majority of its own men in its own work camps and was also able to absorb hundreds of men from other states, particularly in the early years.

The Keystone State was able to provide such abundant conservation work opportunities in part because irresponsible logging in earlier generations had produced environmental damage that needed restorative attention. But also, thanks mainly to Governor Gifford Pinchot, the state's Department of Forests and Waters was able to provide an experienced cadre of trained foresters to supervise most of the conservation work done by the CCC in the state. Moreover, Pinchot's administration had created a new State Emergency Relief Board (SERB), which in 1933 had the trained personnel to identify and recruit needy young men for the camps. The CCC utilized the labor of these young men in a variety of conservation activities in Pennsylvania, including planting trees, controlling erosion, building state park facilities, and restoring historic sites. The beauty and environmental health of large areas of the state still display the beneficial effects of that short-lived program.

But while the CCC provided immeasurable benefits for the unemployed men and the ravaged landscape they worked on, its operation in Pennsylvania also revealed the serious limitations of the entire program. Created as an emergency measure and rushed through Congress in little more than a week, many of its features were not well thought out. Although there is no doubt of the initial general enthusiasm that greeted the CCC, as time went on serious criticisms of the original plan surfaced. In particular, the speedy launching of the program in 1933 required a central role for the army in establishing and supervising the work camps. But the army's role brought with it a pronounced military flavor that soon created problems of image as well as administrative conflicts with civilian administrators and ended up weakening the popularity and effectiveness of the program. Placing the educational activities of the camps, an add-on feature to the original scheme, under the authority of military officers turned out to be a particularly bad misstep.

A more general failing of the CCC was that it was only a partial solution to the problems of unemployment and conservation. It could not take all the young men who wanted to enroll, and a high percentage of those whom it did enroll it could not keep for the full enlistment period of six months. It undoubtedly provided colorful and even important benefits to many young men and their families, and its contributions to conservation were enormous. But its effectiveness would have been even greater if it had adopted a more varied approach to employing young people on conservation projects than the exclusive quasi-military model it followed.

Looked at from a contemporary perspective, the omission of women and the segregation of African-Americans stand out as the most glaring deficiencies of the CCC. Although these discriminations must be seen in the context of the more primitive social mores of the 1930s, they nonetheless weakened the CCC both as a relief measure and as a conservation program. In denying opportunities for women and limiting them for blacks, the CCC passed over many deserving young people and denied the land the benefits of their skills.

Because Pennsylvania had such a large and successful CCC program, it offers an ideal microcosm in which to study the successes and limitations of the CCC idea. It will be useful to begin by establishing the environmental, economic, and political context in which the state's CCC camps were established.

A WOODED LAND

Pennsylvania—"Penn's Woods"—was given its name by King Charles II of England when he chartered the colony to William Penn in 1681. Penn himself, in modest Quaker fashion, would have preferred "New Wales" or "Sylvania," but the king insisted and most inhabitants of the state ever since have thought it a felicitous decision.[3] It certainly was a descriptive name, because at the beginning of European colonization probably all but 2 or 3 percent of the state's 28 million acres were covered with thick forests. Today, about 58 percent of the state is wooded, but in the intervening years wholesale destruction of much of the state's timber resources occurred, especially due to the irresponsible large-scale logging of the late nineteenth century.[4]

The geography and climate of Pennsylvania produced and, for a while, protected its vast forests. The weather is temperate, with abundant rain and snow, and many of the tree-producing regions are in the relatively isolated middle and western portions of the state where two great mountain ranges run diagonally across the state from southwest to northeast—the Blue Mountain Range of ridge and valley in the center and the Appalachian Plateau in the west and north. These have been the areas of white pine and hemlock (the state tree). There is also a narrow range of beech, birch, and red maple along the sparsely settled northern border. Chestnut trees once comprised about 20 percent of all the state's trees, some measuring seventeen feet in circumference and providing highly desirable lumber and bark as well as nourishing nuts. But around 1906 a fungus from China hit the state and the resultant "chestnut blight" destroyed virtually all those prized trees by 1940. It still attacks any chestnut sprouts hardy enough to surface.[5]

Another major feature of Pennsylvania's geography important to its forestry history is its river drainage system. The state has three major rivers with their various tributaries: (1) the Delaware River, fed by the Lehigh and Schuylkill, in the eastern third of the state; (2) the Susquehanna, including the Juniata, in the central portions; (3) the Ohio, created in Pittsburgh by the Allegheny and Monongahela, which drains the western third of the state. These river systems are strongly affected by the forests of the state whose roots and leaf canopies absorb and moderate much of the rain fall, thereby limiting soil erosion and floods. In addition, these rivers historically were linked to the forests as highways of commerce for the logging industry of the nineteenth century: workers floated logs or rafts of logs tied together downstream to the sawmills. The West Branch of the Susquehanna River, carrying logs to Lock Haven and Williamsport, was the most important of these watery boulevards.[6]

The arrival of large-scale commercial lumbering around 1850 began to mar the look of the state and its ecology like nothing before or since. At that time, the small-enterprise timber industry, widely scattered and serving local markets, was replaced by enterprises operating on a hugely vaster scale and serving distant markets with virtually unlimited demand. This new phase of the industry had begun in Maine and then moved on to New York and Pennsylvania before heading to Michigan and other parts west later in the century. By the time the industry centered on Pennsylvania, its new character had evolved in particularly destructive ways. Lumber companies would purchase thousands of acres, set up logging camps and proceed to clear-cut the forests, usually in winter to facilitate the movement of logs across icy and frozen ground to streams soon to swell with springtime melting. After the logging companies had denuded the land of its trees, they abandoned it to tax delinquency sales, thereby leaving vast acres of unsightly stumps, unprotected soil, and volatile brush materials. Heavy rain would not be as easily absorbed by the root systems of trees or interrupted by their vegetation, and the erosion of topsoils would follow, scarring the land and contaminating downstream drinking water. Sudden torrents of runoff waters would also create flooding in downstream communities.[7]

As a consequence of this destructive logging, the state's heretofore isolated and untouched white pines, some rising 150 feet high and containing enough lumber to build a good-sized house, were almost completely eliminated. The state's hemlocks were similarly devastated. Not only was hemlock lumber prized, but the bark was also in great demand by the tanning industry. Loggers would strip the bark, leaving the logs to dry out for months so that they would float better. But what often happened was that these logs would simply provide more fuel for uncontrolled forest fires that would sweep the ravaged areas, fires burning so hot that the soil itself would be damaged. Forests may eventually recover from this kind of damage, but without careful management, it can take up to 120 years for them to return to productive use. The first growths to spring up often are dominated by undesirable vegetation that hampers the return of the more valuable species. In Pennsylvania today there are only a few hundred acres of old growth forest, chiefly in the Alan Seeger Natural Area in Huntingdon County.[8]

Near the beginning of this tragic story, Williamsport, Pennsylvania, on the West Branch of the Susquehanna River in the center of the state, became the lumber capital of the world for a short time. Logs were cut and marked upstream and floated down the Sinnemahoning, the Loyalsock, the Clearfield, and other tributaries to be captured by "booms" down river. The boom at Williamsport served the several dozen large sawmills established there by midcentury. It was an enormous holding pen, eventually six miles around with a capacity of about one million logs. The spread of railroads later made it possible to transport logs without having to float them down rivers. The boom at Williamsport eventually became obsolete, and it was dismantled in 1909.

Fig. 1 The lumber boom of the late nineteenth century led to the reckless clearing of Pennsylvania's forests. Here, migrant loggers pose atop felled trees near the railroad track that runs to their improvised lumber camp in Clinton County. Pennsylvania State Archives

The demand for lumber continued to increase throughout the late nineteenth century, driving the reckless clearing of Pennsylvania's forests. Although Michigan's production surpassed that of Pennsylvania by 1870, the Keystone State continued to produce increasing amounts of board feet, not peaking until 1899. The end of Pennsylvania's short-lived preeminence in the lumber industry was, in part, due to the simple fact that much of its readily accessible forest resources had been used up. It is estimated that by the turn of the twentieth century, only about nine million acres, or one-third of the state's acreage, was still forested.

Of what was left, fires consumed about 400,000 acres a year, and timber was actually being imported into "Penn's Woods." People used language like "desert" or "the Allegheny Briar Patch" in referring to the millions of acres of once prime timber lands then standing in ugly and ecologically dangerous conditions.[9]

Fortunately, some farsighted conservationists began to raise alarms and promote solutions. Among the earliest was Joseph Trimble Rothrock, "the Father of Pennsylvania Forestry." Rothrock was born in McVeytown in Mifflin County in 1839 and educated at Freeland Seminary (which later grew into Ursinus College) and the University of Pennsylvania, where he received a medical degree in 1867. He was instrumental in establishing the Pennsylvania Forestry Association in 1886, the first such state organization in the country, and became its first president. When the Pennsylvania Commission of Forestry in the Department of Agriculture was created in 1895, Rothrock became, logically, the first commissioner.

Although not formally trained as a forester, Rothrock was committed to promoting the new ideas of conservation. Over the next ten years he expanded the activities of his commission, especially in the area of fire protection. By the time he retired from his post in 1906 he had created a separate Department of Forestry in the governor's cabinet, he had helped establish Pennsylvania's first professional School of Forestry at Mont Alto, and he had professionally trained foresters in his employ. Rothrock was also successful in creating state-owned forest reserves, the first such lands being acquired through tax delinquency sales from logging companies.[10]

A NEW BREED OF CONSERVATIONIST

After Rothrock, Pennsylvania was served by several capable and increasingly well-trained heads of the Department of Forestry. Of special note was Gifford Pinchot, who served under Governor William Sproul from 1920 to 1922. After Theodore Roosevelt, there was no more important individual in popularizing conservation ideals than Pinchot, and after Franklin Roosevelt, there was no more important individual in the establishment of the CCC in Pennsylvania.

Light years of social class, money, and education would seem to separate a privileged young man living in a Gilded Age mansion in upstate Pennsylvania from the down-and-out young men in the towns and farms of the same state in the Depression spring of 1933. But the 19,000 men from Pennsylvania who enrolled in the state's first CCC camps that season, and the 165,000 who followed them over the next nine years, can be said to have been started on their adventures when James W. Pinchot recommended that his oldest son, about to head off to college, pursue a career in forestry.[11]

The baronial estate was Grey Towers, built in the 1880s and still standing, overlooking the upper Delaware River just outside the Pocono Mountain town of Milford. It was James W. Pinchot of the family's second generation who built Grey Towers as a summer house. In 1885 his oldest son, Gifford, who had been born in Simsbury, Connecticut, on August 11, 1865, was preparing to enter Yale, soon to become a family tradition. Gifford's mother, Mary, née Eno, could trace her origins back to the founders of Connecticut and was from an even wealthier family than the Pinchots. Prospects were bright and assured for this young scion, but Gifford was still unsure of a specific career goal.[12]

In a conversation pregnant with future significance for American politics and conservation, Father (always "Father" in Gifford's charming and feisty autobiography, published posthumously in 1947) suggested forestry as a field in which the young man might find a career of useful service. Pinchot later recalled that at the time of this conversation, not only were there no forestry schools in the United States, but the country was also in the midst of "the most appalling wave of forest destruction in human history." Although there had been some attempts at national and state levels to *preserve* woodlands, notably in Yellowstone National Park after 1872, *conservation* in the emerging sense of the rational management and utilization of finite resources was still largely viewed as unnecessary and, indeed, "ridiculous."[13]

After enrolling at Yale, Pinchot took as many science and botany courses as he could manage. But if he intended to pursue forestry as a career, he would have to continue his studies abroad. In contrast to America, where woodlands had always seemed limitless, in Europe the need to manage the finite resources of forests had long been recognized. Individuals were no longer allowed to cut and clear at will, leaving the topographical and environmental mess for someone else to clean up. Control of fires, erosion, and flooding were all dependent on the practice of scientific forestry, and there were several well-established schools of forestry in Europe.

Pinchot solicited advice from several quarters and decided to attend the French forestry school in Nancy. He attended classes for thirteen months, not completing the program but judging himself ready to manage forests and anxious to establish primacy in his chosen field. Upon his return to the United

States, he essentially invented a career for himself and became the first American-born forester.[14]

From the start of his career, Pinchot understood forestry as something altogether different from how it was commonly understood in his day. Several forestry organizations already existed in the United States, including the American Forestry Association in which James Pinchot had been active, but they were primarily devoted to the preservation of wilderness areas. In Pinchot's mind, however, forestry was not primarily about preserving scenic beauty; it was about the systematic management of woodlands with a view to maximizing their "sustained yield." It involved, for example, the periodic cutting down of mature trees, rather than letting them rot in untouched splendor. "Forestry is tree farming," he wrote. "Forestry is handling trees so that one crop follows another. To grow trees as a crop is forestry." Later on, when the U.S. Forestry Service produced a handbook on woodsmanship for the CCC, it instructed the young men in the same Pinchot-like philosophy: "Conservation means the preservation of natural resources for economic uses. . . . Forestry is the use of the land to grow a continuous crop of trees. Forestry does not mean the preservation of trees as in a park. . . . Forestry is as much a commercial undertaking as is the growth of farm crops."[15]

Turning down an offer from the U.S. Division of Forestry, Pinchot took the advice of Dr. Dietrich Brandis, a German forester who had become his mentor in Europe, and chose to gain experience in private forestry work before embarking on a career of public service. He did a little consulting work for timber companies and then was hired by George Vanderbilt to manage the forests at his Biltmore Estate in North Carolina. This work earned Pinchot a reputation in his young field, and when Bernhard E. Fernow (another German-born forester) retired as head of the Division of Forestry in 1898, Secretary of Agriculture James Wilson appointed Pinchot as his successor. The position now required a civil service test, which Pinchot was obliged to make up himself! Before he had the opportunity to take it, however, President William McKinley stepped in and waived the requirement.[16]

The next eleven years were busy ones for Pinchot. He oversaw the expansion of the division into a bureau and then into the United States Forestry Service. Meanwhile, he also helped establish the Society of American Foresters in 1900 and set up summer camps in forests to provide work for college students, an interesting foreshadowing of the CCC. He and his family helped establish the Yale School of Forestry in 1900, with summer classes available on their Milford estate. Pinchot continued in his government post under Theodore Roosevelt, and by the end of Roosevelt's second term in 1909, Pinchot had become the acknowledged leader of the young and growing cadre of American foresters and an articulate ally of the president on conservation matters. One of his successors as forester, William B. Greeley, later remembered the aura Pinchot projected in the field: "Pinchot was very much a man's man. He could outride and outshoot any ranger on the force. If camp was within a mile of a stream of any size, he invariably had his morning plunge; and if the stream came from a snowbank a few miles up-canyon, all the better."[17]

After Roosevelt left office, Pinchot kept his position in the new administration of William Howard Taft but was uneasy with some of the new president's appointments from the corporate world. He soon involved himself in a dispute with one of those appointees, Secretary of the Interior Richard Ballinger, over the disposition of some Alaskan lands. The ensuing "Ballinger-Pinchot controversy" resulted in the forester publicly and rashly criticizing the secretary and, implicitly, the president. Taft, described later by Pinchot as "weak rather than wicked," fired him for insubordination and thereby raised a storm of criticism that soon spread to other Taft policies and eventually returned Theodore Roosevelt to the national arena as the Progressive, or "Bull Moose," candidate for president in 1912.[18]

Pinchot, of course, supported Roosevelt in 1912 and in the same year was invited by freshman New York State Senator Franklin D. Roosevelt to give a slide show to the state legislature on the need for forest conservation. This was the beginning of a personal and professional relationship between the two men that continued for the rest of their lives.[19]

The Bull Moosers carried Pennsylvania in 1912, but Pinchot's own political ambitions in his home state were blocked by the Republican machine in Pennsylvania, headed by Senator Boies Penrose. Nevertheless, in time he managed his way into state government when Governor William S. Sproul appointed him Pennsylvania commissioner of forests in 1920. He proved, unsurprisingly, an active commissioner, reorganizing the department and setting up twenty-four forestry districts with a trained forester supervising each. He also created the best forest fire protection system in the country, acquired some 77,000 acres of additional forest land for the state, and succeeded in getting his appropriations doubled, thereby increasing salaries and morale in his department. His nurseries were able to distribute three million seedlings to the owners of private forests for erosion protection.[20]

Pinchot was also helpful in improving the first state forestry school at Mont Alto, which began offering bachelor of science degrees in forestry, thus expanding the pool of trained foresters in the state. Although state purchases of forest reserves during his tenure were modest in scope, the federal government had created the Allegheny National Forest in the western part of the state in 1921, bringing an additional 400,000 acres of the state's forests under professional management. One student of this phase of Pinchot's career sums up his work as commissioner as having provided "strong executive leadership, dynamic public relations, and diversified forest work."[21]

With the death of Penrose in 1921, the political path was cleared for Pinchot to run for governor. Elected in 1922, he moved quickly to implement bureaucratic reforms designed to promote his conservation ideas. He combined the Department of Forestry with some other agencies to create a Department of Forests and Waters. The new department was headed for a while by one of Pinchot's protégés, Robert Y. Stuart, who went on to become forester in the United States Forest Service and an important ally of President Franklin Roosevelt in getting the CCC off the ground in 1933.[22]

This increasingly professional attention to managing Penn's Woods meant that by the time the CCC was created in 1933, Pennsylvania's forests had recovered significantly from their low point at the turn of the century. Forests now covered about sixteen million acres, including about two million under state supervision. Most of the CCC camps would be established on these state-managed lands.

Nevertheless, not all was well in the state's forests. Aside from the chestnut tree blight, there were other dangers arising, chiefly gypsy moth destruction of oak trees and the white pine blister rust. But the most serious problem continued to be the annual scourge of forest fires. Fires were caused accidentally by lightning or careless campers, and sometimes they were deliberately set as protests against large corporate absentee landowners. But the railroads were the chief culprits. Sparks emitted by locomotives and fires set by railroad cleanup crews were the causes of most fires. Although Pinchot had begun to build steel watchtowers and improve communications, fires still burned several hundreds of thousands of acres a year, mainly in the spring after the snows had melted and before the green foliage had matured. The fall was the second most dangerous season, when the leaf protection of the summer fell as potential kindling onto the forest floor.[23]

There would be plenty of forestry work, then, for the young men of the CCC when they began pouring into Pennsylvania's work camps in May 1933. The state's Department of Forests and Waters during Governor Pinchot's second term in 1933 would be ready to cooperate with the program by providing plenty of work projects and trained forester supervisors. With the possible exception of California, no other state was as well prepared to effectively utilize CCC labor as was Pennsylvania. And the Depression, which had hit the state particularly hard, would ensure that there was plenty of labor available for conservation work.

THE GREAT DEPRESSION IN PENNSYLVANIA

When President Roosevelt signed the legislation creating the CCC on March 31, 1933, the Depression was three and a half years old and seemingly worsening with every month. Banks had closed, businesses had failed, and breadlines curled around blocks in the major cities. Among the growing numbers of unemployed, perhaps as many as two million, mostly men under thirty-five, were on the road, riding the rails, hitching rides, or just walking from town to

Fig. 2 Pittsburgh's "Hooverville"—named derisively for President Herbert Hoover—stretched from Eleventh to Seventeenth Streets. The CCC offered hope to the down-and-out in Pennsylvania's urban centers. Carnegie Library of Pittsburgh

Fig. 3 Father James Cox delivering relief to the unemployed in Pittsburgh in 1932. Courtesy Archives of Industrial Society, University of Pittsburgh

town in search of work or simply to give the families they left behind a greater chance of receiving the meager relief help still available. Among these unhappy wanderers were uncounted numbers of teen-aged "tramps" who roamed the country, looking for work or excitement or just escaping domestic squalor. One undercover study of five hundred of these homeless children counted fifty-five of them from Pennsylvania, the highest number from any state in the sample.[24]

The older unemployed tended to stay put, selling apples on street corners, looking for odd jobs, or setting up "Hooverville" housing out of the detritus of a collapsed industrial society. Many discouraged men and women simply idled away, hoping something would turn up, while increasing stress built up within families. Families were staring at "nameless horrors" creeping toward them from "out of the darkness," and reactions wavered over a narrow spectrum from fear through numbness to outright rebelliousness in proportions historians still argue about.[25]

The people of Pennsylvania were especially hard hit. The population of the state was more than nine million in 1930, ranking second in the nation behind New York. It was a curious state in that its urban population of six and a half million ranked it second, again behind New York, but its rural population of three million also ranked second (this time behind Texas). The state's post–Civil War reliance on heavy industry made it particularly vulnerable to the Depression since those industries were harder hit than the service economy. Moreover, most of the people in the rural areas were dependent on the state's farms, and agriculture was, if anything, in even worse shape, accelerating the downward slide begun in the 1920s.[26]

Agriculture was not the only economic sector in the state that had not fully shared in the uneven boom years of the Roaring Twenties. Some industries vitally important to the state's economy, such as coal mining and textile manufacturing, had barely held their own in the decade since World War I had ended. Unemployment in Philadelphia, famed for the diversity of its manufacturing sector, was above 10 percent in the year *before* the Depression started. In the Pittsburgh area employment in steel industries in 1929 was 40 percent below what it had been in 1923. According to the director of industrial relations in Pennsylvania, average wages in Pennsylvania's manufacturing industries were among the lowest in the Northeast and about 33 percent lower than in New York. Sweatshops still existed in the state, paying women $4 a week, less than the standard relief grant.[27]

In July 1932, the Community Council of Philadelphia described unemployment in the city as so bad that it was creating conditions of "slow starvation and progressive disintegration of family life." Tuberculosis rates in the state had recently doubled, and more than one-quarter of schoolchildren in the state were said to be undernourished. Relief funds, heretofore the responsibility of local county boards but now supplemented by the limited funds the state provided after 1931, were near exhaustion with many families receiving less than $3 a week in assistance.[28]

Governor Pinchot's analysis of the causes of the Depression stirred him to righteous anger. He blamed the Depression on "the most astounding concentration of wealth in the hands of a few men that the world has ever known."

Citing a Federal Trade Commission study in 1926 showing that 1 percent of Americans owned 60 percent of the nation's wealth, Pinchot argued that the purchasing power of consumers could not keep up with the rising productivity of the economy. Once the Depression hit and wages fell faster than prices, the problem of underconsumption was compounded and cutbacks and layoffs resulted in further decreases in purchasing power.[29]

By the time Franklin Roosevelt entered the White House in 1933, statistical bottoms were being plumbed in terms of unemployment and business failures. Curiously, in a nation obsessed with size and statistics, there were as yet no reliable United States government figures on unemployment, but estimates by various private organizations (supported by later studies done by the Department of Labor) suggest a national unemployment rate of about 25 percent in March 1933.[30]

The situation was even worse in Pennsylvania. In 1929 Pennsylvania had more than 17,000 individual manufacturing establishments, second only to New York. By 1933 about 5,000 of these were completely gone, and the others operating at low capacity, with devastating effects on employment levels. Governor Pinchot reported in early 1933 that only about 40 percent of the state's workforce was fully employed, with about 30 percent employed half-time or less, and another 30 percent, or 1.5 million people, without any jobs at all.[31]

Among young workers under twenty-four, many of whom were about to be recruited into the CCC, the numbers were often double the general figure. African-Americans, traditionally "the last hired and first fired," were also among the hardest hit. In Pittsburgh, the black unemployment rate was near 50 percent, and 43 percent of black families were on the relief rolls. In Philadelphia, black Americans constituted 13 percent of the city's population but about 33 percent of those on relief in 1932. But relief assistance in the city, faced with unprecedented demand and reduced funds, was providing only 20 percent of what had been given on a per capita basis in 1928.[32]

This matter of relief assistance was about to undergo major changes in the 1930s. Traditionally, relief for the indigent and needy in Pennsylvania had come from private charity groups and was given in kind—food and fuel benefits especially. There was also a small amount of public relief, administered by the state's 425 local boards of assistance. When unemployment was relatively low, relief was generally given only to "unemployables"—the aged, the infirm, and the caregivers of dependent children. Potential recipients would have to be investigated by case workers for worthiness and then provided supervised assistance in managing their meager resources.[33]

But with the economic catastrophe of the 1930s, the numbers of people in need exploded and now included growing numbers of "employables" as well. By 1932 two million of the state's nine million people, were receiving some kind of relief, the highest totals in the country. The private charities in Philadelphia even tried some creative experiments in providing work relief that year but found it to be about three times as expensive as giving relief in kind and productively inefficient as well. Sherman Kingsley, the executive director of the Welfare Federation of Philadelphia, sniffed to Governor Pinchot that some of the unskilled people reporting to work relief projects did not even have "proper clothing."[34]

The need for assistance was so great that by the summer of 1932 the Philadelphia Committee on Unemployment Relief, set up in 1930 to coordinate private charity assistance, had to disband when it ran out of funds to disburse, including the $5 million in public funds granted to it by the city and the state. This collapse of relief in the city left some 57,000 families in the city with no help at all; some reportedly lived on dandelions. This was happening in Philadelphia, the third largest city in the country—Philadelphia, "famed for its quiet wealth, its good food, its day-time naps and its savage conservatism." A similar organization in Pittsburgh, the Allegheny County Emergency Association, set up in 1931, also had to disband in 1932 for lack of resources.[35]

In some parts of the state cases of tuberculosis and pellagra were doubling. Forty percent of the state's schoolchildren were reportedly suffering from malnutrition, and in some counties in the southwestern part of the state many children were eating only every other day.[36] Thousands of coal miners, evicted from company housing after a strike against conditions so desperate that they staged it in the slack demand *summer* of 1931, were reportedly living, three or four families to a room, in hillside shacks, subsisting on weed roots. In 1933, workers all over the state in textile manufacturing and coal mining began staging grassroots wildcat strikes, often in the face of established union leadership opposition. It is impossible to analyze the causes of these 1933 strikes in isolation from the new hope the Roosevelt administration, especially its National Recovery Administration, had kindled in desperate people. On the other hand, without the desperation caused by the Depression, there would have been no fear of lighting the dangerous emotion of hope in the first place.[37]

When the New Deal's Harry Hopkins sent investigators from the newly established Federal Emergency Relief Administration into the state in 1933, they found woeful deficiencies in Pennsylvania's relief system. There was inefficient distribution of food, clothing, and fuel and widespread resentment by workers throughout the state of local relief boards that were dominated by the wealthy and employer classes. Lorena Hickock described the unemployed in Pennsylvania as "right on the edge" in a mood that would not take much more to make communists out of them. With such a Dickensian pall spreading everywhere in the state and no hopeful solutions in sight, it is no wonder some feared that a "Red Menace" might spread.[38]

The patent inability of charities or local governments across the country to meet the unprecedented need for assistance was leading some to look to state governments for help. While still governor of New York, Franklin D. Roosevelt led the way, setting up a Temporary Emergency Relief Administration (TERA) in 1931 and appointing Harry Hopkins, a former social worker from Chicago, as its head. Both Hopkins and his chief firmly believed in the superiority of work relief over direct grants of goods or cash, and the TERA did set up some small-scale work relief projects. One such project involved entraining unemployed young men from New York City up to Bear Mountain for some forestry work. The considerable additional expenses involved in setting up these work projects, however, prevented them from becoming more than interesting previews of later New Deal programs like the CCC and the Works Progress Administration (WPA).[39]

Governor Pinchot was not far behind in involving his state government in the deepening relief crisis in Pennsylvania. In November 1931 he began exchanging ideas with other governors about the problems they all faced. He then called the Pennsylvania legislature into special session (he would do this again in 1932 and 1933) and prevailed upon them to appropriate $10 million of state money for relief. Pennsylvania thus became the third state in the country (behind New York and New Jersey) to bring this new kind of state assistance to local relief efforts. To provide for more effective distribution of this money, the legislature in 1932 reorganized the whole system of public relief in the state. A State Emergency Relief Board (SERB) was set up with Eric Biddle of Ardmore as its first director, and it was now charged with distributing state relief money to local emergency relief boards in the counties.[40]

Like Roosevelt, Pinchot used some of the limited state relief money for small-scale work relief projects. One program set up six work camps for housing some of the 25,000 unemployed men put to work for the Highway Administration, yet another sneak preview of the CCC idea. The state National Guard and the Health Department set up these tent camps, each of which housed between

Fig. 4 Franklin D. Roosevelt with Gifford Pinchot at Governors' Conference in French Lick, Indiana, in 1931. Roosevelt, who was then governor of New York, would be elected president the following year. Pinchot and Roosevelt shared a personal and professional relationship that was critical to the formation of the CCC. Courtesy French Lick Hotel

seventy and ninety men. Unlike the later CCC camps, these were integrated, with blacks and whites living and working together. The number of applicants far exceeded the positions, and men lined up well before dawn on registration days. Those rejected often left in tears. The lucky ones were given thirty days' work and army surplus clothing. The three meals a day the men received resulted in reported weight gains of between five and fifteen pounds.[41]

Pinchot also anticipated the CCC in seeing the woods of Pennsylvania as assets in the attempt to alleviate distress and unemployment. The state Department of Forests and Waters employed 1,100 men to cut 10,000 cords of free firewood for needy families. The men also were engaged in other forestry projects in return for food relief.[42]

Despite this unprecedented state involvement in relief matters, Pinchot realized that the needs were beyond what budgetary and political realities in Pennsylvania could provide. He consequently became one of the earliest and loudest voices in the country for federal relief assistance. He sent a public letter to President Herbert Hoover on August 18, 1931, asking for federal assistance on relief, and he followed the letter up with speeches on the subject in Detroit, Cleveland, and Washington.[43]

Unfortunately, Hoover's ideological rigidity prevented him from formulating any imaginative policy initiatives to combat the Depression. He had, somewhat reluctantly, in 1932 agreed to the establishment of a Reconstruction Finance Corporation (RFC), which was later empowered to make loans to states. Pinchot was able, with the expenditure of much energy, to wheedle $30 million in loans from the RFC for distribution by the SERB, but he was pushing up against Pennsylvania's constitutionally fixed debt limits and was frustrated by Hoover's refusal to provide grants to the states.[44]

By the time Roosevelt took office in 1933, state resources in Pennsylvania were stretched to the limit, no more aid was coming from Washington, and desperation was deepening among Pennsylvania's unemployed. Pennsylvania had to weather the winter of 1932–33 with no additional funds until the establishment in May 1933 by President Roosevelt of the Federal Emergency Relief Administration (FERA), with Harry Hopkins in charge. The FERA was empowered to give grants to the states, and Pennsylvania would receive $196 million from this agency before it was abolished in 1935 and replaced by the federal work relief projects of the WPA, also headed by Hopkins, and the Social Security Administration, which continued the federal subsidies to the states for assisting the unemployables.[45] The creative energy of the New Deal, as expressed in these programs as well as the CCC, was happily greeted throughout the state and resulted in major political shifts.

THE POLITICAL SCENE

The major theme of Pennsylvania politics from the Civil War era down to 1934 is a simple one of Republican Party domination. Democrats were able to elect only one governor in all that time and no United States senators. Republicans also carried the state in all the presidential elections except 1912, when the ex-Republican, Theodore Roosevelt, managed to win a plurality of the vote in a three-way race with William Howard Taft and Woodrow Wilson. In the two major cities, Philadelphia and Pittsburgh, the story was a similar one of long-lived Republican Party hegemony. The party's strengths were rooted in Civil War memories, a large population residing in small towns and on small farms, and an organization that had grown up symbiotically with the big business interests of the state and had learned to tap those interests for whatever campaign funds were needed.

The Democratic Party of the state, in the words of one scholar of the subject, "barely existed" by the 1920s. In the gubernatorial election of 1926 it failed to carry even one of the state's sixty-seven counties. In some places, like Philadelphia, it was a "kept" party, kept around by Republican bosses by means of minor patronage and rental payments on its offices as a means of ensuring the nomination of eminently beatable candidates and useful allies.[46] But the times, they were a-changing.

The Depression, and the widespread perception that Hoover was both unable and unwilling to deal with the problems of mass suffering and insecurity, would provide the Democrats with an opening—if they could seize it and run with it. Electoral success for the party was almost guaranteed in 1932, no matter whom it ran against Hoover, but continued success would demand bold and imaginative departures from the conservative leadership the national party had reverted to in the 1920s. The electoral coalition the Democrats created in the turbulence of the Depression would be a precarious one and one that would have to be exploited with creative intelligence and compassionate rhetoric. Once created, however, it would provide the party with a "permanent majority" that would endure for almost two generations until the white south began to slip away in the 1960s.

The man at the center of this political opportunity for the Democrats was, of course, Franklin D. Roosevelt, often considered the greatest president of the twentieth century. Looking back at Roosevelt from the vantage point of the 1960s, the high noon of twentieth-century liberalism, several New Left historians found him seriously wanting in his commitment to liberal change.[47] Looking back at Roosevelt, however, from the vantage point of this writing, through the denser atmosphere of the "Twilight of the Left," we see assessments of his achievements are bound to be more friendly. More important, if we try not to look *backward* at Roosevelt at all, but rather *forward* with him and the country from 1932 onward, we can perhaps regain a sense of the impressive achievements of his presidency and the indispensable contributions of Roosevelt himself. And nowhere else was his contribution more central than in the creation of the Civilian Conservation Corps.

It is important to remind ourselves of the intense emotions that Roosevelt evoked from his contemporaries, ranging from conservative denunciations of "That Man" to the kind of adulation he inspired in his supporters. One of these stalwart supporters was Senator Joseph F. Guffey, one of Pennsylvania's leading Democrats, who later wrote of him: "I probably saw him as often as anyone. . . . I can only say that in a long and busy lifetime I have never known a greater man, and in the perspective of the years his shadow grows longer as his stature becomes more clearly perceived."[48] Most of the men who served in the CCC would not argue with Guffey's assessment.

Roosevelt and his New Deal had an even more profound impact on the Democratic Party in Pennsylvania than did the Depression. After all, even with unemployment soaring in the state after 1929, Republicans still managed to elect Pinchot in 1930, maintain majorities in both state houses, elect David Reed as United States senator in 1932, win twenty-three of the state's thirty-four congressional seats, and carry the state for Hoover that same year. The Democrats in Pennsylvania had a difficult upward climb ahead of them.

A pivotal figure in this Democratic story is, curiously, the Republican Gifford Pinchot. As an old Bull-Moose Republican and an ardent conservationist, Pinchot's ideological orientation was very different from the laissez-faire conventional wisdom of the triumphal Republicans of the 1920s and closer to that of the two Roosevelts. Moreover, Pinchot and Franklin Roosevelt were linked by personal friendships. The friendship of their wives, Eleanor Roosevelt and Cornelia Bryce Pinchot, was even older, dating from their childhoods.

Pinchot formally remained a Republican in the 1930s, and his relationship with Democrats proved complex and prickly. He welcomed Roosevelt's national policies on relief and appreciated the support the president urged on Democratic state legislators for his own program in 1933. He also cooperated with the Democratic State Committee in the early months of the CCC in helping them get foremen positions in the camps.[49] But when his term was nearing its end in 1934, he engaged in some serio-comical negotiations with state Democrats in the hopes of running for United States senator on a ticket with George H. Earle, the Democratic candidate for governor that year. These hopes were dashed by a bitter dispute that erupted between Pinchot and Joseph F. Guffey, who coveted the Senate seat for himself.[50]

Guffey's election to the Senate in 1934 effectively ended Pinchot's political career. Pinchot made futile efforts to receive the Republican presidential nomination in 1936 and to regain his old governor's seat in 1938, but his health was not good. He suffered from shingles and a series of heart attacks in 1939 weakened him until, at last, he died of leukemia on October 4, 1946.[51]

Meanwhile, the New Deal had an immediate impact on Pennsylvania's economy, which translated into unprecedented success for the Democrats in the 1934 elections. Thanks to successful relief programs, including the CCC, the FERA, and the Civil Works Administration (CWA), not only did Guffey become Pennsylvania's first Democratic senator but George Earle became only the second Democratic governor since the Civil War. The stage was set for Pennsylvania's "Little New Deal" in the middle years of the decade. Roosevelt's New Deal had played the most important role in this revival of the state's Democrats, and the CCC was one of the most popular of its programs contributing to that revival.

1

THE FIRST YEAR OF THE CCC IN PENNSYLVANIA

On Sunday afternoon, June 2, 1933, the Philipsburg American Legion staged a formal flag-raising ceremony, officially opening CCC Camp s-71 in Moshannon State Forest. Two days previously, two hundred young recruits had been trucked from the local train station to their new home. They had arrived in a heavy rain to find no shelter awaiting them, only a field of brush and tree stumps. But they immediately set to work clearing the site and setting up army tents and soon were eating a light supper in the mess hall tent before they prepared for their first night's sleep in the woods.[1]

The saga of the early days at Camp s-71 was being repeated, with only slight variations, all over Pennsylvania (indeed, all over the country) in those late spring days of 1933. Setting up tents, sometimes in the dark, bathing in streams, using ditch latrines—only the high spirits of youth embarked on interesting new experiences can account for all the singing, according to many reports, that went on in these early days of roughing it and "taking it."[2]

The magnitude of placing 300,000 men in CCC camps in less than three months that spring was an accomplishment dazzling in its complexity and colorful in its execution. President Roosevelt's program of Emergency Conservation Work (ECW), the original official title of the CCC, was speedily passed by Congress and signed into law on March 31. On April 3 Roosevelt held a meeting at the White House where the basic organization of the CCC was established. The president, in an off-handed way, drew up a simple chart leading down from Robert Fechner of the Machinists Union, whom he had already appointed as its first director. From Fechner lines went down to the Departments of Labor, War, Agriculture, and Interior. These cabinet secretaries would appoint representatives to an Advisory Council under Fechner. Labor would recruit the young men in cooperation with state relief agencies, the army would condition them and manage the work camps, and Interior and Agriculture would supervise the

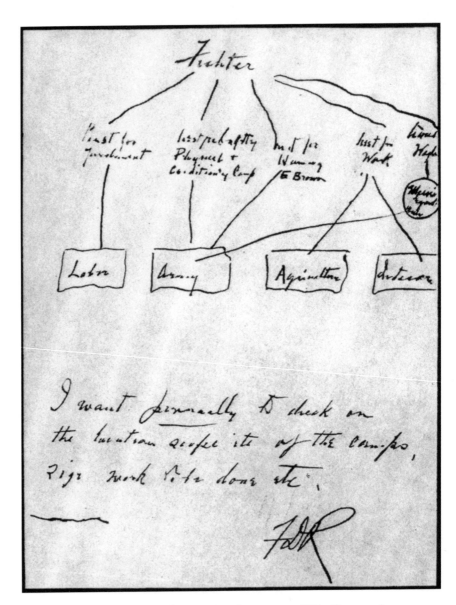

Fig. 5 FDR's sketch of the CCC administration, drawn up at a White House conference on April 3, 1933, wherein Fechner's name is misspelled and the president wrote, "I want *personally* to check on the location and scope of the camps, assign work to be done, etc." Franklin Delano Roosevelt Presidential Library, Hyde Park, N.Y.

conservation work. This Rube Goldberg set-up appears an administrative nightmare on paper and occasionally led to friction, but it was actually an ideal framework in which to get the emergency program up and running in a hurry. It seems a typically New Deal approach—pragmatic, flexible, make it up as you go along, and avoid too much straitjacket precision in drawing lines of authority. And over top of it all was the president, who had conceived the project and almost willed it into existence on his own.

By April 17, in an impressive feat of organization, the first recruits were in the first camp—Camp Roosevelt, of course—in the George Washington National Forest in Virginia. Camps in Pennsylvania began to appear about a week later. The Keystone State provided ideal conditions for the CCC. With a large percentage of its population in economic distress, Pennsylvania could supply abundant recruits for the work camps. In 1933 Governor Pinchot was reporting that two million Pennsylvanians were receiving some kind of relief assistance and he claimed that 12 percent of the nation's unemployed lived in his state.[3] Those unemployed included many young men who were soon to be working in the CCC, receiving salaries of $30 a month. Since most of that money (usually $25 in the early years of the program) would be sent home to the men's families, many of whom were receiving public assistance, the state's relief expenditures could be correspondingly reduced. Dorothy C. Kahn of the Philadelphia Relief Board was expecting savings of $80,000 a month.[4]

Aside from needy people, Pennsylvania also had an abundance of needy forests. Although conditions had improved considerably since the turn of the century, there were still plenty of backed-up maintenance and improvement projects in the state that would easily absorb most of the manpower the CCC would provide over the next nine years. Moreover, the Depression had forced cuts in the operating budget of the Department of Forests and Waters, which would be more than made up for by new federal spending on CCC work.[5]

Pennsylvania also had an abundance of publicly owned land where CCC camps could be placed. The legislation creating the ECW program, in one of its few specific mandates, had required all conservation work done by the CCC to be on publicly owned property, with only a few exceptions made for work on private lands when such work would be crucial to fire and flood protection or to the treatment of tree disease. The ECW office in Washington constantly prodded state officials across the country to begin establishing state parks or state forests or to expand their limited holdings, but Pennsylvania's two million acres of publicly owned lands—the Allegheny National Forest, state forests, state parks and state game lands—were sufficient to keep most of its CCC men occupied and would not have to be added to during the decade of Depression.[6]

LAUNCHING THE CCC IN PENNSYLVANIA

The creation of the CCC created intense curiosity, interest, and excitement throughout Pennsylvania. On April 3, before any specific plans had been set up in Washington, a crowd of two thousand hopeful young men, dressed in their Sunday best, converged on the State Employment Bureau in downtown Philadelphia. The officials there had, as of yet, received no instructions and had to send the disappointed young men home.[7]

After an Executive Order issued by President Roosevelt on April 5 had established policies and procedures, the Labor Department set enrollment quotas, based on the populations of the various states. Roosevelt's early goal was to put 250,000 men in camps by midsummer, and Pennsylvania was initially given 19,500 of these places to fill. These first recruits in 1933 were required to be American citizens, between the ages of eighteen and twenty-five, single, and unemployed, with needy family dependents. The pay of these "Juniors" would be $30 a month, but most of that would be sent home in allotment checks. Young African-Americans joining the CCC would be assigned to separate "Colored" camps.

On April 22 Roosevelt authorized the recruitment of a second category of unemployed men—local experienced men (LEMs). Both Governor Pinchot and General Paul Malone of the army's Third Corps, which included Pennsylvania, were worried about creating dangerous resentment among locally unemployed men by bringing large numbers of outsiders into their midst. Pinchot, in particular, expressed his fears that these jobless men might resort to arson in protest, a tactic with some precedent in the forests of his state.[8]

These LEMs were not subject to age or marital requirements and were not required to allot any of their pay to family dependents. They often served as work supervisors and received upgraded pay ratings. They also were not required to live in camp, although some did. Pennsylvania's CCC quota was adjusted to include 18,200 Juniors and 1,300 LEMs.[9]

Another category of unemployed men for CCC camps was added on May 11 when unemployed World War I veterans, some of whom had come to Washington on a "Bonus March," were allowed to be recruited into separate work camps. In Pennsylvania, the recruitment of 1,950 veterans brought the first summer's total to 21,450. Like Junior camps, Veterans' camps were segregated by race. Their camps tended to be a bit more relaxed than Junior camps. Most of the men were in their mid-forties and tended to remain in the ccc almost twice as long as did Juniors. Beer was sold in their camp canteens and sometimes affected adversely their reputations in rural areas. Moreover, local relief officials sometimes complained about veterans moving their families to communities near their camps where they often became a drain on local relief funds.[10]

As the ccc continued to add categories of the unemployed to its camps, one group of the unemployed notably missing was, of course, women. The need of women for relief and for jobs was critical but not uppermost in the minds of most New Dealers. Eleanor Roosevelt had suggested that some homeless women might be put to work in ccc-run tree nurseries, but nothing came of it. Later, the FERA, the WPA, and the National Youth Administration (NYA) set up some "She-She-She" work camps, but the ccc remained an organization for men only. A very small number of nonresident women did work in ccc camps as secretaries or teachers, and there was enough interest among women that the Labor Department had to draft a "Dear Madam" form letter to respond to queries from unemployed women. Occasionally young women would receive, by mistake, invitations to join the ccc. One such recipient in Northampton County, Pennsylvania, wrote back to the local welfare office: "I ain't no boy I am a girl, but if they have a girls camp let me no at once." Even though that particular office could not fill its quota that month, the girl's application was not accepted.[11]

As a first step in the recruiting process, W. Frank Persons, appointed by Secretary of Labor Frances Perkins to head the selection process, called a start-up meeting in Washington on April 5, to which relief officials of the seventeen largest eastern cities were invited. Philadelphia was represented at this meeting by Dorothy Kahn, director of the Philadelphia County Relief Board, and Pittsburgh by George P. Mills, director of the Allegheny County Relief Board. In addition, Persons invited F. Richard Stilwell, field representative of the recently established State Emergency Relief Board, whom he had appointed state selector for Pennsylvania. Persons assigned quotas for each of these cities: 3,000 for Philadelphia and 900 for Pittsburgh, and the officials returned home to begin setting up the selection process.[12] On May 26, Persons appointed two Veterans Administration officials, H. J. Crosson in Philadelphia and E. R. Bunke in Pittsburgh, as selectors for the 1,950 veterans to be recruited in the state.[13]

In the days following his meeting with Persons, Stilwell meted out the remainder of the state's enrollee quota to the relief boards in the smaller towns. They were instructed to pick men who would agree to send $25 of their monthly pay home as allotments to their families, but this was not always done.[14] They were also told to give priority in their selections to young men whose families were receiving public relief assistance, but this advisory was not always followed either. For example, the family of Bob Ward, who was at Camp s-91 in 1933, owned a dairy farm outside Wellsboro in 1933. Although they were poor, they were never on relief.[15]

Philadelphia sent off the first of its enrollees on April 7, 1933. They were reported as "fine specimens, decidedly under par physically" but "eager to go." Among the first enrollees were Joe Wallace, age twenty-four, 5 feet 2 inches, 98 pounds, the sole support of his parents and sister, and John Phillips, one of seventeen children. Members of the Women's International League for Peace and Freedom provided the young men with box lunches and went down to the train station in a morning rain shower to send them off. In Pittsburgh relief officials had reviewed 2,000 applications for their first 900 places.[16]

What inspired these men to come forward and apply for ccc work encompassed a broad range of motives. Intrafamily tension arising from too many people idling in poverty with no purposive activity undoubtedly was a key factor. Many ccc men later remembered simple hunger as an important motivator. Some parents, eyeing the allotment checks, often drove sons to apply. And, of course, the simple explanation of young men seeking activity, adventure, and structure probably accounted for the bulk of applications. As R. F. Hammett of the Forestry Service pointed out, most of the young men coming into ccc camps in Pennsylvania from the larger cities had never seen a mountain in their life and "they had never seen the woods." At the other extreme were some young men from rural parts of the state who had never seen a black person until their ccc travels.[17]

As time went by and ccc men returned home with improved appearances and stories to tell of camp life (some of them undoubtedly true), other motives began inspiring new waves of recruits. James McEntee, the second director of the ccc, described the appeal of the ccc experience to young men: "They like to see their muscles grow strong, their backs, arms and faces tan from the outdoor work. In sharp contrast to the frail, oft-times undernourished lads who frequently are admitted to the Corps as rookies, are the husky, tanned youth who have been in the CCC for a time—confident young fellows who have learned what a job is and that they are capable of doing it."[18]

When a young man was approved as a CCC recruit by his local relief board in these early years, he would then report to one of the army collecting stations where he would be officially enrolled. In Pennsylvania these were located in Philadelphia, Pittsburgh, Harrisburg, Altoona, Johnstown, Williamsport, Allentown, Easton, Pottsville, Reading, Butler, Erie, Greensburg, Uniontown, Wilkes-Barre, and Scranton.[19] He would have to make his own way there, sometimes a considerable distance for the men from small towns, and he was told to bring a small suitcase of clothing and personal effects as well as a lunch. The first thirty enrollees from Lewistown were dismayed to learn that they would have to get to Harrisburg on their own the following day. The prospect of hitchhiking and spending a night "maybe in jail" did not, however, dampen their determination to sign up. There were other instances of men making their way to army recruiting stations, only to be told that they could not be enrolled that day. These young men would then have to go back home and return on some other day. This often presented hardships for those who had traveled some distance by their own effort and expense.[20]

At the army collecting station the young recruit was given a physical exam and, if he passed, was sworn into the CCC and given a series of inoculation shots for typhoid and smallpox. An experimental shot for pneumonia was offered as an option later in the decade.[21] He was now a "Junior" enrollee and from here on the army would assume responsibility for him. He was then given transportation to one of the army bases in his area that served as conditioning camps for the men before they were assigned to one of the conservation work camps.

For Pennsylvania men, the conditioning camps set up to receive them were: Forts Meade, Hoyle, Howard, Washington, and the Holabird Quartermaster Depot in Maryland; Forts Myer, Humphreys, Monroe, and Story, and Langley Field in Virginia; and the Carlisle Barracks in Pennsylvania. Fort Meade took more of the Pennsylvania boys than the others, especially those from Philadelphia. Although the Aberdeen, Maryland, Proving Grounds were also nearby, that fort's commander warned off the adjutant-general from sending any CCC men there. Not only was sensitive weapons research taking place on the grounds, but the whole base was full of dangerous explosive devices—a very unsuitable place to have large numbers of curious and active boys poking about![22] As time went on, these conditioning camps were phased out and later recruits were received directly into the conservation work camps in the states.

These military bases and all the Pennsylvania work camps were located in the army's Third Corps, which had its administrative headquarters in Baltimore, commanded by General Paul Malone until he was replaced in 1935. Malone was born in Middletown, New York, in 1872, graduated from West Point, and had seen action in Cuba, the Philippines, and France, where he was awarded the Legion of Honor. His Third Corps responsibility also included the camps in Maryland, Virginia, and the District of Columbia.[23]

On the army bases the recruit was given a healthier diet than he was usually accustomed to back home and outfitted with army work clothes. His time, over the next week or two, would be spent in a physical program of calisthenics, light work around the camp, and getting used to the experience of group living. Some men would face problems of homesickness, bad reactions to inoculation shots, and occasional hostility from army recruits on the base who were, fortunately for the CCC recruits, relatively few in number after Depression cutbacks in personnel levels.[24]

Roosevelt had envisioned in a March 31 press conference that the CCC boys would spend, at most, a week or two in the conditioning camps, and then be moved out quickly to the work camps. But the president, who insisted (added on to his famous sketch of CCC administration) that he personally approve of every single camp established, was finding it an impossible burden in the "Hundred Days" rush of other legislation. By early May men were being kept in army camps for more than two weeks and the backlog threatened the president's goal of getting the men to work by July 1. For example, Pennsylvania had enrolled 7,150 men by May 13 and had sent on 4,645 into its work camps. One week later, they had enrolled and sent on to conditioning camps another 4,000 men, but the same 4,645 were the only ones at work in the woods.[25]

Despite herculean efforts being made all over the country, the delays in moving the men into work camps were resulting in discipline problems at some of the conditioning camps.[26] The biggest problem seems to have been keeping the men occupied in the abundant free time they had after they completed the modest amount of training and work they were given. The Philadelphia *Evening Bulletin* on April 27 reported on some of the problems at Fort Meade. There was an acute shortage of recreational equipment at the base, which was creating "rising restlessness and homesickness" among the 3,200 enrollees, most of whom were from Philadelphia. The limited recreational equipment at the fort was claimed aggressively and protectively by army enlisted men there who resented the $30 a month pay scale of the CCC men, considerably more than privates were being paid. Consequently, the young men, with nothing to do after their light duties were completed, were taking to the roads, begging rides to towns, and creating annoyances. The recreational officer was described as "frantic," and he issued calls for help from civic groups like the Playground Association of Philadelphia. When groups in Philadelphia responded with shipments of games and equipment for the camps, the same newspaper reported snidely on the "vacation"-like experiences the men were having.[27]

The CCC administrators were always acutely sensitive to any such adverse publicity, and the burden was now on the civilian administrators of the ECW, both at the national and state levels, to hurry the men into work camps. A series of meetings in Washington to deal with the crisis resulted in Roosevelt's and Fechner's agreeing to streamline administrative procedures, and a torrent of camps began to be approved after mid-May.[28]

The work to be done in Pennsylvania was approved by administrators in the Departments of Agriculture and Interior, working with the state personnel from the Department of Forests and Waters. But consultation with the army was necessary before a camp's specific location was approved. The army had the experience of setting up camps with respect to safe water and sewage, ease of transportation, and suitability of terrain. Finally, the state Department of Health would have to give final approval to the sites as safely habitable.[29]

The work camps in Pennsylvania were arranged into two large administrative districts: an Eastern District, No. 1, which included Pennsylvania east of the Susquehanna River and which was based in New Cumberland; and a Western District, No. 2, headquartered in Pittsburgh, which covered the camps in the rest of the state. In 1933 the Eastern District supervised only twenty-four work camps of the ninety-seven in the state, but by 1936 its area of jurisdiction had grown to control about 60 percent of all the camps in Pennsylvania.[30]

Sometimes idiosyncratic factors had to be considered in locating camp sites. On June 2, Lewis Staley, head of the Pennsylvania Department of Forests and Waters, sent a heads-up note to Lieutenant Hendrix, the commanding officer at Camp s-51 at Pine Grove Furnace in Cumberland County, one of the first three camps to be set up on state lands in Pennsylvania. He alerted Hendrix to the presence of Girl Scout and tourist camps in his area and urged him to make sure no embarrassing incidents occurred.[31]

Another potential problem in locating camps was not on the minds of the CCC people, but it did concern one of the field representatives of the state Bureau of Mental Health, Florence Hackenbush. She worried about the putative dangers presented by some of the indigenous inhabitants of the state. In what reads like some kind of preliminary draft of *Deliverance*, she alerted Persons to the fact that, with so many work camps being established in remote and isolated parts of Pennsylvania, the boys were bound to come in contact with the "deteriorated and degenerative feeble-minded families" living in those parts. She was particularly fearful that the "loose women" in some of these families might take advantage of the young men and abuse them. Ms. Hackenbush singled out Potter County as a particularly dangerous area.[32]

Pennsylvania proved to be one of the more efficient states in setting up work camps because of two major advantages the state enjoyed. First of all, the state was somewhat unusual for an eastern state in that it was home to the half-million acre Allegheny National Forest, established in 1921. The first fifty camps set up in the country were in national forests. These lands were directly under the supervision of the U.S. Forestry Service and locating camps there did not require as much cooperation with state authorities. Moreover, the service had developed a comprehensive plan of forestry work projects that were just waiting for an influx of manpower such as the CCC was about to provide.[33]

Thus the first camp established in Pennsylvania was in the Allegheny National Forest near Marienville, Camp ANF-1, Company #318. Both camps and companies received numerical designations. At the conditioning camps the army had organized the men into companies of two hundred each. Third Corps companies would be numbered 301, 302, and so on, until the numbers ran out, and then there would be companies numbering from 1301 or 2301. Confusing matters somewhat was the CCC practice of giving its own numbers to the work camps in the states. In Pennsylvania, for example, State Forest Camp 119 (S-119) would receive Company #373 in 1933, but in 1936, Company #5471 from the southern Fourth Corps was posted there. In 1937 another Third Corps company, #303-C, a Colored company, relieved Company #5471 and remained there until the camp closed in 1941.[34]

Camp ANF-1 was in business by April 24, 1933, making it the second CCC camp in the country after Camp Roosevelt in Virginia, which had opened a week earlier. Camp ANF-1 later became a Signal Corps outpost for communicating with other area camps. It proved to be of great use during the 1936 floods in Pennsylvania.[35] The men sent to ANF-1 had been organized by the army at Fort Monroe, Virginia. The next three camps established were also in the national forest. These companies, also organized at Fort Monroe, were credited with the same starting date of April 24: Company #319 at ANF-2, near Heart's Content;

Company #320 at ANF-3, near Kinzua and Dunkle Corner; and Company #321-C at ANF-5, outside Kinzua on Sugar Run. The latter was the first Colored camp in Pennsylvania.[36]

The second important advantage for Pennsylvania in these early days was its well-organized Department of Forests and Waters, created by Governor Pinchot in 1923 and headed in 1933 by one of his protégés, Lewis Staley, a graduate of the Mont Alto Forestry School. Staley was responsible for the almost two million publicly owned acres in the state, and his department had plenty of work planned, much of which had been put off by the budget cuts caused by the Depression. While the work done by the CCC on these state-owned lands had to be approved by the federal agencies, the actual work in the state camps was directly supervised by Staley's Forests and Waters personnel.[37]

Staley got the CCC off to a running start. He attended a meeting in Washington on April 6, called by Forester Robert Y. Stuart (Staley's predecessor as head of Pennsylvania's Department of Forests and Waters) to begin coordinating work plans between the federal and state foresters and by the next day had formally sent on 54 work projects to Fechner's office for approval. These were approved by April 21, by which time Staley had a few dozen more in the pipeline. By June 2 Fechner had approved a total of 97 work projects for Pennsylvania.[38]

Only California had more camps—171—and no other eastern state came close to Pennsylvania's 97. Virginia had 48 and New York had 32, for example. Nine of the camps, about 9 percent of the total, were assigned to Colored companies, which was about double the percentage of the African-American population of the state. This was a relatively good record considering that, because of southern resistance, the entire CCC class that summer was only about 5 percent black. Seven camps for 1,400 veterans, who had been enrolled a bit later than the Juniors, were approved by the Advisory Council on June 30, and the men assigned to these camps were in camp by mid-July.[39]

By the end of July 1933, then, there were eighty-nine CCC work camps established on state lands in Pennsylvania, seven in the Allegheny National Forest, and one at Gettysburg Military Park. The conservation work in the Allegheny National Forest was under the supervision of the U.S. Forestry Service, the work at Gettysburg was under the National Park Service (NPS), and the work in the state forests was run by the Pennsylvania Department of Forests and Waters.[40] Despite this frenetic pace of activity by Staley and his department in organizing work projects, the feeling in Washington in early May was that some of the Pennsylvania enrollees, like men from other eastern states, were going

Fig. 6 Lewis E. Staley, a graduate of the Mont Alto Forestry School, was Governor Pinchot's secretary of forests and waters during his second term and played a central role in the successful establishment of the CCC in Pennsylvania in 1933. Pennsylvania State Archives

to have to be sent out west. There were more national forest and national park lands in the West that could more readily absorb the labor of eastern men than could their home states. A small cadre of 337 Pennsylvania men had been sent to Pocatello, Idaho, on May 8 and more were expected to follow.[41]

It is impossible to be precise on the numbers of Pennsylvanians sent west in 1933 because except for Pennsylvania Company #1301, which was sent to Greys River, Wyoming, most of the men who were sent out of state in this early period were distributed, in groups of about twenty, to various companies in camps in Idaho and Wyoming.[42] After the administrative logjam in Washington was broken in mid-May, Staley was able to get enough camp sites approved to occupy the rest of Pennsylvania's enrollment quota. No more Pennsylvania men had to be sent west after May 24. On the president's target date of July 1, the vast majority of the CCC men recruited in Pennsylvania were at work in camps operating in their home state.[43]

The level of activity involved in setting up all these camps in Pennsylvania in May and June 1933 is difficult to imagine and perhaps accounts for the relative scarcity of records on this initial period, especially state records in the Pennsylvania State Archives. Pinchot reported Staley as "swamped" with work, with twenty-six work camps established on a single day, May 30. Staley's deputy, John W. Keller, reflecting later on those feverish weeks, wondered "what we did with our time" before the ECW program began.[44]

Director Fechner complimented Governor Pinchot on Pennsylvania's record, citing it as "one of the very best of our states in cooperating." He recognized the achievement of the Keystone State in setting up enough camps to occupy almost the entirety of the state's enrollment quota and pressed Pinchot, unsuccessfully, to find camps to absorb some of the surplus men from nearby states.[45]

In Philadelphia, far from any CCC camp, there was also frenetic activity in support of the CCC. The program's immediate impact on local business was seen in the rush orders for tents and clothing that the quartermaster general ordered that first spring. From May 15 to June 8 workers at the army's Quartermaster Corps, in the rush to meet the urgent CCC demand for equipment, were kept busy working seven days a week, and women were reportedly working illegal night shifts. The army had doubled the workforce and was still straining to fill orders for 425,000 coats and 200,000 pairs of trousers. Some of the work involved altering sizes of army surplus gear to fit the smaller, often malnourished enrollees. In addition, the workers were producing seventy-five tents a day.[46]

Governor Pinchot expressed concern that widespread violations of Pennsylvania's factory laws were occurring. At first he was told that state laws did not apply on the federal properties, but after the first rush of orders had been filled, the army assured him that it was respecting all relevant standards and was cooperating with the state factory inspectors. By mid-June the workers filling army orders were back to eight-hour days, forty-four-hour weeks, and mutually satisfactory arrangements had been negotiated with private subcontractors in the city.[47] Another violation of fair labor practices occurred when a private company in Delaware, paying substandard wages, provided the Quartermaster Depot in Philadelphia with 15,000 cots. This episode resulted in Fechner asserting his authority over all CCC purchases of over $2,500.[48]

Once the work projects and sites were established and the men equipped and housed in the work camps, there was a whole new set of shake-out problems. Poorly chosen sites, faulty tents, and shortages of proper clothing and tools plagued the early camps. The site chosen for Camp s-101 near Ridgway was full of boulders and tree stumps that had to be cleared before the tents could be erected. Clarence J. McMaster was among the first group of men to arrive at the camp. He remembered clearing the woods for the tent site, bathing in the Clarion River, and using a latrine ditch behind the tents. The original tent site in the picnic area at Promised Land State Park had to be moved to the Deerfield area ten days later, and it was not until June 5 that the men were ready to do forestry work. Philadelphia boys assigned to Camp s-51 at Pine Grove Furnace lived in railroad cars for a few days and had to walk two miles every day to the camp site until they had it prepared for tents. Occasionally camp sites were placed where water supplies soon proved inadequate. At the early Heart's Content camp in the Allegheny National Forest, the men had to dig a 120-foot-deep well when the stream in camp could not supply the needed amount of water.[49]

Delays in getting the White House to authorize the purchase of tools for the earliest Pennsylvania camps were among the most important factors leading to Roosevelt's Executive Order of May 12, streamlining procedures and breaking the logjam of early May.[50] Three camps in Somerset County had no adequate tools for the first three months, and the men busied themselves in cleaning up roadside trash to minimize the dangers of fires.[51]

The question of trucks was particularly crucial. They were essential in the conservation work because they brought supplies to camp and transported the men and equipment to the work sites. Governor Pinchot did what he could to supplement the number of ECW trucks out of state supplies, but Fechner pleaded with him for more. By midsummer the ECW had bought or rented eight hundred trucks for the ninety-seven Pennsylvania camps.[52]

One little wrinkle was added to camp organization on July 21 when the Advisory Council approved a Forestry Service proposal for "side camps," established and supervised by the technical services outside army jurisdiction. Some of the conservation work, particularly clearing fire lanes, began taking the men farther and farther away from base camp, necessitating longer transportation time and thus less work time. The army had resisted this new arrangement but finally agreed to allow a maximum of twenty workers to be detached to side-camps in the field.[53]

CAMP SUPERVISORS

Camp supervision reflected the general overlapping of administration for which the CCC was notorious. Supervising the two hundred enrollees, usually including about a dozen LEMs, were the military men and the technical people. A typical camp in the organizational set-up period in 1933 had a commanding officer (CO), usually a captain from the regular army, assisted by two subalterns and several army enlisted men. Third Corps army regulations required at least one officer to reside in camp. Others could reside outside the camp if they received permission and if "the interest of the government and the CCC will not suffer."[54]

Fig. 7 An early enrollee, young and apprehensive, in his oversized work clothes at Camp s-51, Pine Grove Furnace (Cumberland County). Located in the Michaux State Forest District, Camp s-51 was one of the first three camps to be set up on state lands in Pennsylvania. The caption on the photo calls this young man a "typical forest worker." Pennsylvania State Archives

Fig. 8 Securing enough trucks to transport men and equipment to work sites was a challenge in the early months of the CCC. Here, Pittsburgh boys pose around a truck in Camp S-51, Pine Grove Furnace, in May 1933. Pennsylvania State Archives

Regular army officers were mostly replaced by men from the huge pool of 100,000 reserve officers beginning in late 1933. Occasionally, in a small number of camps, officers from the other armed services would serve as COs or as assistants. In some camps there would also be a resident army surgeon or an army chaplain. Later in the decade the army rotated its officers every six months or so to make the experience of camp command available to as many as possible and to broaden officers' experiences.[55]

Questions of camp discipline were delicate matters for COs. They lacked the firm and formal authority over the men that the Uniform Code of Military Justice would have provided them for army recruits. As there were no military police (MPS) in camps, officers were forced to rely primarily on their "command" abilities, and the army came to appreciate the value of this CCC experience for its

Fig. 9 Commissioned and noncommissioned officers in charge of Camp s-95, Forksville (Sullivan County), in May 1933. Pennsylvania State Archives

officers. Mild penalties of extra duty, small fines, and confinement to camp on weekends could be administered. The ultimate punishment could be dismissal from camp with a dishonorable discharge. By November the army had set up a system of hearings and appeals for men about to be dismissed.[56]

Somewhat paralleling the army co in authority was the camp superintendent, usually a forester appointed by the Department of Forests and Waters and approved by the U.S. Forestry Service or the National Park Service. He was in charge of the work projects and had supervisory authority over the men when they left camp to work in the field, leaving behind about twenty men under the co's jurisdiction for camp and kitchen duty.

The general lines of responsibility between the army and the technical super-visors were defined in broad terms, but disputes could arise in the interstices. For example, disagreements occasionally arose on questions of awarding ratings and extra pay to certain enrollees or on which ones would be allowed to re-enlist. Relations between supervisors could become quite formalized. In the Camp s-107 records at Michaux State Forest there is extensive correspondence between the CO and the superintendent on such issues as truck availability, charges for meals taken in camp, and the rating of enrollees. The CO even admon-ished the superintendent for allowing his personnel to enter army offices with-out permission.[57]

Because the army had general responsibility for the health and safety of the men, disagreements could arise on whether a certain work project was appro-priate or whether the weather was suitable. If weather forced a cancellation of a workday, it was usually made up on Saturday, a day partially reserved for camp maintenance, and that could cause friction. When emergencies arose, such as fires or floods, the CO could assume total authority over the men and dis-rupt normal work routines. There were many issues that could not be resolved in written regulations and had to be worked out on the ground. But usually the officers and supervisors cooperated amicably. They lived together and ate together and had a common interest in keeping camp operations running as smoothly as possible.[58]

The superintendent was variously assisted by two foresters, eight foremen, a blacksmith, and an engineer, as well as by the presumably helpful LEMS. These work supervisors, unlike the army men, were not required to live in camp, but many did and had their own separate quarters. They were expected to pay nom-inal fees for meals taken in camp. Salaries for these positions ranged over scales but at Promised Land State Park, Camp s-139, in 1933, the superintendent was paid $148 a month, the engineer $136, the blacksmith $96, and the eight fore-men $102 each. By 1936, the superintendent at this camp was being paid $216 a month, the six foremen were each receiving between $100 and $166 a month, the engineer was paid $166, the blacksmith $110, and a mechanic $120.[59]

There was no civil service protection for most of these skilled people and the forestry services had no reserve force in readiness as the army did. Therefore, these positions had to be filled with local workers, and political influence often affected their appointment. An early inspection by Fechner's office reported that Camp s-108, Big Pond, near Shippensburg, was badly run, mostly due to several frequently drunk foremen who had been appointed on the recommendation of the local Democratic congressman.[60] In contrast, at the very start-up of the program, Senator Guffey's sister, Mrs. Emma Guffey Miller, who sat on the Democratic National Committee, was receiving complaints from her people in Pennsylvania that they were being shut out of these jobs by state and local Republicans. She reminded President Roosevelt how important those jobs would be in building up the party base in the state.[61]

A similar complaint was directed at Governor Pinchot three weeks later. Pinchot received an angry letter from a Democratic congressman from the Stroudsburg area about the influence that the Pike County relief boards, dominated by Republicans, were having on the appointment of foresters to the camps. The congressman charged that Staley was working closely with relief board officials to make sure that only Republicans got those jobs. Pinchot looked into it and found that there had actually been an equal number of Democratic and Republican foremen appointed in Pike and in adjacent Monroe County.[62] This, however, would not be the last time that Staley would be accused of heavy-handed politics in CCC matters. After he went to work for the U.S. Forestry Service in 1935, Senator Guffey tried to get him fired, claiming that Staley had used his people to oppose Democrats in the elections of 1934 while he was head of the Department of Forests and Waters.[63] On the other hand, after the Democrats elected Governor Earle in 1934, it was the turn of Republican congressmen to complain about being shut out of CCC appointments.[64]

Political influence rarely affected the selection of enrollees. Nor was there any politics involved in the skilled personnel who worked for the Departments of Agriculture (U.S. Forestry Service and the Soil Conservation Service) or Interior (National Park Service). But when these so-called technical people needed other skilled or experienced workers, such as blacksmiths, mechanics, or foremen, local congressmen usually recommended appointees from lists of locally qualified men drawn up by the services. These lists were known as "Friant lists," named after Julian N. Friant, an official in the Department of Agriculture who initiated the system. Superintendents supposedly had the right to reject outright incompetents, but there were many complaints from the foresters that they had been pressured to hire unqualified people. In Pennsylvania, the Department of Forests and Waters needed permission from Washington to fire incompetent foremen.[65]

A critical report on this matter of political influences on the CCC was published by the *Forestry News Digest* in March 1936 and was picked up by the *New York Herald-Tribune*. The resultant publicity was embarrassing to Fechner's office.[66] The political side of the CCC was a murky area, one that cannot be investigated with any precision, although a study done for the American Council on Education in 1942 claimed that 60 percent of the skilled positions in CCC camps were filled by improper political influence.[67]

CAMP LIFE IN THE FIRST YEAR

For the enrollees, life in the work camps continued some of the patterns they had experienced in the army conditioning camps. The young men had gotten acquainted with their Company comrades in the army camps, but now they began to learn the ropes of life in their very different work camps in the woods. City boys were treated to their first sights of bear, deer, porcupines, groundhogs, and beaver, and lectures on rattlesnakes were a vital part of their initiation into a forest environment. Tony Cellini from South Philadelphia was not untypical of city boys. Before his time in the CCC, he had known of two kinds of trees— Christmas trees and all the others.[68]

Some of the daily routine was similar to the regimen they had adjusted to in the conditioning camps. Reveille was usually bugled at 6:00, followed by a flag-raising ceremony and breakfast. After making their beds with an army-style tightness that could bounce a quarter upon inspection, they were trucked out to the work sites around 8:00. They worked till noon, ate lunch in the field— sometimes a hot meal, but usually sandwiches—and then worked until 4:00 or so, depending on travel time.[69] Back in camp, there would be some free time to clean up and relax before the flag-lowering ceremony and dinner at 5:30, in dress uniform. Evenings were spent in classes, recreation, watching an occasional movie, or on a trip to town if that was feasible. Taps were blown at 10:00 for lights-out and a bed check made before 11:00.

Weekends and holidays were work-free, unless bad weather had prevented work during the week. On Sundays, church services were offered to those who wanted to participate. It was the rare work camp that had a resident chaplain, but between the army's full- and part-time itinerant chaplains and the community-based clergymen, the men had ample opportunity to attend services at camp or in town.[70]

The Quartermaster Department of the army was not initially prepared for the prodigious appetites of the young men, previously undernourished and now ravenous after hard labor in the woods. One camp inspection report on S-71 in

Fig. 10 Evening wash-up at Camp s-141, Indiantown Gap (Lebanon County), in August 1933. Pennsylvania State Archives

Centre County reported the menu for a typical and randomly picked day, October 16, 1934. For breakfast, the men had bacon and egg omelets, fried potatoes, prunes, cereals, coffee, milk, and bread and butter. Lunch brought to the men in the field that day consisted of beef stew, kidney beans, potatoes, bread and butter, and coffee and milk. In case anyone was still hungry for dinner, the menu was macaroni and cheese, creamed green beans, lettuce, tomatoes, bread and butter, hot chocolate, sugar, evaporated milk, and chocolate pudding. Of course the camp PX was open for late evening snacks as well.[71]

In most work camps in Pennsylvania in the first six months in 1933 the enrollees lived in army tents. These were usually of World War I vintage with wooden floors, and most of them were designed to sleep six men with a portable

Fig. 11 Mess call at Camp s-56, Licking Creek (Mifflin County), in May 1933. Pennsylvania State Archives

heating stove inside. They were easily set up, depending on the site chosen. One camp reportedly completed the job in one hour! In contrast, at the early camp at Hillsgrove, two hundred men from Philadelphia arrived at "camp" to find that there would be no shelter until they had cut down trees to make a path for the trucks to deliver the tents. It was such a rainy week that they even had to buy dry wood from local farmers to cook with, but *Happy Days* assured readers that "the men sang" through it all.[72]

Some of the tent canvas had deteriorated in storage, and leaky roofs resulted in some unpleasant nights in the mountains of Pennsylvania for recruits, even in the comparatively mild early summer. The weather had been a concern when the program began, with Fechner worrying in May that work camps in the northern states might have to be moved south when the hard weather came. Some of that hard weather hit Pennsylvania earlier than expected, in late August. A terrible storm swept through the state, devastating nine of the tent camp sites and drowning one enrollee, George Kester of Company #383, at Camp s-95, La Porte.[73]

Fig. 12 Mail delivery at Camp s-51, Pine Grove Furnace, in May 1933. Pennsylvania State Archives

CCC camps were usually located in rustic and isolated settings. A student of the CCC educational program in 1934 provided a picturesque description of his experiences in looking for camps that still rings true today for people seeking old camp sites: "These little villages show on no map that can be purchased in a city shop. . . . I have ridden behind an Army chauffeur with a Corps Area map

Fig. 13 CCC enrollees outside their tents at Camp s-95, Forksville, in May 1933. Pennsylvania State Archives

as his guide, and seen him hunt his camp for an hour. Only by questioning at country filling stations, by nosing up dirt roads, by guessing hazardly at rude forks can one stumble at last upon the more elusive of them."[74]

Few camp buildings of the CCC era remain in Pennsylvania today. The best preserved camp complex is that of s-70 in the Michaux State Forest, leased and admirably maintained since the 1940s by Methodist church groups. Parker Dam State Park has a well-preserved barracks building, which houses a CCC museum. Promised Land State Park has a few utility buildings and an officers' quarters that now houses an attractive display of CCC artifacts and memorabilia. Laurel

Fig. 14 Mess hall under construction at Camp s-141, Indiantown Gap, in August 1933. Pennsylvania State Archives

Hill State Park claims to have more original CCC camp buildings than any other state park, including some barracks.

But at most of the CCC camp sites today, curious or pious pilgrims looking for places where CCC men, sometimes their ancestors, lived, worked, and gamboled with youthful energy beyond imagining, will find themselves driving on poorly marked gravel roads, traipsing through dark forests, overgrown and snake infested, or gazing across open meadows now devoted to playground equipment. Sadly, the site of Camp Joyce Kilmer, s-148, in Union County, now serves as a junk yard for the State Forestry Department.[75]

The camp site of s-51 near Pine Grove Furnace State Park in Cumberland County is more typical. It sits off the road on Michaux State Forest land. Intrepid visitors hiking through tangled underbrush will need a vivid imagination to re-create the camp life of the hundreds of young men who spent formative months of their lives there. One can still see a few macadam foundations of buildings off to the side of a trail, and the more adventurous can hike their way upstream to a dam and sluice channel built by the men. A small pond that served as a swimming hole does not look very inviting today, but the inspired tourist might be able to close his or her eyes and conjure up ghostly images of young men splashing and frolicking after a hard day's work. Perhaps the most

Fig. 15 Entrance to Camp s-129, the "Governor Pinchot Camp" in English Center (Lycoming County), in September 1933. Pennsylvania State Archives

Fig. 16 Temporary quarters and mess tent at Camp s-51, Pine Grove Furnace, in May 1933. Pennsylvania State Archives

poignant relic of the CCC presence at Pine Grove Furnace is an intricately designed water fountain, now decrepit and unused, that clearly was a work of skill and pride.

The creation of the CCC and then the arrival of CCC camps were, with very few exceptions, warmly welcomed by Pennsylvania communities nearby.[76] Indeed, the members of some communities were not content with only one camp in their vicinity but pleaded with Pinchot to set up more and complained when camps were shut down. The camps meant increased business for local contractors and merchants because the policy of the CCC was to make purchases in local areas whenever possible. These purchases of food, gasoline, and hardware profited local depressed economies, and even some of the $5 a month available to the two hundred men in camp to spend on weekends in town was appreciated. Communities usually welcomed the arrival of CCC men, contributing recreation equipment, arranging sports competition with local teams, and hosting weekend dances.[77] There was very little hostility, let alone violence, toward camps in the neighborhood, although the recent laying off of sixty employees in the Clearfield State Forest produced some resentment when men at the CCC camp located there seemed to be doing some of their old work.[78]

Meanwhile, the men were amusing themselves in camp after work hours. One camp crowned as bread-eating champion "Fats" De Carlo of Uniontown, who ate an impressive twenty-three slices in one sitting. Another camp created a kind of fraternity, the "Order of the Hairy Lip," open only to those whose mustaches were visible at ten yards. Other camps organized minstrel shows in blackface, still a popular entertainment in those years. Company #1322 at North Bend started a vegetable garden with seeds provided by local relief organizations. They planted a variety of vegetables, but no "spuds" (KP peeling duty being one of the more unpleasant aspects of camp life).[79]

An important activity, almost universal in the camps, was the publication of some kind of camp newspaper, about five thousand of which eventually appeared for runs of various length. The typical paper was several pages of mimeographed reports on camp life, editorial essays, poetry, and sometimes advertising. Many of them tried to come up with snappy titles, such as "The Cammal's Hump," put out by Company #365, S-124, at Cammal. *Happy Days,* the unofficial national newspaper of CCC activities, encouraged these efforts, gave them some professional advice, and occasionally ran contests for the best papers. An early Pennsylvania paper, "The Barracks," put out by Company #1301, Camp SP-3 at Broughton, was judged the best paper in the Third Corps and tied for the best in the country in 1934.[80]

These camp newspapers provide interesting information about camp activities and personnel and are an invaluable source for anyone looking for information about individual camps or relatives or friends who served in the camps. Unfortunately, extant copies of CCC camp newspapers exist only in scattered sites—at some State Park offices, in Archival files with CCC material, in private hands. The most extensive collection, garnered from many sources, including the Library of Congress, is in the hands of the Center for Research Libraries in Chicago in microform. Unfortunately, the fees charged by this organization make it practically inaccessible to most researchers.[81]

Fig. 17 Scenes from Camp s-141, Indiantown Gap, August 1933. Boxing (top) was one of the recreational activities at camp. The lower photo shows an evening parade. Pennsylvania State Archives

Fig. 18 Noncommissioned officers pose for the camera at Camp S-141, Indiantown Gap. Pennsylvania State Archives

Deer hunting season that first year, and in subsequent years, presented special problems. In some of the camps the men were ordered to remain inside when the fireworks began on the first day. John J. Graham, who was stationed at a camp in the Allegheny National Forest, remembered it as sounding like the Battle of Gettysburg. Lewis Staley, in the absence of instructions from Washington, recommended that COs purchase plenty of red cloth to mark their men in the woods, put up perimeter signs around work crews, and surround their camps with chest-high chicken wire as legal protection against roving hunters. One enterprising commanding officer reportedly rented out to hunters, at $3 a night, the bunks of men who went home for weekends![82]

What the CCC Means to Me

In 1937, Fred C. Jacobs won first prize in a camp-sponsored contest for his essay on "What the CCC Means to Me." Jacobs's winning essay was forwarded to President Roosevelt by the assistant educational adviser, along with a copy of a letter of congratulations to Mr. Jacobs from Assistant Field Director Fred Kurtz. Excerpts from the essay (which can be found in the FDR Library at Hyde Park) follow. Spelling and punctuation appear as they do in the original.

To me, a veteran of the World War, the CCC means early to bed and early to rise, feeling fine when I get up in the morning and fine when I go to bed at night—a ravenous appetite, plenty of pep and enthusiasm and the satisfaction of being a live.

After the days work I usually spend the early evenings in our recreation hall playing checkers, reading the papers and chatting and joking with the men. I call most every man I know "Doc" and they in turn call me "Doc." "Doctor" for a change and the man always smiles. This is indicative of the good fellowship in the CCC.

Twice a week we have movies and the men eagerly anticipate movie night. The United States Department of Agriculture has shown a number of interesting educational films in conjunction with the regular movie program—films of forestry, agriculture, oil, mines and progressive cities, states and industries of the United States. . . .

Five days a week the lights in our camp go out at 9:15 p.m. and Saturdays and Sundays 10:00 p.m. I go to bed as lights go out and in five minutes am sound asleep. On week days I am up at 6:00 to 6:15 a.m. and usually feel good and anxious to eat and get going. During the week we breakfast at 7:00 a.m.; Sundays at 8:00 a.m. Work of the day for all hands starts at 8:00 a.m. sharp, with an hour off for lunch and quitting time 4:00 p.m. Saturdays there is no work in the woods; the men police around the Camp area, inspection at 11:00 a.m. and duties for the week are ended. . . .

I think men here do less drinking than on the outside; this is no doubt due to a well balanced food menu, getting the right amount of exercise, sleep and following regular habits in daily routine.

Upon the completion of my present six months enrollment period I will have $135.00 in the hands of the Quartermaster Department. Other men in the CCC during the same period will have sent home that much or more. I consider this probably more than I could have saved on a job in some city drawing $90.00 or even $100.00 per month. When you consider that board, clothes, lodging, medical *and dental service are free, and many other services and articles at reduced rates, in the CCC,—well, it would be a lot worse. . . .*

As I view my life here, the CCC has meant to me, above all else, freedom from worry, moderate comfort and an outlet for my stored-up energies. To know that you have warm raiment, food in the larder, coal in the bin, a roof over your head, good cheer in camp and something to do makes life worth while. . . .

The CCC means that the country man meets the city man and learns of city life. He hears stories of the night life on Broadway, the old Barbary coast in San Francisco, the dens of hell that existed in the Klondike during the gold rush days, the flying fish off the sunny shores of California, the Everglades in Florida and the rock-ribbed coast and seafaring towns of Maine.

Since entering the CCC I have seen many projects undertaken and brought to completion. Men blazing trails, building levees, dynamiting rock, curbing turbulent streams, fighting fires and doing everything humanly possible to cherish and nourish nature. In this Camp we work principally to save and conserve one of her greatest gifts to mankind, the trees. I am reminded of a line from the poem "Trees"— "Fools like me write poems but only God can make a tree.". . .

Finally, the CCC means a movement fostered by our great Government for the upbuilding and moulding of character and health in boys who were undernourished, unemployed, down in morale and looked forward to the future in hopeless despair. It all means that if there is anything good in a man or a boy the CCC will bring it out and make better him a better citizen for the future.

When we consider that our Government has generously and magnanimously made the CCC movement possible, it means respect and reverance for this good old U.S.A.; that we, as members of the CCC, in big things, in little things and in all things, stand out for all of that which makes America First.

(The End)

Because the men's work day was set at eight hours, including transportation to and from the job sites (unlike the technical supervisors from Interior or Agriculture whose work day did not include transit time), camp supervisors began to raise concerns very early on about how to occupy the men for the rest of the day. General Paul Malone was concerned that, with an effective workday of six hours, there would be too much leisure time for "active young men." He intended to fill that time with "useful pursuits" and had been working with Pinchot and Staley from an early date in getting forestry educational materials into the camps—pamphlets, filmstrips, and a few motion pictures.[83]

Commanders and supervisors in the camps did what they could to fill up the men's free time, but in the summer months, at least, outdoor recreation was usually their first choice. With the approach of fall and fewer hours of daylight, the scattered calls for a more formal camp education program received a more serious hearing, and the president authorized such a program in December 1933.

The educational program of the CCC always had the quality of an afterthought about it and was not clearly conceived nor well structured. Many CCC supervisors thought that the on-the-job training the men received was sufficient, but other administrators, like Frank Persons, were concerned with providing more useful and employable skills than forestry work for men who would be returning to city lives. The program that emerged in 1934 offered voluntary, after-work instruction in a variety of academic and vocational subjects, enabling a certain number of motivated and ambitious men to acquire useful skills and even career paths, but it left many others without any meaningful instruction.

Clarence C. Marsh was appointed by the Interior Department's Office of Education to be director of CCC education in early 1934. Marsh served only about a year in this position before he resigned out of frustration caused by the apathy, and even outright hostility, to the program that he received from both Fechner and the army. In Pennsylvania, Marsh selected two prominent educators, James Rule of Harrisburg, and M. S. McDowell of State College, to make the appointments of educational advisers for each of the camps.

Marsh sent along to Louis Howe, the president's closest political adviser, the first list of adviser appointees, mostly unemployed teachers, together with the names of those who had recommended them.[84] Howe was very anxious lest these appointments might be influenced by partisan (read: Republican) politics. Responding to a complaint by Democratic Congressman Mees of Pennsylvania, Howe sent the list of educational advisers appointed to Pennsylvania camps, each adviser on a salary of $2,000 a year, to Democratic officials throughout the state, asking them to scrutinize it for evidence of adverse political influence in the appointments.[85] Political patronage did not exactly control these appointments, but it was a picture in chiaroscuro style.

The educational program got off to an uneven and shaky start. Although some camps were able to expand course offerings from the solid base they had established on their own that first summer, others lagged behind. A camp inspection of s-139 at Promised Land State Park reported that, as late as June 1934, no educational adviser had yet arrived and no formal classes were offered at night, just a few films.[86]

The educational advisers were under the supervision of the commanding army officers once they were in camp, one of the many administrative confusions in the CCC organization. And because the educational program in the camps was thereby under the army's jurisdiction, the attitude of camp commanders was crucial. One educational adviser was introduced to the men by the CO with a somewhat less than enthusiastic endorsement: "Boys, the Government has decided to give you an educational program. You don't have to take it unless you want it, and I don't know that it will amount to anything. But here's Mr. Smith who will have charge of it, and he can talk to you."[87]

Over the years an amazing variety of subjects taught after hours in the CCC camps evolved, and a popular image emerged of young Abe Lincolns studying into the nights after long hard days of log splitting. Lessons taught covered almost every conceivable academic topic as well as arts and crafts and highly technical subjects like auto mechanics or metalworking. The courses taught were as varied as camp personnel felt qualified to offer, and instructors included not just the educational adviser but also the military, technical personnel from Interior or Agriculture, and even enrollees themselves. By 1938, for example, there were 603 different subjects being taught in camps. Of the 23,168 people offering this instruction, only 1,537 were the educational advisers. Army personnel giving classes numbered 3,033, 9,895 were technical people, 688 local citizens volunteered their services, and 5,767 of the camp instructors were the enrollees themselves![88]

ANOTHER SIX MONTHS

By October 1933, as the initial first six-month enlistment period drew to a close, the conservation work done by the men had made an impressive start, and the CCC penchant for collecting and reporting mind-numbing statistics on its work projects had begun. In Pennsylvania, some two million gooseberry and currant bushes, the most important hosts for the fungus that causes white pine blister rust, had been uprooted and burned; six new steel fire observation towers, each 80 feet high and linked by telephone, had been erected; some 850 miles of forest roads and 900 miles of trails had been built or improved; and 80 miles of telephone wires strung up.[89]

With the CCC off to such an impressive start and Pennsylvania's experiences being replicated, more or less, throughout the country, Roosevelt decided to extend the program for an additional six months and issued an Executive Order to that effect on August 19. Director Fechner was given the go-ahead to build more permanent structures for winter quarters, and he told Howe that he had decided that wooden structures would make the cheapest and most suitable type of buildings.[90]

That fall the army quartermaster oversaw the letting out of contracts for lumber and building materials for the construction of more substantial living quarters for 1,443 camps across the country, a task that was described as the biggest housing project in history. Local contractors, using teams of about thirty workers, were hired by the Corps headquarters, usually at union wage levels. The design of buildings and camp sites varied considerably from camp to camp as did the number of buildings. Fechner reported an average of nineteen buildings per camp in 1936, with construction costs usually at $20,000 per camp.[91]

Politics, of course, played a role in these building contracts. The ECW assistant director, James McEntee, wrote a contractor in Camp Hill, advising him to contact local Democratic Party officials for information on how best to obtain this work. Preference was also given to union contractors. McEntee, who, like Fechner, had come from the trade union movement, defended this practice by citing the need for speed and reliability in letting out these contracts, and working through local building councils was the method usually adopted. By Thanksgiving, most Pennsylvania men were in the newly constructed barracks.[92]

By 1936 the CCC had worked out a system of precut supplies of wood for prefabricated and standardized buildings, to be laid out in more or less standardized U-shaped pattern of barracks, supervisors' quarters, mess hall, recreation hall, bathhouses, and utility buildings. This system made it easier to pack up and move camps when work projects were completed, although the resulting uniformity lacked the charming individuality of the earliest camps.[93]

Although most of the early CCC buildings were built by local skilled contractors, the CCC men themselves, of course, built many buildings, such as mess halls, officers' quarters, recreational buildings, and storage sheds. Though few CCC men had skilled backgrounds, with supervision and direction they were capable of impressive construction work. The handsome and sturdy tourist cabins still in use at many state parks in Pennsylvania are clear evidence of this.

But those kinds of buildings were intended to be permanent and were labor-intensive projects, unlike most camp buildings, which were always thought of as temporary.

The extension of the CCC for another six-month term not only resulted in extensive building projects but also required that the process of approving new work projects and camp sites had to start up again. Fechner warned Pinchot that winter weather might require shutting down some of the work in Pennsylvania unless he could get his forestry people to obtain speedy approval for new projects for the next six months. He also recommended that Pinchot contact Pennsylvania congressmen, asking them to back projects in which they had an interest. As early as August 28 Pinchot was able to reply that Pennsylvania had submitted seventy-one work proposals, with another seventeen on the way.[94]

Once new work projects had been lined up and the number of work camps established, the state selecting apparatus had to be cranked up again with an eye toward filling October quotas. This was a bit more complicated now, because not only would recruits have to be enrolled to replace the men who had not completed, for one reason or other, their six-month tours, but rough estimates had to be made of how many of the men in camp would re-enlist, as they were allowed to, for another six-month term. Approximately 175,000 of the original class eventually decided to re-enlist, and the enrollment in October was finalized at 125,000 replacements. When many camps subsequently became a little light, it was decided to have an intermediate enrollment in January 1934 of another 25,000 recruits. Thereafter enrollments would take place four times a year.[95]

Persons's office at the Labor Department assigned Pennsylvania a quota for what was now called the second enrollment period in October 1933. The number of men in Pennsylvania camps, which had hovered around 18,000 that first summer, increased to 20,400 by January 1934. By now Eric Biddle, executive director of SERB, had turned over the CCC selection responsibility to his assistant field director, J. Fred Kurtz, who began meting out quotas to the local Emergency Relief Boards throughout the state and issuing policy guidelines as well. When the October enrollment was completed, Pennsylvania had its entire quota of men in its own camps, the men who had been sent west in the first enrollment period having been recalled.

Most of the camps were continued from the first period and a few were brand-new. Of the total 104 Pennsylvania camps in the second enrollment period, 85 were on state forest lands, 6 on state game lands, 7 in the Allegheny National

Forest, 2 at Gettysburg, 1 on state National Guard lands, 2 in state parks, and 1 in the city park in Reading. Because Pennsylvania could provide work, four companies of men from the Second Corps (New York, New Jersey, and Delaware) who had gone west in the first period were now moved back east and occupied new camps in eastern Pennsylvania for the next six months, after which those camps were filled with Pennsylvania companies.[96]

In the midst of all this activity surrounding the extension of the CCC, Governor Pinchot received the tragic news of Forester Stuart's death. Stuart had apparently committed suicide, falling from a seventh-floor window in an office adjacent to his own in the Department of Agriculture building in Washington on October 23. Stuart, a former protégé and friend, had headed the Department of Forests and Waters during Pinchot's first term as governor and had moved on to become head of the U.S. Forestry Service in 1928. He had experienced a nervous breakdown in early 1932 but had recovered to become one of the key men involved in the planning and implementation of the CCC.

William Terry, a messenger for the Forest Service, was approaching the building shortly after 8:00 A.M. when he saw Stuart crash onto a car parked below the window. The window had a low sill, and the initial speculation was that Stuart might have experienced vertigo and fallen out. There was puzzlement, however, over why he was in that particular office. The window in his own office had a fire escape, which would have obstructed jumping, but the window from which he fell provided a clear fall. He left behind no suicide note, but he had been complaining of ill health and nervous fatigue due to overwork.

Pinchot was devastated by the news and rushed off a telegram of condolence to Stuart's wife. In addition to his widow, Stuart left behind two young daughters. His successor at the Forestry Service was J. Fred Wilcox, who served until his own death in 1938.[97]

The new year of 1934 found Pennsylvania's CCC men hunkered down in permanent buildings with plenty of cut wood to keep the barracks warm during long winter nights and more food than most of them had ever had in their lives. They also had been supplied with winter clothing and bedding through another impressive effort by the army quartermaster. The men were given paid leaves on Thanksgiving and Christmas when they could return home or simply relax and enjoy the special holiday meals in camp—for many of them the first time they had tasted turkey.[98]

Fechner worried that heavy snows in the mountains of Pennsylvania might cut off and isolate some of the camps, but he had to turn down Staley's request

Fig. 19 Pleased with the early success of the CCC, President Roosevelt extended the program for another six months in August 1933. This meant that enrollees would be working through the winter. Here CCC men from Camp S-94, Edgemere (Pike County), burn brush along Porter Lake in March 1934. Pennsylvania State Archives

for fifty-eight snowplows for lack of funds. The governor's office assured Fechner that the state Highway Department would do its best to keep the roads around the camps clear and passable.[99] The first heavy snow fell in early November, and Camp S-140 in Lackawanna County, for one, was ill-equipped for such weather. Finding conditions intolerable, twenty-six boys left camp. Persons assured Eric Biddle that emergency supplies of stoves and bedding were being rushed to the camp and, if the AWOLs returned soon, their offense would be overlooked.[100]

Robert Ward, who was spending his first months at Camp S-91 at Watrous that winter, remembers the weather as being particularly severe. When temperatures

Fig. 20 Robert Ward at Camp s-91, Watrous (Tioga County), in 1934. Ward was from Wellsboro, where his family owned a dairy farm. Photo courtesy of Robert Ward

dropped to forty degrees below zero, the men objected to being transported to work sites in trucks with only light canvas protection. A few dozen of them went on strike, but most changed their minds when the camp commander threatened to discharge them.[101]

Of course, occasional complaints arose from the men, usually about food or dictatorial cos.[102] But "well begun is half done" goes the old saw. The ccc camps in Pennsylvania would expand and contract over the next eight years. Some would be shut down, sometimes reopened later, and others would be erected anew; work projects would be completed, new ones conceived, and by the end, some 184,000 young Pennsylvania men would have moved into the camps, gained some weight as well as some work experience, maybe learned a useful skill, and then moved out to start on an amazing variety of work experiences and life stories. The remainder of this book can sample only a few chapters of this epic tale.

2

ENROLLING PENNSYLVANIA MEN FOR THE CCC

Pennsylvania's admirable record in the first year of the CCC owed much not only to Governor Pinchot and his well-trained foresters in the Department of Forests and Waters, but also to the efficient process of selecting enrollees set up by the State Emergency Relief Board (SERB). Over the next nine years more young men from Pennsylvania would be recruited for CCC camps than from any other state except New York. And in some years in the late 1930s, Pennsylvania ranked first in numbers enrolled. A close examination of how the process worked and of the diverse difficulties faced by the state's selectors will provide important insights into how the organization evolved in a changing economic environment.

J. FRED KURTZ

The man chiefly responsible for selecting Pennsylvania enrollees was J. Fred Kurtz. In 1933 Kurtz was the assistant field director of SERB, and by summer 1934 he had clearly emerged as the principal operational manager of the CCC selection process in the state. Kurtz later claimed that he had been involved from the beginning, but most of the early correspondence to and from the SERB office on CCC matters was in the name of Field Director Richard Stilwell or Executive Director Eric Biddle.[1] Whatever Kurtz's role in the first year, by the second summer of the program he had assumed charge of selecting Pennsylvania enrollees. Kurtz would provide the Pennsylvania side of the CCC story with its only thread of continuity. Governors would come and go, as did their cabinet secretaries for relief and conservation; camps in the state, with their enrollees and supervisors, also came and went. Through it all, up to the end of the program, Kurtz continued to supervise the process of selecting Pennsylvania's seemingly inexhaustible supply of unemployed young men.[2]

In earlier years, Kurtz had owned and operated a number of businesses, including some coal mines, but he faced ruin in the Depression. In 1930 he went to work for the Pennsylvania Bureau of Corrections, but he transferred to SERB in 1932 where Richard Stilwell appointed him as his assistant field director.[3]

As a CCC administrator, Kurtz impressed people with his intelligence and energy. But he also came across as inflexible and lacking in tact in interpersonal matters. Part of his problem in dealing with people was undoubtedly caused by the insecurity he felt over his position, which had no civil service protection.[4] Kurtz was always in fear of his frequently changing superiors. When the Democrats came into power in 1935, he became "jittery about my future." He began to importune the Office of Selection, headed by Frank Persons in the Labor Department, for a position in Washington, assuring them that even though he was a registered Republican, he voted Democratic as often as not.[5] When no position was offered him in the national office, he begged Persons to recommend him to his various superiors who rose and fell over the next few years with the changing political winds in Harrisburg. Persons was happy to oblige these requests, but one detects notes of impatience and even bemused condescension in his correspondence to and about Kurtz.[6]

Kurtz also had strained relations with the military people involved in the CCC. Any complaints that young recruits had with their camp experiences were often directed to the local relief officials who had selected them. These officials would send these complaints to Kurtz who in turn usually passed them on to Persons. Because many of the complaints about camps centered on the CO, the War Department came to resent Kurtz for these reported criticisms.[7]

For example, in early 1935 Kurtz received a particularly serious charge from the Bedford office about a CO in Camp S-71 who was reportedly drunk half the time and who had the men sledgehammering rocks all day. The young complainant wrote, "I would sooner trap rats yet." The investigator sent to check out the allegations found nothing amiss at the camp and thought the charges might be related to the Republican politics of the officer. Other complaints that Kurtz forwarded to Persons involved alleged drunkenness at some of the Veterans' camps, which he felt was giving the program an unsavory image and hurting recruiting.[8]

Persons encouraged Kurtz to cultivate closer relations with the Third Corps military personnel and to pursue these kinds of complaints more amicably with the army supervisors before making allegations. But, despite these occasional criticisms, Persons clearly respected Kurtz's opinions on policy matters and occasionally adopted his suggestions as national policy.[9] Moreover, no one ever questioned Kurtz's ability or effort in running the country's second largest CCC selection system. Persons wrote to Fechner in 1936, "Mr. Kurtz is one of our most alert, enthusiastic and capable selecting agents."[10]

THE SELECTION PROCESS

The program of Emergency Conservation Work (ECW) was hastily cobbled together in the crisis months of 1933 and never quite lost that "emergency" characteristic. It was originally authorized for six months by Executive Order on April 5, 1933, the date that came to be celebrated as the birthday of the CCC. It was given a six-month extension, also by Executive Order, on August 19, 1933. In January 1934, the president told Fechner that he wanted ECW for another year and asked Congress for $275 million to run it until April 1935.[11] The following year, 1935, Congress gave the program more of a legislative foundation and a full two-year term. In 1937, Roosevelt and Fechner proposed to make the CCC a permanent agency, but Congress granted it only a three-year extension. The Corps, then, was subject to annual budgetary authorizations, and when Congress failed to appropriate funds for it in June 1942, the CCC simply faded out of existence with no formal execution rite.

But the birth of the CCC with that original six-month authorization in 1933 created an imprint that would ever mark its administration. Men would continue to be enrolled for six-month periods, work projects were authorized for the same periods, and every six months the whole camp structure would change. Camps would close; new ones would be opened; and old companies of men would receive new members, be disbanded, or be moved to other camps or even other states.

Because of fairly alarming rates of attrition in CCC camps in the first year, Frank Persons decided to allow enrollment of replacements in the months of January and July, halfway through the regular turnover of men and camps, which occurred in April and October. At first, in January 1934, the technical work supervisors in the camps were allowed to recruit locally for whatever number of men they required. The precedent of allowing the camps to recruit directly ended in June 1934 when Persons, faced with replacing 68,000 of the original men whose maximum enlistment tours were about to expire, decided to use the state selectors for the intermediate periods as well as for the regular enrollments.[12]

But that early practice of accepting replacement recruits at the camps continued on a small scale and proved an irritant to the selectors. Finally, in 1941, in the last summer of the program, as the number of recruits dried up, applicants were officially allowed to enroll directly at the camps, to the chagrin of state selectors.

Kurtz supervised the July 1934 selection process for replacements in which Pennsylvania easily met its quota of 7,047.[13] The assigning of state quotas had become more complex after 1933. Persons and his office had to determine the number of camp vacancies that would open up across the country and then assign each state a portion of this number. Much guesstimating seems to have been involved because the assigned quotas for states were partly based on population, partly on the number of people out of work, and partly on the track record of the state selectors.[14] Occasionally Persons would respond to political requests and allow selectors like Kurtz to increase the number of recruits in certain areas.[15]

When the first year of CCC work had been completed, Persons asked the state selectors to survey local attitudes toward the new program.[16] Eric Biddle of SERB sent the request on to his local relief boards, and their findings constitute a kind of early report card on the CCC. The responses were overwhelmingly positive. Some of the early fears that the CCC would promote militarism or bring rowdiness to local communities had been allayed. To be sure, there were still a few reported complaints about this "expensive experiment" (Bucks County), this "New Deal artificiality" (Schuylkill County), as well as reports of too many greedy parents whose only interest in the CCC seemed to be the allotment check they received every month. But the positive responses far outnumbered the criticisms. Most relief officials reported parental satisfaction in the "changes in the health, appearance, attitude and spirit" of their sons when they returned home (Montgomery County). Philadelphia relief officials conducted the most extensive sampling of 722 enrollees and their parents. Among the young men who had served in camp, 74 percent said they liked it; among their parents, who hadn't, the approval rate was 83 percent.

One concern, expressed by many, touched on the most trenchant criticism of the CCC: what would the boys do when they returned home to economic conditions not so different from the ones that had attracted them into the CCC in the first place? The CCC was effective in providing short-term relief assistance for a portion of unemployed youth and their families, but its impact on the general economy was always minimal. The work experience and the education the CCC provided were no guarantees of employment for the young man discharged back to his home community. And the CCC never developed programs for following up and assisting his re-entry.

Consequently, many men regretted having to leave camp. Over the life of the program, about 16 percent of them would re-enlist for another tour. But from 1933 to 1935, the maximum enlistment period allowed was one year, which seemed too short for many of the boys who had had "a wonderful experience"(Allegheny County). One boy, who had been at Camp s-82 in Waterville, wrote to his local recruiter: "It is a swell place to spend the summer in the mountains with fresh air," the work was "none too hard," and "we have well balanced meals which is the most important part."[17]

PEAK YEARS: 1935–1936

There were important changes for the CCC in 1935, both in Harrisburg and Washington. Newly elected Governor Earle replaced Biddle with Robert L. Johnson as executive director of SERB. Kurtz was left, albeit anxiously, untouched by Johnson to continue doing the actual work of CCC selection.[18]

Changes in Washington that year, in the form of three pieces of legislation, had a more profound impact on the CCC. These were: (1) the 1935 extension of the ECW program for two more years and its expansion to what became its peak levels; (2) the creation of the Works Progress Administration (WPA), the massive public works program that was the capstone of New Deal work relief efforts; and (3) the creation of the Social Security program.

These programs combined to make the Federal Emergency Relief Administration of 1933 redundant, and it went out of business in December 1935. Now the only direct relief given by the federal government was in the form of work relief for "employables." The WPA and CCC provided the bulk of those jobs. Relief for nonemployable people—the blind, the aged, the disabled, mothers with dependent children—now fell entirely on the states, with some assistance from Social Security on matching-fund bases. Such, at least, was the new theory, but the expensive work relief projects of the New Deal never succeeded in employing everyone who was out of work, and thus many "employables" had to be continued on direct relief by the states.[19]

For the CCC this meant that, in the judgment of Roosevelt and his advisers, the jobs programs of the federal government had to be reserved *exclusively* for those who were not only needy and unemployed, but actually on state relief rolls. Moreover, the relief requirement for families of CCC applicants was restricted to those receiving *public* relief—WPA work or county poor board assistance. It did not apply to those receiving assistance from private agencies like the Red Cross.[20]

In Pennsylvania, CCC selectors had been giving priority to young men from their relief caseloads, but many unemployed young men whose families were not actually on relief were recruited as well. Indeed, in March 1935 Kurtz was complaining to Persons about reports he was getting of the army allowing the technical services to directly recruit local boys who sometimes were from wealthy families. And one CO was allegedly recruiting Philadelphia prizefighters to help him police his camp.[21]

Now this tightening of eligibility requirements for CCC enrollment was curiously working at cross-purposes with the dramatic expansion of the ECW that Roosevelt and Fechner were planning. Their projected goals for 1935 were to build 1,276 new camps, making a total of 2,916, and putting 600,000 men in them by summer.[22] As it turned out, these goals were unrealistic and could not be met. But still, the period from late spring 1935 into early 1936 saw more than 500,000 men in 2,652 work camps, numbers never approached before or after.[23] To help meet the demands of new camps, some 3,000 army reserve officers, as well as some navy and marine reserve officers, were now assigned to supplement and sometimes replace the regular officers still in the program.[24] To help fill the new camps, the Junior eligibility age was raised from twenty-five to twenty-eight and a bit later lowered from eighteen to seventeen. Moreover, the Veterans Administration was now allowed to recruit men who had been drafted in 1917 and 1918 but rejected for actual service.[25]

In Pennsylvania the number of camps peaked at 141 in 1935.[26] Filling these camps with Pennsylvania men presented enormous challenges to Kurtz and his selectors. Even the modest efforts at liberalizing eligibility standards for recruits did not compensate for the requirement that they all be from the public relief rolls. The pressures on selectors to find more CCC recruits from this diminished pool of eligibles was intense and resulted in Pennsylvania being unable to meet its quotas for the first time.

The crisis brought Dean Snyder, Persons's assistant, to Harrisburg on June 6, 1935, for three days of meetings with Kurtz. In these meetings, Kurtz fretted that he would be able to get only about half of his quota of 29,254 men from relief rolls, and he feared the loss of CCC moneys to the state if he could not fill the camps with Pennsylvania men. He whined that other states, with lower standards for relief eligibility, would more easily be able to recruit. He asked for permission to recruit among men from other states who were temporarily residing in SERB-run transient camps, but Snyder vetoed the idea because transients usually had no dependents to receive allotment checks.[27]

Kurtz pleaded, again unsuccessfully, with Persons to make CCC work compulsory for young men in relief families.[28] And he complained again when, because of low recruiting in the state, the War Department was forced to cancel its already announced transfer of some Pennsylvania boys to California. He feared that the disappointment of the boys, some of whom were looking forward to "the trip of a lifetime," would result in bad publicity and damage even more his recruiting tasks.[29]

Kurtz received some support in his attempt to loosen the eligibility standards from the Third Corps headquarters, which feared a dearth of men in the camps. And there is some evidence that younger and less experienced men were being brought into camps as LEMs by the technical supervisors. The policy, however, remained inflexible for the next two years.[30]

Pennsylvania was able to raise only a bit more than half of its projected quota that summer—15,788 enrollees. Although a few areas of the state were able to provide more men than they had been assigned (Cambria, Potter, Somerset, and Lackawanna Counties), most fell far short, and SERB director Johnson ordered selectors who had not reached at least 50 percent of their quota to explain to him and Kurtz why their numbers were so low.[31] In response to these selectors' observations and recommendations, Kurtz urged the local relief boards to start publicizing the CCC and suggested that they encourage local newspapers to publish excerpts from letters included in the SERB's 1934 survey of attitudes. He also recommended that they try to persuade local civic groups to provide eyeglasses for boys who were rejected for vision defects but qualified in all other respects.[32]

Things improved with the November enrollment when Kurtz's people were able to exceed their 8,704 quota by 1,700. This new class had 2,180 seventeen-year-olds, starting a trend toward ever-younger recruits. As a result, despite all the obstacles and griping, Pennsylvania actually enrolled more new recruits in the fiscal year 1936 (July 1935 to June 1936) than any other state—26,371.[33] Kurtz had put together the most efficient recruiting machine in the country.

This great surge in the number of CCC camps and men in 1935 was only a little less impressive than the 1933 effort. But the gains made were not sustained, and force levels soon dropped back to around 300,000 men. Roosevelt was facing an election year in 1936, and he began looking for ways to curb federal spending to ward off conservative critics. He therefore ordered dramatic and wrenching cutbacks in the ECW program for 1936. This announcement met with the kinds of congressional protest that the later shutting down of military bases in the cold war produced. More than two hundred congressmen signed a petition urging him not to close camps, and others threatened to block pieces of the president's legislative agenda unless he relented. As a result, Roosevelt was forced to back off a bit and promised to close only those camps whose work was completed.[34]

With the sharp cut in the number of camps in 1936, there was no January enrollment. Despite that break in signing up men, Kurtz's recruiters still missed filling their quotas when enrollments resumed in April and November. This shortfall in the number of Pennsylvania recruits meant that, for the first time, a significant number of enrollees from out of state (twenty-four Fourth Corps companies from the Southeast) was needed to fill up Pennsylvania's still high number of 119 work camps.[35]

Kurtz, always looking for ways to ease the constraints on his recruiters, gave approval for them to take up two boys from families with particularly strong needs, and he lobbied Persons to liberalize re-enlistment policy. Recruits had been allowed to serve a maximum of one year since the program began. But the Veterans Administration allowed men with one year of service to re-enlist for a second year, provided that they "sat out" for a year. Kurtz pointed out to Persons that many of the boys returning home from camp became discouraged when they could not find work and would like to re-enlist. He recommended a waiting period of sixty days for Juniors wanting to re-enlist for a second year. Persons received the suggestion as "interesting" and soon modified Labor Department policy to conform to that of the Veterans Administration. Enrollees were now allowed to re-enlist for a second year after a one-year period of sitting out, provided that they had served at least four months of their original enlistment term.[36]

Still looking for more ways to attract recruits, Kurtz obtained clearance from Persons to allow all enrollees to allot only $22 to their families, arguing that the standard camp allowance of $5 a month spending money was not enough for weekend entertainment, post exchange purchases, or trips home. Some boys were forced to ask for credit at the camp exchanges to such an extent that payday often brought them no real money. The adjutant-general warned COs that this was bad for morale and that they should see to it that every boy received at least some cash on payday. Kurtz made a small impact on national policy when his suggestion of allowing enrollees to keep $8 of their monthly pay became uniform policy, rather than being left to individual choice as had been the case. Kurtz tried to press his luck and asked for a new policy that would allow the boys to stay in camp until they received a job offer, but this suggestion was ignored in Washington.[37] Yet in spite of the problems in 1936—the reduction in the scale of the program, the continuing difficulties in recruiting—Kurtz and his people had managed to bring more enrollees into the CCC than any other state during the fiscal year, and by the end of June 1936 there were 17,737 men at work in Pennsylvania's 119 camps.[38]

CCC CHANGES: 1937–1939

Meanwhile in Washington big changes were in store for the CCC. Toward the end of 1936 Fechner recommended to the president that the CCC become a permanent agency, not just an *emergency* one. He had asked the Departments of Agriculture and Interior to study whether there was enough conservation work available to justify the continued existence of the CCC, and they responded that there was work enough to occupy 300,000 to 350,000 men "for many years to come."[39]

Roosevelt adopted Fechner's recommendation and made it part of his Annual Message to Congress in January 1937. He proposed making the CCC a permanent agency at a force strength of 300,000 in 1,500 camps. He argued that there was an ongoing "need for providing useful and healthful employment for a large number of our youthful citizens."[40]

Roosevelt sent his legislative request to Congress in early April where it immediately ran into trouble in the House. Despite the president's landslide re-election in 1936 and the tremendous popularity of the CCC—a Gallup poll reported 82 percent support for it that year—Roosevelt's mishandling of the Supreme Court issue in 1937 encouraged stronger political opposition than he had experienced in his first term. His critics saw another opportunity to limit the power of the president in this debate over extending the life of the CCC, the president's "pet project."

What finally emerged in June was not a permanent agency but a three-year extension for the program with some important modifications.[41] First of all, the name "Civilian Conservation Corps" became official and "Emergency Conservation Work" was swept into the dustbin of historical trivia. (Even Fechner, the most faithful user of "ECW," had abandoned the phrase in his recommendations for a permanent agency.) Second, Congress for the first time set down in law certain policies and procedures that heretofore had been left to the discretionary authority of Roosevelt and Fechner. The statute confirmed the salary level of $30 a month for enrollees and even specified the number and the pay of those who could serve as leaders (6 percent of the company at $45), and assistant leaders (10 percent at $36). The age of recruits was limited to between seventeen and twenty-three, and they were now allowed to serve up to two years in the Corps. The law mandated that enrollees in camp who so desired should be provided a minimum of ten hours of educational instruction. In addition, five enrollees in each camp would not be bound by the age or marital restrictions: a camp leader, a mess steward, and three cooks. Most important for Kurtz and other selectors, the requirement that recruits be selected from the relief rolls was dropped and the more liberal standard that the young men simply be "unemployed and in need of employment" was adopted. Finally, in a petty assertion of power, Congress cut Fechner's salary from $12,000 to $10,000, in part because he had supported the president's Supreme Court plan, in part because he was making more than members of Congress.[42]

Another somewhat delicate matter had been touched on in the 1937 law. Congress allowed the CCC to recruit young men who were on probation or parole. Fechner had been sympathetic to the idea of using the CCC to further the rehabilitation of such young men, but selection policy had always excluded them. Knowing the sensitivity of this matter, Fechner called a conference in Washington on November 12, 1937, presided over by one of his assistants, Charles H. Taylor, to discuss the issue. But no vote was taken and nothing was ever done to enroll parolees. The dominant fear was that allowing "roughnecks" into the CCC would hurt its reputation and arouse fear and hostility from parents toward the program. In 1939 Snyder reprimanded Kurtz for apparently allowing two Philadelphia boys who were on probation to slip through the screening process and to be sent to a camp in Virginia.[43]

In contrast to the political friction in Washington, 1937 was a very good year for the CCC in Pennsylvania. Kurtz received a bit more job security, although not civil service protection. The Labor Department was now allowed the right to appoint the state selectors for the CCC, and Kurtz was logically chosen for Pennsylvania. Kurtz proudly began using his new title, "J. Fred Kurtz, State

Supervisor of CCC Selection," in correspondence with the Labor Department in July.

Moreover, Governor Earle had established a Department of Public Assistance (DPA) to replace SERB in 1937, and Kurtz's position was below that of the director of assistance administration and above the fifty-five local directors who supervised the more than 3,000 caseworkers. Later in the year, on November 15, 1937, Kurtz was given a new title, director of federal programs, when the functions of CCC selection and surplus commodity distribution were merged into one position. Kurtz thereafter devoted half of his time to the CCC and the other half to the distribution of federal surplus commodities for the Commodity Credit Corporation. The only people in Pennsylvania receiving state salaries for working on CCC selection were Kurtz himself (half his salary coming from the DPA, the rest paid by the Commodity Credit Corporation), his administrative assistant, a secretary, and a file clerk. The selectors in the counties performed CCC work on top of their ordinary duties of administering relief. The other expenses of the CCC in Pennsylvania—building, maintaining, and supplying camps; paying recruits and supervisory personnel—were assumed by the federal government.[44]

With the relief requirement now abolished, Kurtz's job of meeting Pennsylvania's heavy enrollment quotas was considerably eased, and the state once again was able to fill its camps with its own men and was also able to send large numbers of recruits out of state as work projects were completed. Kurtz instructed his recruiters to continue giving priority to young men from families receiving public relief from the state's DPA, followed by those receiving federal relief in the form of WPA work. Families receiving some form of private relief came next and, finally, the category of young men who were simply out of work could be tapped to fill up remaining slots.[45]

The continuing high rates of unemployment in the state also made Kurtz's job easier. In the Pittsburgh area, 56 percent of steelworkers were still idle in 1937. Only 20 percent of the high school class of 1938 found jobs in New Castle, where obsolete and shut-down steel mills littered the landscape. A school official there remarked on the class of 1939 that they were not competing for jobs but rather "fighting to get into the CCC."[46]

The process of getting recruits to work camps was now formalized and streamlined a bit, as some evolutionary changes had crept into the process since 1933. Recruits were now examined by army-appointed physicians at local relief offices, instead of at army stations, and, if accepted, were transported by the army directly to a work camp. Paul Slovan, who passed the physical in Sharon in April 1938, was immediately loaded into a truck with other new enrollees and, without notifying his family or knowing where he was headed, spent a scary day traveling up to the Allegheny National Forest.[47]

Once in camp the "rookies" would join the resident company and be given a few days of light work and conditioning before assuming regular duties. The army conditioning camps had been gradually phased out and now played no role except for recruits who would be sent west. These young men were now sent to the army bases at Tobyhanna or New Cumberland for the outfitting and conditioning thought necessary for the different environment and types of work they would be doing out west.[48]

Kurtz, with his new position and some increased clerical help, was pushing a lot more paper and collecting a lot more data than had been possible in the early years.[49] He was regularly reporting on the ages of recruits, their geographical backgrounds, their employment histories, and their heights and weights, as well as the number of recruits who were rejected and the reasons why.

He also found time in 1937 to write a report explaining in some detail how the process of enrollment worked. After getting the state's quota from Persons four times a year, Kurtz would mete out district quotas to the fifty-five local DPA officers based on the numbers they had on their relief rolls. A publicity campaign would ensue, advertising the openings via Boy Scout troops, schools, and the local clergy. Newspaper and sometimes radio ads were placed. Some recruiters mailed out CCC information with relief or WPA checks. The DPA caseworkers were instructed to see to it that the men selected were good candidates, needy and with determination and motivation to complete their hitch in the CCC. Kurtz suggested to Persons that enrollees who had been loaned money by local civic groups to purchase eyeglasses so that they could pass the physical be allowed to have $2 deducted from their pay for repayment, and this idea was adopted.[50]

If a local district could not meet its quota, Kurtz would assign the remainder to other areas, and if the state could not meet its number, he would report that to army officials at Third Corps headquarters, which would seek recruits from other states in the Corps. Once the number of local recruits was known, the army would contact the relief offices to make arrangements to examine and enroll the men and then transport them to the camp where they were needed.

The relaxed eligibility requirements and continuing high levels of unemployment among the young resulted in 1938 being another boom year for CCC recruitment.[51] In Pennsylvania, Kurtz enjoyed the reduced pressure in meeting quotas, but yet another potential job crisis threatened him in early 1938. His superior at the DPA, Karl de Schweinitz, resigned as director in a messy political squabble with Governor Earle and Senator Guffey.[52] Kurtz worried that the new DPA head, Arthur W. Howe, might prove to be more partisan than de Schweinitz and possibly jeopardize his position. Once again, he solicited "unsolicited" letters of recommendation from Snyder and Persons. The crisis passed, and Kurtz set about energizing his recruiters for the upcoming enrollment periods.[53]

Interest in and support for the CCC had never been greater than during these years the late 1930s. The Gallup poll found approval rates of well over 80 percent in Pennsylvania for the CCC, and Governor Earle reported widespread support for the program.[54] The Department of Forests and Waters was getting letters like the following one from a District of Columbia visitor to World's End Park: "Your CCC boys are making an excellent showing here and it is gratifying to see some of our youth so healthy and well disciplined when they might otherwise be engaged in occupations less useful."[55]

The persistent Depression kept attracting men to the Corps, and Persons was reporting about four applicants for each opening. Although the general economy was improving slightly, it had not done much to improve the high levels of unemployment among the very young. According to Persons, there was 40 percent unemployment in the fifteen-to-nineteen age group, the category now providing the bulk of CCC recruits, and 24 percent among those aged twenty to twenty-four.[56]

Although recruiting young men into the CCC was getting easier after 1937, Kurtz, along with national officials, was growing more concerned about a new problem—the large number of recruits who were not completing their enlistments and were deserting camp.[57] The national office kept pressing the state selectors to adopt orientation programs for new recruits that might reduce the high attrition rates in the camps.

Kurtz's response was that of a busy man with other priorities. He composed an introductory letter for enrollees, telling them what to expect and warning them that the first week's loneliness and homesickness would be the worst. He reminded them that they were not the recipients of charity but rather were being given a chance to work. His advice to the young men included the following admonitions: "Keep agitators at arm's length. Be a man. Stand on your own feet. Don't ruin your chances." He then closed with upbeat congratulations to them on being chosen from so many applicants.[58]

Somewhat more positive words came in later letters. In June 1938 his message for new recruits was decidedly more upbeat: "Congratulations! You have landed yourself a job. It will last at least six months. . . . There may be few opportunities in your lifetime that will profit you so greatly, train you so thoroughly, benefit you so much in so many ways, as will be afforded you by a period of enrollment in the Civilian Conservation Corps."[59]

Dean Snyder complimented Kurtz on keeping his state near the top in its number of enrollees, but he urged an even greater effort to ensure a better quality of recruits given the high rates of desertion in the program.[60] Kurtz, in turn, kept the pressure on his selectors to pick only boys of good character who were willing to serve. "The CCC is not intended as a dumping-ground for any county's mis-fits, agitators, or malcontents," he wrote them. He warned against recruiting boys still in school who viewed the CCC as a "summer vacation" between grades.[61] He kept reminding them of the importance of *selecting* men, not *collecting* them, and gave them a scolding: "The CCC is *not* an organization to enable you to sweep undesirable locals away from your town; *not* a scheme of rehabilitation primarily; *not* a temporary set-up to give casual assistance for a few weeks to boys who would like a short vacation at government expense without giving anything in return." County recruiters were encouraged to arrange send-off ceremonies for recruits, with speakers, music, and lots of hoopla. Kurtz thought such ceremonies would lift the morale of the boys as well as provide helpful publicity.[62]

The combination of successful recruiting and shutting down some Pennsylvania camps resulted in the transfer out of state of growing numbers of men over the next few years—to New Mexico, Texas, and Arizona in the Eighth Corps; to California, Montana, and Idaho in the Ninth Corps; and to Maryland, Virginia, and the District of Columbia in the Third Corps. While Pennsylvania had the second highest number of enrollees in the country in 1938—18,310—the number of camps in the state was down from its high of 141 in 1935 to a new low of 58. Most of the men transferred out of state were current enrollees who would be outfitted and conditioned before heading west.[63]

Pennsylvania in 1938 not only had an abundance of enrollees, it also had the distinction of producing the "ideal enrollee," at least in the opinion of the editors of *Happy Days*. They selected Richard G. Annutis of Company #1381 at Camp

Fig. 21 The army base at New Cumberland was a conditioning center for CCC enrollees who were being shipped out west and was also the site of a cooking school. Here men are training to become CCC camp cooks. National Archives

s-60, Petersburg, as the winner of their contest. Annutis had been valedictorian in his Catholic high school in St. Clair, had served in two other camps in Pennsylvania, s-57 and s-112, and had lately been promoted to assistant educational adviser at his camp. The DPA did all it could to publicize the distinction achieved by one of its recruits.[64]

Mr. Annutis was a bit exceptional in that he was a high school graduate. Only 564 of the 3,560 Pennsylvania recruits enrolled in October 1938 could claim that distinction. But 1,903 members of that class had completed at least one year of high school. Persons reported similar national figures for the educational level of recruits. The lack of jobs was not only attracting young men into the CCC but also keeping American boys in school longer.[65]

In many ways the good times for the CCC continued into 1939. Enrollments

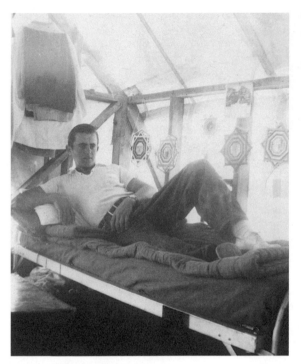

Fig. 22 Steve Bubernak in his tent at a side camp in 1938 in New Mexico, where he worked as a cook. Photo courtesy of Steve Bubernak

were strong, the experienced administrators were at their most efficient, the introduction of new spruce green uniforms boosted morale a bit, and Congress extended the life of the Corps until 1943, although it was still subject to annual funding.[66] But it was also an eventful year for the ccc, bringing some changes that damaged administrative morale.

The agency lost the independence it had enjoyed from its inception. Roosevelt had long been trying to get Congress to allow him to reorganize the federal bureaucracy, and with the Reorganization Act of spring 1939, Congress passed some of what he wanted. Under the new arrangement, the ccc became part of a new Federal Security Agency under Paul McNutt, the former governor of Indiana. Fechner resisted the idea of putting his organization under anyone but the president directly. When he then found out that the ccc would be part of a "welfare" agency rather than a "work" agency with wpa and pwa, he resigned, sort of, in a letter to the president on May 22 and regretted it almost immediately. He was then embarrassed to tell Roosevelt of his change of heart. After some mediation, the president returned Fechner's resignation letter on June 2.[67]

It was not a good year for Fechner. Professional and personal problems were piling up, and his health was failing. His administration of the ccc had always had its critics, but his efforts to centralize more and more authority in the director's office swelled the chorus of complaints and created more irritability in the organization than had existed at any time, even in its jerry-built days.

The Advisory Council met rarely now, usually only to learn of decisions made by the director. In May, Fechner moved the Division of Selection out of the Labor Department and placed it under the jurisdiction of his own office. Persons, with the new title of special assistant to the director, and his small staff (usually six people) continued to do the same work but were more closely scrutinized by the director.[68] Fechner then proceeded to assign all auto repair work for the work camps to a series of regional shops set up under his authority, taking the work away from the technical agencies and local businesses. The number of employees under the director's supervision jumped from 76 to 1,876 in the next two years, and tighter control of CCC expenditures as well as more intrusive field inspections by the director's office contributed to a loss of morale on the part of the technical services.[69]

Cooking for the CCC

Steve Bubernak was sixteen when he enlisted in the CCC in 1938. Originally from Old Forge near Scranton, he did forestry work at Camp s-82 in Waterville (Lycoming County) for about a year before he volunteered for the cooking school at New Cumberland (Cumberland County). Upon completing the course he was sent to camps in New Mexico. He wasn't completely happy out there and left the CCC after completing a six-month tour. In a May 2004 letter, Steve recalled his CCC experience.

I was inducted into the CCCs, April 12, 1938, from Scranton, PA. I was sent to s-129, Waterville, PA. I was from Old Forge, PA, and was underage. The justice of the peace made me a fake birth certificate for 50 cents.

My duties were planting trees and building roads in the mountains as fire trails. Our camp was in a valley with a stream running nearby. After a few months we had a torrential rain and our camp was flooded by about a foot. That was the first time that I had ever seen water snake eels. While working building roads in the mountains we saw mother bears with their cubs crossing the road ahead of us and plenty of rattlesnakes and deer.

They immediately moved our camp approx. 8 or so miles to higher grounds to s-82 Waterville. I took a K.P. job as steady work and later became a 2nd cook. After being a 2nd cook for approx. 6 mos. a request came through for cooks to volunteer to go out West. I jumped at the chance because I wanted to see the West.

I was sent to New Cumberland, PA, to a Cook and Baker School. The School was mainly a hub for new recruits and cooks going West. The cooks would cook on the train and feed the new recruits.

After approx. 4 to 5 wks. I was put on this train of new recruits and two others, one fellow approx. 5'9" tall was given the rate as mess sergeant. The other fellow approx. 5'8" tall was rated as 1st cook. Me being 5'2" tall was given the rate of 2nd cook. As the train started to pull out of Harrisburg, the mess sergeant said to the two of us that he knows nothing about cooking. The first cook said that the nearest he had come to cooking was doing K.P. *They both looked to me and I told them that I was a cook. They both uttered a sigh of relief and told me that they will be glad to do the* K.P. *work and take trays of food out to the new recruits on the Pullman cars. They both said that they wanted to go out West. . . .*

Discharged 12-14-39 from New Cumberland. Discharge paper states that I was an excellent cook and worker.

Fechner also acquired new critics in the War Department. In 1937, the army had begun rotating its officers in CCC camps in order to spread around the valuable experience. Reserve officers were given six-month probationary assignments, and if they proved satisfactory, they would be rotated to another camp after eighteen months. When many of the officers, most of whom seemed to have enjoyed their CCC postings, complained about the new policy, Fechner stepped in to support them, Roosevelt backed him up, and the result was a wrangled compromise whereby only about half of the officer staff in the camps would be rotated.[70]

More discontent for the military came in 1939 after Congress sweetened the pension and disability provisions for reserve officers on active duty. Roosevelt was alarmed at the additional cost this would add to CCC expenses and ordered that, as of December 1939, all camp COs would have to be given civilian status. This change had little practical effect, because about 95 percent of the reserve officers in the camps simply resigned their commissions, reverted to civilian status, and kept at their posts with new CCC-style uniforms and reduced benefits. Moreover, the War Department kept its administrative control of the camps. But the change did save the government more than $2 million a year, and as time went on, some "real" civilians, including former CCC enrollees, served as camp COs. These civilian COs did not rotate but served in their assigned camp during good behavior, with no civil service status. They were now supposed to be addressed as "mister" instead of "captain" or "lieutenant," but old habits die hard.[71]

In Pennsylvania, Kurtz and his selectors went about their business largely untouched by these disputes in Washington. The state enrolled 20,159 men in the fiscal year ending June 30, 1939, keeping it second to New York, which was not too surprising given the very large number of people in the state still receiving some form of public assistance.[72] The state DPA put this number at 1.6 million, about the same as it had been in late 1934. Moreover, unemployment rates for young people, especially those in their teens, still ranged between 40 and 50 percent.[73] Consequently, there were many more applicants for the CCC than places available. But because the number of approved work projects for Pennsylvania was decreasing, more and more Pennsylvania boys, almost one-half of those recruited in 1939, were sent to camps in the West.

Shipping large numbers of Pennsylvania boys west, especially to New Mexico in the Eighth Corps, caused new worries for Kurtz. He was aware of the costs involved in sending men by train across country, and if the enrollee became homesick or unhappy with his camp assignment, there was the additional and wasted expense of bringing him home. Therefore, Kurtz urged his selectors to pay special attention to recruits whose parents signed the necessary form allowing their sons to be transported out of Corps. (No permission was needed to assign an enrollee to any camp in the Third Corps.) He warned them off immature seventeen-year-olds, who were more inclined to get homesick.[74]

Kurtz instructed the selectors to temper the excitement of young men, anxious to travel and see some sights, with warnings about the isolation of camps in New Mexico and the sparsity of towns. He had received a report from an "Eighth Corps Official" describing the erroneous expectations many young men from Pennsylvania had of the West. They would find "nothing glamorous" about cowboys and Indians, but, he observed, the mountain scenery, comfortable camps, and interesting work would be satisfying to some recruits.[75]

It was mostly city boys who ended up in New Mexico, and it took some cultural conditioning for them to adapt to the different environment. One camp at Fort Stanton named its newsletter "The Lonely Pennsylvanian." Leo Murphy of Philadelphia complained about the food, especially the sour milk and cement-hard biscuits. A few Scranton boys who ended up at Las Cruces were reported as "intractable" and refusing to work. Some camps saw Pennsylvania boys attempting to organize strikes, always strongly resisted in CCC camps, and others engaged in refighting the Civil War with Texas boys. Tragically, one young man from Pottsville, Lawrence Schulz, was missing for two days before his body was discovered in an arroyo where he had apparently been drowned by one of the flash floods peculiar to that area. But overall, most Pennsylvania boys seem to have adjusted well after some early problems with the altitude and the heat. Jim Duffy at Apache Creek Camp kept warm memories of attending Christmas Eve Mass at a Spanish chapel and singing "Silent Night" in the town square outside.[76]

Kurtz touted the success of his selection process by pointing to the smaller percentage of Pennsylvania men being prematurely discharged from Eighth Corps camps than those from Pennsylvania ones. Overall, though, fewer Pennsylvania men re-enlisted for the western camps. "Too much sand, too many Indians, too few girls," was the common complaint.[77]

In spring 1939 an interesting but short-lived experiment was tried in the selection process at Fechner's instigation. Selectors were encouraged to identify boys with particular aptitudes or interests and, without informing recruits, were instructed to code their applications with symbols that the army could consult when making camp assignments. The idea was to send enrollees to

Fig. 23 CCC enrollees from Pennsylvania Company #3350 buying candy, cigars, and cigarettes from the company canteen in Orogrande, New Mexico, December 1940. National Archives

camps that might have educational or vocational programs or work projects of particular interest to the men. Persons was lukewarm to the plan and warned Kurtz to keep the whole thing out of the public light as only a small number of enrollees would be given this kind of placement. In October, Pennsylvania selectors coded 820 applications for special placements but only 279 were accommodated. There seems to have been no local enthusiasm for the idea, and by December Kurtz told the selectors that they should no longer bother coding applications for Eighth Corps assignments.[78]

When James McEntee succeeded Fechner in 1940, he tried to continue this scheme, but Kurtz found that it was not working very well. He was getting reports from selectors who had succeeded in getting their boys into specific camps that then turned out not to be at all capable of providing the training they were supposed to. The agricultural training at Gordonsville, Virginia, proved particularly disappointing to boys sent there. Elsewhere in the country there were many complaints about recruiters promising more than they could deliver, such as courses in aviation or trade instruction. The program continued for another two years before it was canceled in December 1941. Kurtz later eulogized it as an idea with good intentions but totally impracticable and, in the end, a wasted effort that benefited only a very small number of recruits.[79]

In the midst of these flush times when there were still three to four times as many applicants as openings in the CCC, Howard L. Russell, the new director of the state DPA, requested that Kurtz make a study of recruits from the state. This was the largest self-study made by CCC officials in Pennsylvania since the one done in summer 1934. The result, "Some Characteristics of CCC Enrollees," was put out by the DPA in May 1939.[80]

The typical CCC enrollee, the study generalized, was a white boy of seventeen or eighteen, from a city family on relief, with six or more people in the household. The boy had never worked at all, was 5 feet 7 inches tall, and weighed 143 pounds. Surprisingly, about one-quarter of recent enrollees had graduated from high school, although most had only gotten to eighth grade. This profile was similar to the occasional studies done by the national office or other groups that attempted to draw national profiles.[81]

The most striking change in Pennsylvania's enrollment figures in the last few years of the CCC's existence was the increase in the numbers of seventeen-year-olds. The following figures are taken from Kurtz's circular letters to his county selectors.

ENROLLMENT OF SEVENTEEN-YEAR-OLDS IN THE CCC IN PENNSYLVANIA

Date	Number of seventeen-year-old enrollees	Percent of all enrollees
April 1937	1,141	40
July 1937	1,958	46
October 1937	2,350	39
January 1938	808	38
July 1938	2,023	38
January 1939	1,522	32
July 1939	1,720	29
October 1939	1,612	34
January 1940	2,177	34
April 1940	1,376	36
July 1940	3,309	43
January 1941	3,768	50.6
February 1941	501	60
April 1941	1,870	61
May 1941	901	65.5
July 1941	2,507	69.9

As young as the CCC was getting in the official records, there is considerable evidence to suggest that the average age of enrollees was even younger. Steve Bubernak, who entered from Old Forge in 1938, remembers paying 50 cents to a justice of the peace for a forged birth certificate when he enrolled in the CCC at age sixteen, a practice he claims was common in his area. He had to eat six bananas the morning of his examination to meet the minimum weight of 104 pounds. Stanley Oravecz was admitted to Camp SP-14 at Blue Knob in summer 1941 when he was only fifteen, and he remembers several boys being only thirteen at that time. Robert Allen Ermentrout, who served as an army officer in several CCC camps, claimed that most camps had underaged enrollees. He himself allowed one fourteen-year-old boy, who had a mother and seven sisters at home, to remain in his camp.[82]

Interrupting the succession of strong enrollment periods in Pennsylvania was an ominous, if barely perceptible, blip in October 1939 when the state fell short of its assigned quota. The shortfall was only two, but given the recent large reservoirs of applicants, it arrived with the kind of suddenness with which the European war had begun in September. Kurtz attributed the falloff in applicants to both the industrial pick-up stimulated by the war and the fear on the part of young men and their parents that the CCC would become a fast track into the army. In Washington, Fechner was trying to allay such fears and was resisting suggestions for military training in the camps. He stressed that, in the event of a military draft, the enrollees in the Corps would be on the same footing as everyone else. But worries and rumors spread.[83]

The year 1939 ended amidst the misleading calm of the "phony war" in Europe. In retrospect, we can see that the good years of the CCC were now behind it. Robert Fechner, who had labored so hard to establish a conservation program he had not conceived of nor had any interest in before his appointment by President Roosevelt in 1933, died of heart failure on the very last day of the year. Death, absurd and indomitable as it is, would at least spare Fechner the last few troubled years of the organization he had midwived and grown to love. The looming problems of declining enrollments, rising desertions, and creeping militarism would become the responsibilities of his longtime friend and associate, and now successor, James J. McEntee.[84]

THE LAST GOOD YEARS: 1940–1941

The steps that Fechner had taken in his last years to centralize CCC administration had been criticized by Harold Ickes in Interior and Henry Wallace in Agriculture, and on Fechner's death, they proposed abolishing the office of the director altogether. Roosevelt took the easier route and kept the system intact. While McEntee simply continued the centralizing policies begun by Fechner, he received even more criticism for them. He did not have the prestige of his former friend nor his folksy demeanor and seems to have been an abrasive figure.[85]

Kurtz was one of many who came in for early scrutiny by the new director. McEntee began prodding the state selectors to upgrade their administrations, and even Kurtz with his excellent track record received a poor grade. McEntee sent an investigator to Kurtz's offices in May 1940. The subsequent report was critical of Kurtz's failure to cooperate with the State Employment Service and the technical services in the camps. The investigator singled out, in particular, the weak efforts Kurtz had made to provide some form of precamp orientation for recruits. And, while he commended Kurtz for meeting regularly with the 3,800 local caseworkers, he noted in his report that Kurtz was "not very good at leading" these meetings. But Persons continued to commend Kurtz for his efforts, especially in the area of publicizing the educational opportunities provided by the CCC.[86]

Official CCC figures on enrollments testify to the ongoing efficiency of Kurtz and his selectors. Pennsylvania enrolled 22,003 men in 1940, more than any other state. There were also more young men from Pennsylvania in the CCC in mid-1940 than from any other state. But because of the improving economy, Kurtz and his people were both recruiting younger boys and digging deeper into the nonrelief population, recruiting larger numbers of so-called border-line cases from the needy unemployed.[87]

Because fewer recruits were coming from families on relief, McEntee's office introduced changes in the allotment system. If there was no one at home dependent on a boy's monthly checks, he was now allowed, as single veterans had been from the beginning, to deposit $22 a month with the army and receive the money saved when he left the Corps. Later in the year McEntee proposed more changes. He wanted men with dependents to have $8 a month to spend, to send $15 home to family members, and to deposit $7 with the CCC, to be returned to him as a lump sum when he left the Corps. He had Persons solicit opinions from selectors on this idea before adopting it as policy, and after getting mostly positive feedback, the new system was adopted in November.[88]

In Pennsylvania, Kurtz and his people were in the minority of those strongly opposed to these changes in the allotment system. Howard L. Russell, director of DPA, wrote to Persons in August after Kurtz had surveyed his selectors. Russell pointed out that Pennsylvania was meeting its recruitment quotas quite nicely without this added incentive for enrollees, and he feared the loss of income to the families of enrollees still on relief. He proposed a compromise of $10 spending money and $20 allotment payments, but to no avail.[89]

Because ever-younger boys were being recruited, more enrollees were coming into the Corps with no work experience at all. The percentage of inexperienced new men jumped from 49 percent in July 1939 to 68 percent in April 1940. McEntee boasted that his boys were getting "scholarships in work experience." As a result, the director tried to make job training a more pronounced feature of the CCC. He announced that the mission of the organization had changed priorities: short-term work relief for the unemployed would remain its primary purpose, but job training would now rank higher than conservation work.[90]

WAR AND THE CCC

Long before the Japanese attack on Pearl Harbor forced the United States to abandon its traditional isolationism once and for all, the "last European war" that was fought from 1939 to 1941 was already having a heavy impact on the American people.[91] The country had relaxed its Neutrality Laws on trade with belligerents (November 1939), had geared up the first peacetime draft in its history (August 1940), and had begun to give Lend-Lease assistance to Britain and others (March 1941). Young men from Shamokin and Coudersport and all the other cities, towns, and rural areas of Pennsylvania that, geographically and culturally speaking, seemed worlds removed from Bastogne or Tarawa were soon to have their lives touched by events in places they would be hard pressed to find on a map. And many of these young men who were serving in the CCC felt the war's impact even earlier.

After the fall of France in June 1940, Congress passed a resolution directing the CCC to train its men in work skills that would be useful to the military in time of war.[92] During the next two years, the CCC would try to walk a fine line between touting its usefulness to military defense and attempting to retain its civilian character. There would never be any weapons training in CCC camps, but Director McEntee intensified efforts, begun under Fechner, to provide on-the-job training in skills useful to the military, such as cooking, first aid, radio operation, and demolition. After Pearl Harbor, the boys were also given fifteen minutes of marching drill every day and a mandatory twenty-hour course in Red Cross first aid.[93]

Even the CCC's conservation work was now getting wrapped in military khaki. McEntee bragged that 73 percent of the work the CCC did was similar to that of the Army Corps of Engineers. Men in the CCC were learning to drive tractors, "which are first cousins to tanks." As McEntee searched for justification for keeping the Corps in existence in a time of decreasing unemployment, he stressed how the work skills the men were learning would make them good "material" for the military.[94]

The last year of the CCC would see the line between the military and the CCC blur even more as eighty companies were assigned to spruce up and ready military bases.[95] Examples of this kind of work in Pennsylvania included cutting out of a side camp from Hickory Run's NP-6's Company #1324, which spent six months improving the artillery range at the army base at Tobyhanna, and the assignment of Company #329 to work on the army air force grounds at New

Cumberland in 1942. Amidst growing fears that the CCC was simply a boot camp for the infantry, Kurtz urged his selectors to impress upon enrollees and their families the argument made by Senator James Byrnes of South Carolina. Byrnes had argued that the kind of military-related skills the CCC was giving its men were noncombat in nature and made it *less* likely that someone with that kind of training would end up with a rifle in his hands.[96]

The year 1941 would turn out to be the last full year of operation for the CCC. In hindsight, although the organization has come to be seen as part of an earlier, more innocent epoch when young men were allowed the luxury of spending their days planting trees, the pressures of a prewar culture were having an impact on the core identity of the CCC. It was still technically *civilian* and it still did *conservation* work, but more and more it was looking like a paramilitary *corps*. The Corps spent its last year struggling to keep its recruits in camp and struggling to maintain its identity.[97]

The recruiting of Pennsylvania men continued strong through 1941, outperforming all other states. But this record was made only by dint of extraordinary efforts by Kurtz and his selectors, who reached more deeply into the teen-age population than ever before. Moreover, the effort had a Sisyphean quality to it because enrollees were leaving the camps faster than new recruits could replace them.[98]

The January 1941 enrollment in Pennsylvania of 7,432 men was unusually high because more than 1,200 men did not complete their camp assignments in the last quarter of 1940 and had to be replaced, in addition to the regular turnover. Kurtz urged his recruiters to remind their boys that a dishonorable discharge for desertion or refusing to work would have no bearing on their draft status nor would it disqualify them in any way from serving in the armed forces.[99]

Because of the increasing number of vacancies in the camps, due to men securing employment and leaving with honorable discharges or just leaving on their own, many camps were undermanned in the weeks between enrollment periods. To fill the camps, the CCC shifted to a system of "intermediate" enrollments in between the scheduled ones. Kurtz was opposed to this new system, fearing it would simply make meeting his quarterly quotas that much harder.[100]

The CCC was, almost desperately, trying to make its service more attractive in a number of ways. Enrollees were promised that they would not be sent out of their own Corps area unless they agreed to it.[101] Kurtz didn't think this would help much because, in his experience, most Pennsylvania boys were eager to serve in the western Eighth and Ninth Corps, and it had always been his practice to secure such permissions in the past. Besides, with the reduction in CCC camps taking place, by July 1941 all of Pennsylvania's fourteen companies of men serving in the Eighth Corps were brought home as well as three of the nineteen companies in the Ninth Corps. Kurtz thought that a better incentive for recruiting was to stress the opportunities for advancement offered in the CCC. He publicized the fact that 3,120 former Junior enrollees from Pennsylvania were now serving in the Corps as civilian COs, project superintendents, or foremen.[102]

McEntee was pressing the state selectors to produce more favorable publicity like this. He declared the week of February 16 "Know Your CCC" week and urged camp COs to invite local communities to open houses as part of a more active public relations effort. Kurtz did what he could to cooperate and urged his selectors to place some "Earn While You Learn" spot radio ads, promoting the job training opportunities in the CCC.[103]

Despite the 10 percent reduction in the size of the Corps in spring 1941, recruiters were exhorted to "stimulate" the flow of applicants, and more liberal standards were afforded them. Selectors were now allowed to sign up as many brothers as were available from families on relief (two per family had been the previous limit) and up to two from families not on relief (one had been the limit before). A year later Kurtz was proudly able to report that one Pennsylvania family of twenty-four children had seven sons in the CCC with several younger boys hoping to join up soon. Men were now allowed to re-enlist after only a three-month sitting-out period, instead of six. Recruiters were also allowed, for the first time, to take seventeen-year-olds who were still in school but had no interest in remaining there. Even though the spring enrollment was short by 840 and Pennsylvania's few remaining camps were falling below minimally acceptable strength levels, Kurtz commended his people on their "splendid record under existing circumstances."[104]

Kurtz provided retrospective totals for Pennsylvania in June 1941. So far, 177,176 Pennsylvania Juniors had served in the CCC. The counties that produced most of the recruits were Philadelphia with 39,889; Allegheny County (Pittsburgh area) with 24,464; Luzerne County (Wilkes-Barre area) with 12,486; and Lackawanna County (Scranton area) with 10,959.[105]

Director McEntee, faced with a numbers problem all over the country, opened up the selection process and ended the process of enrollment periods and quotas. Selectors were instructed to enroll on a continuous basis, and the army would accept all they could muster. He also antagonized Kurtz by sending an army officer to several Pennsylvania counties to act as a recruiting agent. More controversially, McEntee allowed the army to begin accepting enrollees at the camps, bypassing the selectors. He backed off somewhat when state selectors protested, and he agreed that if the selectors could keep their camps at a minimum strength of 185 men, the army would stop recruiting applicants at camp.[106]

Kurtz bitterly criticized this new system of bypassing the selectors' screening procedures for enrollees. He charged that the camp COS were enrolling too many men who were ineligible, especially those under age. Kurtz had his selectors check on 207 of the 400 enrollees signed up by the army that summer. They found 90 of them ineligible and had them dismissed from camps.[107]

For any admirer of the CCC project, studying its records over this last year of existence makes for melancholy reading. Knowing, as we do, that the end is rapidly approaching, there is a certain pathos in this last act of men desperately trying to keep the story moving along while the clock ticks ahead to a closing time they do not even know exists.

The number of CCC camps in Pennsylvania continued to drop and numbered only 16 by the end of 1941. Nationwide, the CCC had started the year with 183,000 Juniors in camps. Even though 252,000 new men were enrolled in 1941, at the end of the year there were only 93,000 still in the program. Men were leaving at the rate of 28,000 a month.[108] The camps were hemorrhaging. The end was not far off.

3

THE CCC IN PENN'S WOODS

The men of the CCC generation must often think that sometime after 1945 they were whisked away in a time-travel machine to live in a world so radically different from the one in which they spent their youth. Later generations have been so impressed with the exotic and outsized experiences of those men that they have called it "the Greatest Generation." One of the men from that generation was Leo Ruvolis, who enrolled in the CCC in Wilkes-Barre in 1938.

Leo was the youngest of four children in an anthracite coal mining family. His parents had emigrated from Lithuania, and because jobs were so scarce, he was allowed the luxury of finishing high school in 1937. Also because jobs were so scarce, he went into the CCC in January 1938 and stayed for a year. He entered the CCC at a time when most Pennsylvania enrollees were being sent out of state, and he was sent directly to a camp in Virginia manned mostly by Pennsylvanians. His high school education enabled him to move from outdoor work on the Blue Ridge Parkway to an office position as assistant company clerk, "swapping a pick for a pencil," as he puts it. He also worked as editor on the camp's newspaper and took some courses in civil engineering and surveying, sparking interests that led him to a degree in that field when he finished college on the G.I. Bill after the war.

His experiences in the CCC, including contacts with college students from nearby Virginia Military Institute and Washington and Lee, had expanded his horizons to a much larger world than he had known back home. After leaving the CCC, he enlisted in the Army Air Corps and eventually trained as a bomber pilot in the famed Eighth Air Force. He left a young wife to head a bomber crew that helped to soften up the D-day beaches, and his plane was later shot down over central Germany. He spent the last ten months of the war in a German prison camp.

After the war Leo advanced quickly in that time machine that was accelerating his generation forward so rapidly. His education prepared him for high-tech jobs in photogrammetric engineering and eventually training in early generation computers with IBM. He finished his varied working career as director of the computer center at York College in Pennsylvania and, finally, as a professor there. Reflecting back on how he was able to walk through so many new doors and fulfill so many ambitions, he wrote: "I really believe the dream began in the CCC."[1]

Leo Ruvolis was only one of the 184,916 Juniors and Veterans recruited for CCC work from Pennsylvania over the nine years of the program's existence. (An additional 9,656 supervisory personnel were also employed in camps within the state.)[2] The vast majority of these Pennsylvania enrollees worked in Pennsylvania camps where most of the work was related, directly or indirectly, to forestry conservation. But recreational development, soil conservation work on farms, and historic preservation provided for an interesting mix of CCC activity in the state. In addition, an undetermined number of Pennsylvania men like Leo, especially in the 1937–41 period, were sent out of state to work in sometimes radically different environments. For all these reasons, the history of the CCC in the Keystone State provides more opportunities than any other state to study how the organization operated in the field and to appreciate the great variety in the work and camp life of CCC men. There was no typical CCC enrollee or CCC camp, but this chapter, by looking at some of the varied experiences of Pennsylvania men, will try to provide a representative sampling of CCC life.

THE NUMBER AND TYPES OF CCC CAMPS IN PENNSYLVANIA

It is difficult to determine exactly how many individual CCC camps there were in Pennsylvania. The Corps credited Pennsylvania with having an average of 78 camps a year, ranking it second to California, but it never published totals of individual camps in the various states. CCC records make it relatively easy to identify the number of camps operating in the state at any point in time— 97 in July 1933, 4 in May 1942, for example—but it is much more difficult to determine how many different individual camps operated in Pennsylvania over the nine-year life of the organization. Very few camps operated continuously. Most were open for only a few years, closing when the work assignments approved for the camp were completed. Others would open when new conservation projects were approved, and sometimes new companies reopened old camp sites. Camp names changed frequently, and some camps had different numbers at different times. Near the end of the program, camps were being closed during enrollment periods instead of waiting for the end, as had been the case in earlier years. A further complication came in 1934 and again in 1936–37 when several Pennsylvania camps were housing companies from other states.

Only by examining the individual camp histories and keeping track of openings and closings can one arrive at the total number of CCC camps in Pennsylvania.

Based on available camp histories, *Annual Reports of the Director of CCC*, camp directories, camp inspection reports and station and strength reports in the CCC records, and the recorded number of camps for each enrollment period in the NPS records, it appears that there were 152 different CCC camps in Pennsylvania over the nine-year life of the organization.[3] The highest number of camps at any one time was 141 in the fifth enrollment period in the summer of 1935, by which time 5 of the earliest camps had already been closed—S-92, S-106, S-115, S-142, and SP-3. After that peak period, camps in the state began to close, but it seems that only 6 new ones opened: 2 new Soil Conservation Service camps—SCS-12 and SCS-13; an army air force camp at New Cumberland—AF-1; 2 state park camps—SP-14 and SP-19; and a state forest camp—S-158. This total number of 152 is offered with tentative confidence more than with absolute certainty.

Fig. 24 Leo Ruvolis enrolled in the CCC in 1938 at Wilkes-Barre. He was sent to a camp near the town of Buena Vista in Virginia, which was manned mostly by Pennsylvania recruits. Photo courtesy of Leo Ruvolis

The Pennsylvania camps can be organized into five categories according to which technical agency supervised the work: (1) 14 were "F" camps, all located in the Allegheny National Forest under the U.S. Forestry Service; (2) 18 were supervised by the National Park Service of the Interior Department, including 2 "MP" camps at Gettysburg Military Park, 8 "NP" camps in the 5 recreational development areas at French Creek–Hopewell, Hickory Run, Raccoon Creek, Blue Knob, and Laurel Hill, and 8 "SP" camps developed in cooperation with the state Bureau of Parks located within state forests and a few cities;[4] (3) 11 were "scs" camps run by the Soil Conservation Service of the Department of Agriculture; (4) 3 were "A" camps established on army bases at Tobyhanna, Carlisle, and New Cumberland; and (5) the remaining 106 were "S" camps run by the Pennsylvania Department of Forests and Waters on state-owned or private forest lands. Camps were located in 48 of the state's 67 counties, with a heavy concentration in the central counties of Clinton (10 camps), Potter (9 camps), and Centre, Elk, and Lycoming (8 camps each).

The following table charts the fluctuations in the number of camps in Pennsylvania during the life of the Corps.

Enrollment Period	Camps by Category					Total Number of Camps
	F	SCS	A	NPS	S	
July 1933	7			3	87	97
November 1933	7			6	91	104
April 1934	7			7	82	96
November 1934	7			8	82	97
April 1935	14	9	2	15	99	139
September 1935	14	9	2	15	101	141
November 1935	12	9	2	13	86	122
January 1936	10	9	2	12	75	108
April 1936	8	9	2	12	75	106
November 1936	7	9	2	12	69	99
April 1937	7	9	2	12	60	90
November 1937	4	8		9	36	57
April 1938	4	7		6	33	50
November 1938	3	7		6	33	49
April 1939	3	7		6	33	49
November 1939	3	7		6	33	49
April 1940	3	7		6	32	48
November 1940	3	7		6	33	48
April 1941	3	7		6	32	48
November 1941	2	5		6	20	33
January 30, 1942	1	3		4	9	17
April 30, 1942		1	1		4	6
May 31, 1942			1		3	4

THE WORK OF THE CAMPS

The primary purpose of all these camps was, of course, conservation work. In the minds of both Roosevelt and Fechner, this work was not only going to repair much of the damage that greed and neglect had inflicted on the natural resources of the country, but it was also going to restore the physical and mental health of young men ravaged by idleness and poverty.

The task of describing the work done by the 194,572 men who passed through the CCC camps in Penn's Woods is too daunting for words, and this perhaps explains the penchant for the dizzying array of statistics that CCC officials produced regularly for a quickly sated public. A little past the halfway mark of the CCC's life, the state Department of Forests and Waters included in its report covering the period from 1933 through 1937 a two-page list of categories of work the men had accomplished. A brief sampling follows: 390 foot bridges, 617 vehicle bridges, 83 cabins, 1,414 other buildings, 2,115 miles of truck trails, 692,036 acres of forest improvements, 14,061 acres of reforesting, 53 recreational dams, 12 million trees planted, and so on.[5] By the end of the program in 1942, the major accomplishments of the CCC men in Pennsylvania included: 791 miles of telephone lines strung, 3,386 miles of truck trails and 3,483 miles of foot and horse trails blazed, 61,046,160 trees planted, 102 large dams constructed, 254,974 man days of nursery work, 510,465 acres cleared of forest diseases and pests, 31,585 acres of forest fire hazards cleared, 1,783 fish-rearing ponds stocked.[6]

Fig. 25 CCC men hand-grading Clear Run Road (Jefferson County) in June 1935. Pennsylvania State Archives

Within these large categories, the work done by the men in Penn's Woods was about as varied as informed imaginations could conceive doing in woods and parks. Some work went even beyond that elastic limit. One commanding officer of Company #1377 at Camp s-102 at Mehoopany organized a small work team around the camp to construct a nine-hole golf course, which was then opened to the public at $.25 a round with the proceeds going to the camp recreational fund. Camp f-3 in the Allegheny National Forest scattered poison around 20,000 acres to eliminate porcupine damage. Another camp, sp-13, Camp Buffalo in Lehigh County, worked on a game preserve, feeding the animals and constructing access roads for the public to drive around and see deer, elk, and bison. And there was one atypical camp: s-145 in Lycoming County, where Company #367 spent two years constructing a five-mile road simply providing access *to* the camp, work finally judged as "excessive" by the camp inspector.[7]

The popular nickname of the ccc was "Roosevelt's Tree Army," and most of the work done was "in the woods." But work was also done in city parks and on farms, and some of the camps like scs-5 in Sligo, scs-7 in Glen Rock, and sp-4 in Reading were located inside town limits or just on the outskirts.[8]

In addition to "pure" forestry work, ccc men worked in the related area of soil conservation. In 1933, Hugh Hammon Bennett, a chemist in the Department of Agriculture who had done much to publicize the misguided practices of many farmers, cooperated with Harold Ickes in getting the Public Works Administration (pwa) to establish some pilot soil conservation projects. The next year thirty-four ccc camps, listed with Soil Erosion Service (ses) numbers, were set up to perform this type of work. Bennett, however, became convinced that soil conservation really belonged in the Department of Agriculture, and he was able to convince the president on the matter. One day when Ickes was out of town, Roosevelt transferred the service out of pwa.[9]

The Department of Agriculture, taking advantage of the great expansion in the number of ccc camps in 1935, began to establish Soil Conservation Service (scs) camps throughout the country. These camps usually worked on private farm lands with the cooperation of the owners who had to promise to maintain any improvements made for at least five years. The ccc men worked under scs engineers to halt the erosion of topsoil into streams and rivers. The work included building and seeding contour furrows in pastures, constructing diversion ditches and fences, bulldozing tree stumps, and planting seedlings. In Pennsylvania there were eventually eleven scs camps, all working on private land.[10]

Farmers were given instruction and assistance in contour plowing, and ccc men spent much effort in building "check dams," small barriers built in hillside gullies to prevent torrents of rainwater from dislodging soil and sending it downhill into streams. The check dams would divert and dissipate the flowing waters across a wider stretch of hillside, where it could be absorbed more easily as ground water. Crews would then seed and sod these gullies, allowing root systems to utilize the excess water and fix the soil.[11]

The development of facilities in state parks was another important category of CCC work. Only eighteen states had set aside money for state parks before the arrival of the "tree armies," but the rapid influx of labor now resulted in many more states creating recreational areas in the woods. Pennsylvania was one of the states that had parks before 1933. Valley Forge was the first, dedicated in 1893 and made a national park in 1976. The first recreational parks in the state were established by Joseph Rothrock in 1903 at Mont Alto, Promised Land, and Caledonia on state forestry lands. But for many years the parks were the "stepchildren" of the Department of Forests and Waters and underfunded. With the growth of automobile travel, the demands for camping, picnicking, and recreational facilities resulted in the development of more facilities in forestry lands for such purposes and the creation of a Division of Parks within the Bureau of Forestry in 1929.[12]

Although the Depression forced drastic cuts in the budget for parks, help was soon forthcoming from federal work relief projects. The CCC was the first of these, of course, and Robert Stuart, who had supervised Pennsylvania's extensive forests before becoming head of the U.S. Forestry Service, argued for including CCC camps on state-owned lands, not just in the national forests. Since so many CCC camps were located on state forestry lands in Pennsylvania, CCC work projects inevitably expanded to include recreational improvements in addition to the traditional forestry work. The Civil Works Administration also provided a short-lived but efficient source of manpower for state parks during the winter of 1933–34. By 1935, when the number of CCC camps in the state was at its peak and an abundance of WPA labor was also available for park improvements, Governor Earle created a separate Bureau of Parks within the Department of Forests and Waters, independent of the Bureau of Forestry. The people of Pennsylvania responded to these newly available facilities, and the number of visitors jumped from two million in 1930 to nine million in 1935.[13]

Much of the forestry and soil conservation work done by the CCC in Pennsylvania is now part of the landscape and as such is not as immediately visible as some of their enduring construction projects. (The lines of neatly planted

Fig. 26 CCC men constructing a fish dam in Cedar Run (Tioga County) in July 1935. Pennsylvania State Archives

hemlocks along Route 144 at the entrance to Ole Bull State Park is one obvious exception.) CCC men, working with and instructed by skilled carpenters, engineers, and masons, sometimes furnished by WPA, supplied the labor for the building of cabins, picnic benches, pavilions, and dams. The largest single construction project of the CCC in Pennsylvania was the Laurel Hill Recreational Development Area dam, built by Company #2332 to provide a sixty-six-acre recreational lake.[14] But there were many other such dams (see Appendix 2), still providing recreational waters for state park visitors today.

While the Department of Forests and Waters worked with the CCC to improve recreational areas throughout state forestry lands in "S" camps in Pennsylvania, the National Park Service undertook the direct supervision of work crews in eight "SP" camps: SP-1 and SP-3 in Allegheny County; SP-2 in Cooksburg State Forest (originally this camp was called s-100); SP-4 in Mt. Penn Park in Reading; SP-5 in Johnstown; SP-11 in Pymatuning State Park in Crawford County; SP-12 at Fort Necessity in Fayette County; and SP-13 in the Trexler-Lehigh Game Preserve in Lehigh County. The NPS also took over the work started at S-107 near Scotland and developed this as SP-18 at Caledonia State Park.

The NPS also assumed control of five recreational development areas (RDAS) and supervised the work of CCC and WPA labor in them: French Creek–Hopewell, near Philadelphia; Hickory Run, between Allentown and Scranton; Raccoon Creek, near Pittsburgh; Laurel Hill, near Johnstown; and Blue Knob, near Altoona. These RDAS were intended to provide recreational opportunities closer to metropolitan centers than the more remote state parks. The Resettlement Administration within the Department of Agriculture undertook the purchase of submarginal farmlands and turned them over to the NPS to develop for outdoor recreational purposes. The labor of the CCC and the WPA was then put to use by the NPS to develop these areas, which were turned over to the states after World War II. They exist today as state parks.[15]

What is not clear is what work was done by the CCC and what was done by WPA on park lands. Sorting out which improvements were made by these two separate organizations at places like Promised Land or Hickory Run State Parks would require untangling the copious work order files that are still stored in drawers in those two parks. The projects completed by these two work relief agencies seem to have been similar in nature—building cabins and pavilions and improving picnic areas and recreational waters.[16]

Two of the state park projects worked on by CCC men were in the metropolitan centers of Johnstown and Reading. (The work done at Stackhouse Park in Johnstown was terminated when the local authorities failed to cooperate with maintenance work on the improvements made.) There was also park development work at Fort Necessity, the site of George Washington's hapless defense against French and Indians in 1754. Part of this work involved restoring Braddock's Trail, which had led to his disaster in 1755. The work done there by Camp SP-12 over a two-year period had to be terminated in 1937 because of disappointing progress and little public interest. Today it is run by the NPS as a national battlefield site.[17]

The historic preservation work done by two African-American companies at Camps MP-1 and MP-2 in Gettysburg Military Park was also done under NPS supervision. The two companies worked to restore the battlefield to its 1863 appearance, and when the last great reunion of Civil War veterans met for the seventy-fifth anniversary commemoration in 1938, the park had been made into

Fig. 27 In 1933 the CCC boys set up Camp S-73 at the intersection of Tyler and Mud Run Roads in Clearfield County. They planted trees, built roads and trails, and constructed Parker Dam, which was designated a recreational reserve in 1936. Today their handiwork can be seen in the sandstone pavilions and CCC Interpretive Center near the breast of the dam. Pennsylvania State Archives

a showcase of historic restoration work. Other historic preservation work was done by SP-17 at Hopewell Village, a colonial iron foundry that was on a site replete with Revolutionary War relics serendipitously discovered in the course of developing the French Creek Recreation Development Area in Berks County.[18]

The planning, execution, and reporting of this enormous quantity and variety of CCC work produced an almost equal quantity of record keeping. The state Department of Forests and Waters in its planning for CCC work required each of its four regional conservationists to report three times a week on the work that was being done, and this was on top of reports compiled at camp level and parallel with reports going to Washington, all of which were separate from the army's own camp records. In the development of state park facilities district foresters were required to file particularly detailed reports on development projects, reporting costs of materials and skilled labor hired and on the income potential of improvements.[19]

The bureaucratic procedures underlying CCC work could be truly byzantine. For example, the directive that an NPS inspector wrote to the project manager at Hickory Run in 1937 has the sound of parody but was typical of what went on behind the scenes of CCC men at work: "We are in receipt of 10-352's for Job 149, Fences, CCC 131. A study of this job application shows that you have not tabulated the types of work under various CCC classifications as stipulated in Washington Office Memorandum R-11 (Numbered Paragraph 3, Pages 2 and 3 which says 'It will be necessary to record in the job application after the justification a tabulated breakdown of the job in accordance with CCC form 7')."[20]

At some parks, CCC men would occasionally be put to work providing assistance to the visiting public. The NPS was sensitive about this work and urged local officials to be very selective in picking men for these kinds of public contacts: "Care should be taken to use neat and courteous enrollees only, those who will enlist the cooperation of camp visitors and patrons . . . in training enrollees for duty emphasis should be placed against the use of rough, commanding and forcing methods of acquainting the public with the regulations."[21]

Winters in Pennsylvania could tax work schedules and vary work routines. Camp supervisors must have looked at heavy snows with the same dread as parents facing snow days for their school-age children. The 1936 winter was particularly bad in the Northeast. Fechner called it the "bitterest winter of a century." Camp supervisors were hard pressed to find activity for the men in Pennsylvania. Some used their manpower to distribute feed for wild animals. Others, like Company #1329 at Camp S-97 near Salisbury, went to work indoors, painting and sprucing up the camp buildings. Company #1394 at S-68, Weikert, was simply sent to the library. The heaviest snows in decades, more than two feet, isolated Company #381 at S-52, Wells Tannery, and fifteen of the men were cut off from camp and had to be put up in the nearby town of Todd. Company #301 at S-80, Masten, reported forty-one inches of snow and spent some days skating and sledding. The CO of Company #1357 at Camp S-135, North Bend, organized a log-chopping contest. Howard "Slim" Miller was the first to chop through a fourteen-inch log and was awarded a carton of cigarettes. One desperate CO at Hillsgrove organized a snowball fight between work platoons

Fig. 28 The company office at Camp Sun Valley scs-13 in Sunbury (Northumberland County). ccc work required an enormous amount of record keeping. In this photo, Commanding Officer Lt. W. A. Kelley is seated at the large desk. Around him, from left to right, are clerks Dominick Pedaline of Rochester, Pa.; William Blughter of Bloomsburg, Pa.; and Mike Kocopi of Clymer, Pa. National Archives

and gave out ice cream afterward. But even without snow, extreme cold would stop construction work. Some forestry work could go on in even bitter cold, with the men keeping warm both from the hard work and from making fires from fallen branches. Cord wood, with its noted twice-warming quality, could always be cut, and local roads cleared and cleaned up.[22]

Winter Reverie

Outside my window the snow is softly drifting down in feathery-white clouds, covering the bleak landscape with a beautiful whiteness. Through its haze I can dimly glimpse the background of the near-by mountains, those wooded hills whose beauty has never ceased to impress me with their magnificence. It brings back memories of that day which, if judged by time, means nothing, a mere interlude, but if judged by the wealth of experience, and the gain in mental and physical attributes, a lifetime, that day when we first viewed this camp of ours. We were new to the game then, wondering what the future held in store for us—if we would be able to stick it out—or, as we learned to call it afterwards, "take it." Little did we realize then that there was untold happiness awaiting us in this forest refuge, away from the artificial pleasures of the city.

—from an essay written by an unnamed Pennsylvania man, included in Ray Hoyt's early study of the CCC, *We Can Take It*, published in 1935

The heavy snowfalls of 1936 brought disastrous flooding to the central and western parts of Pennsylvania with the thaws of mid-March. More than one hundred people died and thousands were left homeless. The *Pittsburgh Press* called it the worst flood in the city's history, and Williamsport reported the Susquehanna River at a record flood level of thirty-five feet.[23] Several CCC camps were called to help in the tasks of rescue, relief, and clean-up work in the aftermath. Ordinarily, the CCC men were released to the supervision of the technical services for the workday, but when disasters like these floods created widespread devastation and suffering, Fechner would order the army to assume full-time authority over the men in responding to the emergency. The 1936 Pennsylvania floods warranted such assistance, and Fechner ordered the army to make use of all available CCC manpower in the regions affected.[24]

Almost overnight, 7,000 CCC men were mobilized to help in rescue and clean-up work. They were often the first ones arriving to give help, hope, and confidence to shocked and depressed local populations. A black company, #2336, from Camp S-146, was the first to arrive with truck-borne assistance to Renovo, one of the most damaged towns. In Johnstown, another hard-hit area, more than

400 CCC men were put up in Cochran Junior High School while they shoveled mud and helped with all the other necessary clean-up work.[25] This disaster relief work earned grateful plaudits from Governor George Earle. The governor acknowledged that "without the CCC the floods would have undoubtedly taken a much higher toll in human life and property. Its work was outstanding." Fechner called the CCC efforts "spectacular." Local community leaders greatly appreciated the help and remembered it long afterward.[26]

Despite the great variety of work done by the CCC, the popular image of the Corps as a "Tree Army" doing forestry work is certainly not a false one, especially in Pennsylvania. The vast majority of the CCC camps in Pennsylvania were in state and national forests, and the principal work done in those places involved reforestation, the harvesting of seeds, the planting of seedlings, and the promoting of healthy growth in existing forest stands. The Department of Forests and Waters in 1938 credited the CCC with advancing forestry work in the state by twenty-five years.[27]

Some of the most important forestry work involved the collection of seeds for the four state forestry nurseries. Camp s-139 at Promised Land collected 457 bushels of tree seeds in one six-month period in 1938. About 60 million seedlings from the nurseries were planted by the CCC in Pennsylvania. The plantings were done in areas that had been made barren by shortsighted logging or by fires or in areas subject to soil erosion runoff.[28]

Tree planting was sometimes done by individuals who were assigned quotas and sometimes by men working in pairs under the supervision of a forester who would establish lines for planting. (He would always carry a snake-bite kit as rattlesnakes were an ever-present threat in the woods of Pennsylvania.) One man would dig the hole, a second would plant the small six- to eight-inch seedling, and they would switch jobs after completing a row. Teams could work with great efficiency, planting about four to five hundred trees in a day. This back-breaking work was among the most difficult the CCC men had to do, and they were almost too exhausted to get to the mess hall after a day spent at it.[29] But CCC men not only planted trees, they also cut them down. To maximize healthy forest growth, supervisors would go through the woods and mark the smaller or less healthy trees that were crowding the growth potential of the better specimens.

Other important stand improvement work involved fighting various tree diseases. Much of the effort was devoted to fighting the white pine blister rust. This fungus arrived from Europe around 1905 and attacked the valuable lumber-producing white pine trees of the state. The fungus has its primary host

Fig. 29 CCC men did a full range of forestry work, including collecting tree seeds and planting the seedlings. Here, men roll seeds into nursery beds at the Clearfield Tree Nursery in May 1934. Pennsylvania State Archives

in currant or gooseberry plants, small bushes with needle-sharp thorns, and has to pass through those hosts before affecting the trees. It does not spread from tree to tree directly. In the 1920s, groups of Boy Scouts and schoolchildren were occasionally mobilized to uproot these plants in local areas. The CCC provided much larger teams of workers, often working in crews of eight men moving through the forest in straight lines, wearing heavy gloves and wielding mattocks. The men would tear up the plants by the roots and burn them in piles or hang them to dry and rot. The goal of the U.S. Forestry Service was to remove all the host plants within one thousand feet of tree stands. This was one of the major work activities of CCC forestry work crews, and it is a bit poignant to learn that today foresters no longer consider this disease as a major threat and devote no effort toward its eradication since it is not considered "a consistent killer of trees."[30]

CCC camps devoted considerable time and energy in combating the ever-present threat of forest fires. Thanks to the CCC and its organized fire brigades, supervised by experienced foresters, the amount of acreage lost to fire dropped by half between 1933 and 1938, with losses cut to "the lowest in the history of the Commonwealth."[31] The network of observation towers, which Pinchot had promoted in the 1920s, was expanded and linked by telephone lines. The men blazed miles of roads and truck trails through forests to allow access for fire-fighting crews. They also devoted considerable effort in cleaning out fallen trees and underbrush that could serve as kindling for fires as well as breeding grounds for harmful insects.

This latter activity was, and continues to be, controversial. Critics accused the CCC of eliminating the natural cover for forest animals and making the forests too "park-like." Hunters, in particular, thought the CCC was ruining things for them. Other critics of the CCC accused it of destroying the "natural equilibrium" of nature when it sent "misguided and enthusiastic young men" to invade the woods and introduce new alien shrubs and trees. Such activity was deemed contrary to the ideal of *conservation*. Experienced foresters, however, tried to strike a balance between fire prevention and keeping natural cover undisturbed.[32]

The Enchanted Forest

The woods were full of a great variety of animal life, some of which ended up in camp "zoos." The memoirs of former CCC men are replete with anecdotes about snakes and bears in particular. It is not uncommon to hear the men tell stories of companies adopting bear cubs and keeping them as company mascots until they grew so big that their playfulness became dangerous. The relatively tame adult bear kept at Camp S-91 was later shot by a farm woman who misinterpreted the animal's behavior.

Snakes, especially rattlers and copperheads, were almost always killed on sight. The men would sometimes bury the venomous heads or collect the rattles as trophies.

Less commonly, strange wayfarers would show up in the middle of the woods. One night in the hard winter and deep snows of 1934 a man appeared at Camp Watrous, asking for food and lodging for the night. He said he had some business across Cedar Mountain and was gone the next morning before reveille. The men tracked him and discovered he had taken a wrong turn onto a circular road. By the time they found him, his feet were frozen and he had to be taken to a hospital. The men never did find out what his business had been but, whatever the real story was, it improved in the retellings.

Another mysterious wanderer showed up at this same camp, claiming that he could make doughnuts. He was given a kitchen position without pay for a few months before he resumed his travels.

SAFETY AND HEALTH IN THE CAMPS

The inherent dangers of fires, coupled with inexperienced young men trying to deal with them, occasionally resulted in tragedy. Fires of all types, in camps and in the woods, were responsible for the deaths of forty-seven CCC men, forty-two enrollees, and five foremen in the nine years of the program, many fewer than died in motor accidents in a single year.[33] But the tendency for fires to kill men in clusters, coupled with the emotions that death by fire always produces, resulted in the extra attention that fire-related deaths in the CCC were given.

Forest fires, of course, occur regularly, set off either by lightning or by man. Ordinarily, fighting forest fires was the job of local voluntary fire wardens and fire crews. The CCC camps would also have small cadres of trained men to battle fires in their vicinity or to help the local men. Occasionally, however, large-scale fires spread beyond the capacity of the trained crews to contain them, and then the entire camp would be mobilized for emergency support.[34] The worst single fire disaster for the CCC occurred in the Big Horn National Forest in Wyoming in August 1937 when fifty CCC men were burned, fifteen of whom were killed.[35] The second deadliest fire in CCC history occurred in Pennsylvania, and it was the single worst disaster in the history of the CCC in the state.

This "Pepper Hill Fire," a fire of unknown origin, broke out along the Sinnamahoning Creek in Cameron County on October 19, 1938. The area had experienced a drought and the dry conditions taxed the efforts of the men from Camp s-132 who were sent to fight the fire. They had spent long hours fighting another fire the day before, and some were near exhaustion. In the evening a small squad of seven enrollees, led by Forester Gilbert Mohney of the State Department of Forests and Waters, became encircled by fire whipped up by swirling winds, and the men were burned to death.[36]

Besides Mohney, the dead included: Basil Bogush, 19, who had been in the CCC for almost a year; Ross Hollabaugh, 18, also in for about a year; Stephen

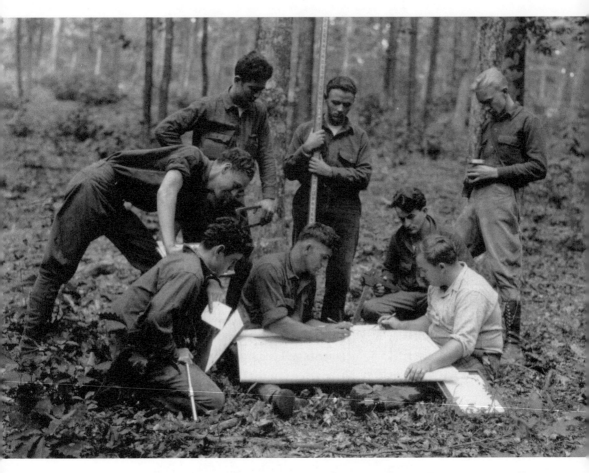

Fig. 30 CCC forest stock survey crews at work in Mont Alto State Forest, August 1934. To maximize healthy growth, these men cleaned out fallen trees and underbrush, cut down small or unhealthy trees, and uprooted diseased plants. Pennsylvania State Archives

Jacofsky, 17, in for six months; George Vogel, 17, in for three months; John Boring, 19, in for six months; Peter Damico, 17, in for three months; and, perhaps the most poignant case, Howard May, 18, who had been in camp for only thirteen days. May was from Erie and had signed up for the CCC despite his mother's objections. She described him as a "happy go luck fellow" who was trying "to help the family." After a tragically absurd late rain subdued the fire, May was found in a kneeling position with his arms and head on a rock.[37]

Five of the men were killed at the site and three died soon after in nearby hospitals. A coroner's inquest was held in Cameron County on October 31, and

the six-man jury ruled the deaths accidental. But they also charged the camp officials of s-132 with "laxity and negligence" and recommended that the three-man safety committee at the camp, headed by the CO, Second Lieutenant Rodman Haynes, be disciplined for not having provided adequate training for the young men before they were allowed to participate in firefighting. The three "rookies" who had entered camp since July had not received any Forest Service instructions on fires at all. The project superintendent, Earl F. Getz, was faulted for allowing Mohney, fatigued after a long day and not a CCC designated "fire warden," to lead a crew not specifically trained in firefighting into a difficult and treacherous area. No one was indicted and no one person was held responsible, but the jury clearly blamed the deaths on the general negligence of both the army and the forestry personnel.[38]

Even before this inquest was held, the army had quickly convened its own panel of officers and conducted a hearing at the camp on October 20. The panel sat for four days, heard witnesses, and prepared a fifty-six-page report. The army board concluded that the fire had freakishly jumped behind the men, cutting them off. They assigned responsibility for the tragedy almost entirely to the technical service people. Mohney, they reported, was exhausted from a long day of activity, and his crew was described as "disorganized." Although Lieutenant Haynes was cited for "administrative neglect" for his failure to properly organize safety training in camp, the superintendent was found equally at fault on this matter and, moreover, bore the primary responsibility of making sure that the men were properly trained before they were released to him by the army. The board emphasized that once the men were out of camp, the foresters had complete responsibility for them.[39]

In Washington news of this "most disastrous fire" was shocking and, it was feared, potentially damaging to the reputation of the CCC. Fechner sent one of his camp investigators, Charles Kenlan, to the coroner's inquest and, after studying the records, they both concluded that the camp CO shouldered the primary responsibility for what had happened. Fechner found himself frustrated, not for the first or last time, by his lack of authority over camp personnel. He thought the CO should be removed, but he was powerless to do so and came up against the army's tendency to defend its own.[40]

Lieutenant Haynes's superior, General J. K. Parsons, commanding general of the Third Corps, saw no evidence of culpability on the part of the army; he put the blame on the project superintendent for any training deficiencies the men may have had. Parsons's superior, army chief of staff General Malin Craig, in a confidential letter to Parsons, agreed with his exoneration of Lieutenant Haynes and opined that no amount of safety training could have prevented the freak accident. He did suggest that Parsons have all his COs re-read the safety regulations. Craig's superior, Secretary of War George Tyner, also backed up the army's point of view, and Fechner was left no recourse except to issue a directive to the effect that camp commanders were to be responsible for making sure that the men had adequate safety training before they were released from camp to fight fires. He also complained to the president about his lack of disciplinary authority over supervisory personnel, but nothing was changed and all the supervisors at Camp S-132 were kept in their positions. Under the administrative arrangements of the CCC, Fechner had no authority over the appointment or disciplining of camp commanders. Although they were paid by his CCC, any orders he sent out to them had to go through War Department channels.[41]

Fechner's authority was equally weak in dealing with the technical services. He was as stymied by the Department of Agriculture as he was by the Department of War in trying to affix responsibility for the loss of the lives of seven of his enrollees. The Forestry Service refused to find any fault with the forestry personnel for the deaths.[42]

Again, and not for the first time, Fechner felt his helplessness when it came to dealing with the technical services. In 1935 he had complained to the president about his inability to remove a number of incompetent technical people from Camp s-140 in Lackawanna County in Pennsylvania, including a project superintendent and two foremen who were allegedly often drunk. The Forestry Service refused to cooperate. The "muddling through" administrative apparatus of the ccc generally got the job done, but there were many instances like these when things fell through cracks.[43]

The ccc tragedy of 1938 is commemorated by a memorial plaque to the fallen men, located off Pennsylvania Route 120, southeast of Emporium. The memorial site, built by the men of Camp s-132, was dedicated in a ceremony on October 11, 1939, attended by five companies of ccc men from nearby camps, along with Assistant Director McEntee. The tragedy did lead to some improvements in ccc fire safety training. Fechner ordered that all camps have trained fire brigades of twenty-five men who would be first responders, that all enrollees be given some fire training, and that no one under eighteen be released from camp to fight fires.[44]

Death by fire always arouses emotions of horror but, in fact, relatively few ccc men died that way. There were many dangers when large numbers of inexperienced young men were placed in the woods with potentially dangerous tools, heavy equipment, and high spirits. The ccc actually developed an admirable safety record, but it had to work at it. In 1933, the accident rate was 288 per 1,000 men working in camps, counting accidents serious enough to result in lost work time. In the first summer of the ccc, Fechner appointed George Weidenfield of the Labor Department to oversee safety issues. Weidenfield received accident reports from camps and encouraged cos to establish first-aid training programs.[45]

When these measures failed to reduce the number of accidents, Fechner appointed, in May 1934, an industrial safety expert, Samuel M. Lauderdale, to head up a new Division of Safety in his office. Regulations and safety posters were distributed to the camps and a monthly *Safety Bulletin* was published, as well as other various publications from time to time. In 1935 every camp was required to have a safety council, consisting of the camp commander, the project superintendent, and the medical officer or contracted physician. The council was to meet at least once a month and was charged with overseeing all aspects of camp life and work that posed potential safety hazards. Regular fire drills were required, and training in handling tools and equipment, driving vehicles, and fighting forest fires all came under the purview of the council.[46]

In Pennsylvania, the Department of Forests and Waters also sent periodic safety bulletins on various issues involving the handling of tools and dynamite. "A wrench is not a hammer, a pick is not a crowbar, an axe is not a wedge" were some of the safety tips foremen were instructed to impress upon their charges.[47] All these efforts resulted in a markedly improved safety record. The accident rate dropped steadily in every year and by 1941 was down to 81 per 1,000. At the end, the death rate for CCC men was not only below that of the army, but it was lower than that of young men in the general population as well.[48]

Motoring accidents killed more CCC men than anything else—in 1940, for example, 154 of the 297 men killed died in such accidents.[49] The men were in trucks almost daily, traveling to and from work sites, picking up materials, going into town on weekends. Pennsylvania camp records are replete with records of truck-related deaths. An early accident on June 28, 1933, at Camp s-54 occurred when one of the thirteen men riding in a truck fell out and was

Fig. 31 The CCC had its share of accidents, but for the most part it had an admirable safety record. Here, a CCC boy with sunstroke is carried off to camp on a stretcher in Logan State Forest, May 1933. Pennsylvania State Archives

driven over. The camp was briefly known as Camp Fox in honor of the man killed. Another sad instance, attracting some national news interest, involved three World War I veterans from Veterans' Camp SP-16 in Beaver County near McDonald. The men were in town, with no supervision, celebrating Armistice Day in 1936 and were killed driving back to camp in a truck.[50]

Unfortunately, the health records of CCC recruits did not improve as dramatically as the accident rates. As recruiting agents delved into an ever-younger population, problems of communicable diseases proved nettlesome. All recruits were, upon enrollment, inoculated against typhoid, paratyphoid, and smallpox, but of course there were many other ways to get sick, and the later classes of CCC men were about two and a half times more likely than army men to fall ill. Pneumonia, in particular, was a serious problem, although fewer died from it as time went on. Appendicitis and, somewhat surprisingly, coronary disease were the principal causes of death by illness in the camps in 1940. In that year, 282 men died of those two causes, almost as many as the 297 killed in accidents.[51]

Contributing to the sickness rates among CCC recruits was undoubtedly their generally poor physical condition upon enrollment. A 1941 study showed that 70 percent of the boys were below acceptable weight levels when they were enrolled. During a six-month tour, weight gains varied somewhat depending on backgrounds. White urban boys put on about nine and a half pounds, white rural boys a bit more. Black urban boys put on still more, and the biggest gains, sixteen and a half pounds, were seen among black rural enrollees. Of course there were exceptions. Edmond Dochod, who was from the town of Nanticoke, claims he put on forty pounds of muscle in the two years he served at S-80 from 1937 to 1939. As one officer put it, the men "have grown more rapidly than the trees which they have planted."[52]

Occasionally disease outbreaks forced the quarantining of camps. A camp near Bloomsburg was closed because of diphtheria in 1933, and another, outside Reading, was quarantined for fifteen days in 1934 because of a case of spinal meningitis. When Camp S-107 was quarantined in 1935, the CO gave strict instructions to the project superintendent about the transportation and isolation of the work crews.[53]

With so many health dangers potentially capable of sweeping through entire camps, it is not surprising to find the stress that CCC officials placed on cleanliness. Water supplies were regularly monitored and frequently chlorinated, regular army inspections of food and kitchen sanitation occurred, and the men were required to bathe weekly, clean their teeth daily, and keep their hair short.

Complaints about bedbugs were rare but received serious attention when they appeared. The Third Corps awarded camps like s-134 for having low sickness and accident rates.[54]

Venereal disease was another worry for the ccc authorities. In some camps the army provided some elementary education for the men and condoms were available in some of the post exchanges. But in other camps there was nothing apart from the occasional "short-arm" surprise inspections in the barracks or before showers. Disease rates grew alarming enough to force more drastic action in 1938. All serious cases of syphilis were sent to local hospitals, and, once cured, the recruit was given a dishonorable discharge, sent home, and his local board of health was notified.[55]

A study sponsored by the American Council on Education in 1941 found that, of 4,450 men given the Wassermann test, 1.8 percent showed positive for syphilis. The more sensitive Kahn test was given to 3,040 men and it showed a 3.6 percent rate. Overall, venereal disease rates for ccc men averaged 18.3 cases per 1,000 men, compared to the army's record of 87 per 1,000 in World War I.[56] But, then again, the ccc men were not in France.

Relations of enrollees with young women from nearby towns varied greatly. At one end, a young Leo Ruvolis, who had gone from Wilkes-Barre to a camp near Buena Vista, Virginia, had virtually no relations with the local people, except for some store clerks. He sums up the behavior of ccc men in town as "keeping your britches zipped and your mouth shut." In contrast, not a few enrollees met their wives on ccc excursions into local towns. Edwin Smith from McKeesport, who signed up at age fifteen in 1938 and was stationed at Camp s-155 in 1940, met his wife in nearby Wellsboro and settled there after his tour.[57]

Attitudes of local young women toward the ccc boys plunked down in their midst varied, of course, but there seems to have been a common concern among many of their parents about their daughters getting involved with poor young men with seemingly poor prospects.[58] The investigators for the American Council on Education seemed to provide support for these parental fears when they undertook an in-depth survey in 1941 of the moral attitudes of 419 ccc men, taking several hours for each interview.

The council found the men "not high in moral quality," and on matters of gambling, sexual behavior, and the use of alcohol, they concluded that the "majority of ccc enrollees might almost be described as immoral." Gambling went on in the camps, especially around paydays, and under the noses of camp commanders, most of whom seemed to have had the philosophy that "boys will be boys." Masturbation was commonly confessed by the men interviewed, although homosexuality virtually unheard of. More than 90 percent of the men boasted of having had sexual intercourse, and most of them claimed their first experiences at ages fourteen to sixteen.[59] Those who can remember what adolescence was like, at least in the pre-sixties era, may be forgiven an arched eyebrow on hearing of these self-described exploits and a more cynical receptivity to the entire study than the educators who undertook it in 1941 seem to have had.

Fig. 32 Tony Frattini of Blairsville, Pa., spends downtime with a local ranch girl named Nancy Brown while serving at a CCC camp in Orogrande, New Mexico, in December 1940. National Archives

FREE TIME IN CAMP

While it is safe to say that the most important and longest lasting legacy of the CCC was in the work that the men performed, they actually spent more of their time in camp. The hours after dinner or on weekends were spent in relaxation, recreation, or education. Relaxation could mean anything from reading materials in the camp library, writing letters home, listening to the radio, playing music, or just hanging out and "chewing the fat." Some camps put on theatrical shows and the Federal Theater Project of WPA visited more than one thousand CCC camps after 1936, bringing a variety of professional productions.[60]

It is difficult to imagine but for many of these CCC boys, camp life was much richer than their home life had been. Not only was there usually more, and better, food, but according to an extensive study begun by the American Youth Commission in 1936, 12.6 percent of the boys came from homes where there were no books, and 37.1 percent lived in houses with no running water. Surprisingly, however, there were pianos in 15.7 percent of the homes.[61]

Recreational activities after work included outdoor sports in the long daylight hours of spring and summer or on weekends. Indoors, games of checkers, pool, or ping-pong helped pass the time. Intercamp athletics became highly organized, with district and Corps championships at stake. Major league baseball scouts were known to attend ccc games and signed twenty players to contracts. Sometimes the men would be trucked to college football games on Saturday afternoons.[62]

Of all the leisure-time activities in camp, the one that held the most potential for helping the ccc to make a serious contribution to public policy was its educational program. But although the ccc offered marvelous opportunities for many boys, the educational program has to be counted as its greatest disappointment. Recruits typically came into the ccc with eight or nine years of schooling, but many had fewer than that, and about 3 percent were classified as illiterate. Instruction in the three Rs benefited many of these boys, and even the more formally schooled gained from vocational instruction in typing, auto mechanics, and a wide variety of other skills taught in ccc courses. An indeterminate number of the men, but probably a low percentage, launched themselves on lifelong careers with their ccc training, but for most recruits the general work experience—often their first paying jobs—was the most valuable education they took away from camp.

The idea of providing education in ccc camps had not been part of Roosevelt's original grand idea, but it was talked up by both national and state administrators very early in the set-up phase. An organized program of camp education, however, did not begin until January 1934 when the newly established Division of Education, under Clarence C. Marsh, began to place educational advisers in the camps. This took a while. In 1936 there were only 116 educational advisers for the 195 camps in the Third Corps.[63]

Holding classes in rooms where other activities were going on was not ideal either. It was not until 1937 that a separate building for education was required in the camps, and as late as 1939 the building used for classes at Camp sp-18, near Scotland, Pennsylvania, had no stove and everyone had to wear overcoats and gloves during winter classes. The educational adviser assigned to the camp spent most of his time organizing recreational activities. At Promised Land in the Pocono Mountains, Camp s-139, there was no adviser until June 1934. The camp had no electricity until 1935, and although studying by lantern may sound charming and even Lincolnesque, it was also discouraging to young men who were tired from a day of hard physical labor.[64] Pennsylvania boys sent out West ran into other problems. For example, those at a camp near Las Cruces, New Mexico, found the language barrier impossible to bridge between the English spoken by the adviser and their own variety.[65]

The educational adviser was normally a college graduate, often an unemployed teacher, always male. (Women, however, often worked in camps as teachers of individual courses.) The job of educational adviser tended to be a lonely and isolated position of low prestige, resulting in high turnover rates. Although the adviser earned about $2,000 a year, that was less than the CO or the project superintendent.[66]

One of the camp educational adviser's regular jobs, usually working closely with the enrollee he had selected as the assistant educational adviser, was to supervise publication of the camp newspaper. Usually a dozen or so of the men contributed to the issues, and some of them clearly aspired to journalism. "The Mountain Eagle," put out by Company #1385 at Camp S-64 in Milroy, for example, contained drama reviews of camp plays and book reviews of current best sellers, as well as the usual camp news about work and sports. This paper also included comics, a crossword puzzle, and ads for both national and local products. At Richmond Furnace, S-54, the "Co. 305" was a sixteen-page mimeographed collage of camp news, jokes, cartoons, essays, and a "Sympathetic Sally" advice column that was periodically awarded the "honor banner" as the best camp paper in its subdistrict of nine camps. A staff of fourteen put it out, with the educational adviser listed as its "censor." It took thirteen men to put out "Bunker Hill Bunk" for S-51 at Pine Grove Furnace.[67]

The adviser, the CO, and the project superintendent constituted the Educational Advisory Committee within each camp. They were responsible for approving the courses to be offered and for lining up instructors to teach the courses. (It probably worked in the reverse order more often than not.) The educational advisers were part of the camp personnel and as such came under the administrative authority of the camp commander. But army attitudes toward the whole project were often less than enthusiastic. General Paul Malone of the Third Corps was typical of army officers in his limited interest in camp education. He wanted the illiterate boys taught how to read and write, and the rest of the men to be advanced one year in grade level. In addition, he thought that all the enrollees should be given some sort of on-the-job training in simple vocational subjects. And that would be enough for young men whose principal reason for being in CCC camps, in his opinion, was to perform useful conservation work.[68]

But the educational opportunities in camps quickly outgrew these kinds of modest expectations. The variety of courses that came to be offered for enrollees was limited only by the imaginations and interests of instructors and students. In addition to resident camp personnel, after 1935 the WPA paid unemployed teachers to work in CCC camps. At Pine Grove Furnace in 1936, for example, there were five WPA teachers giving classes, including two women.[69] A report on the CCC educational program in 1938 revealed that instruction was being given by 10,629 work project technicians, 5,643 enrollees, 4,286 military personnel, 1,826 educational advisers, 1,745 assistant educational advisers, 1,671 WPA teachers, 381 regular school teachers, and 79 National Youth Administration (NYA) teachers. The most popular subjects were auto mechanics, office skills, and carpentry.[70]

In a few places, such as Williamsport, Pennsylvania, the Corps was able to take advantage of the vocational educational facilities of school districts, but this was exceptional. Although some CCC boys, like Leo Ruvolis, embarked on life-long careers because of their camp experiences, this happened rarely. A critical study of the educational programs of a small sample of camps in 1939 found that despite initial enthusiasm, enrollees dropped out of programs in disheartening numbers. The average enrollee received only twenty-seven hours of instruction over a two-year enlistment period. Moreover, the costs of camp education were higher on a per capita basis than they were in public schools.[71]

Except for the educational adviser and the WPA and NYA teachers, the instructors were unpaid. Foremen pressured into giving classes often resented having to return to camp after having their dinner at home to give unpaid instruction. They often tried to squeeze their classes in before dinner, and they sometimes ran out of subject matter for the time allotted.[72]

Attendance at classes was, in theory, optional. In 1935 the participation rate for enrollees was about 60 percent, but in later years subtle pressures were placed on enrollees to sign up for courses and the voluntary nature of the program was not always advertised. Although claims approaching 90 percent participation were sometimes made toward the end, those numbers seem to greatly inflate the true picture. It is impossible to determine how many boys stayed with a subject for more than a few days. Summertime classes competed with outdoor recreation. Nor did the different educational levels of enrollees make for ideal instructional environments. As an incentive, certificates were awarded to those who persevered in some defined course but these, of course, had no significance outside camp. The American Council on Education's in-depth survey of the attitudes of 395 enrollees in 1941 found that 30 percent liked the classes they took, 44 percent took them only because they seemed to be "required," 24 percent took nothing at all, and 2 percent reported that there were no classes at all offered at their camp.[73]

Fig. 33 For many men, an important part of the CCC experience was the vocational training they received for life after the CCC. These two photos show some of the educational opportunities. Men receive training in auto mechanics at the Williamsport Vocational School (top) and take a radio class at Camp F-4 in the Allegheny National Forest (bottom). Top, National Archives; bottom, Franklin Delano Roosevelt Presidential Library, Hyde Park, N.Y.

Camp libraries could enrich the free time of enrollees, and Clarence C. Marsh took an early interest in upgrading the quality of literature they offered. The original books supplied by the army to the camps in 1933 seem to have been of the Zane Grey Westerns variety. Marsh made sure the men had access to more serious literature if they so desired. He also began what became a very elaborate publication program of CCC course manuals and how-to books. By 1939, the Educational Division had produced workbooks for English and math and had prodded the technical services to produce instructional booklets on various topics relating to the kinds of work being done. There were also self-teaching manuals for camps with a shortage of teachers. In the Third Corps, a monthly newsletter called "The Adviser" was published for the benefit of the camp educational advisers.[74]

In the politically volatile 1930s, the CCC walked a fine line between its goals of promoting good citizenship and its attempts to discipline the free and open discussion of issues. As the American Council on Education critique put it, "Obedience is not the supreme virtue in a democracy." But Fechner tended toward a more fearful and cautious approach. He forbade left-wing publications, such as the *New Republic* and the *Nation,* in the camps. In 1934, apparently on the recommendation of an assistant, he stepped in to remove copies of a book entitled *You and Machines* that the Educational Division had distributed to the camps. Read today, it seems an innocuous discussion of the advantages and disadvantages of the impact of machines on employment, but Fechner thought it conveyed too discouraging a message. His heavy-handed action was the last

Fig. 34 Relaxing in the library at Camp s-80 in Masten (Lycoming County). National Archives

in a series of discouraging slights to Director Marsh, who resigned soon afterward and was replaced by Howard Oxley.[75]

One booklet that did meet with Fechner's approval was entitled *A Manual for Instruction in Civilian Conservation Corps Camps.* It was published by the Vocational Division of the Office of Education in July 1935 and had a chapter on "How to Avoid Dangerous Issues." The author had come up with ingenious techniques for deflecting or postponing indefinitely any discussion of sensitive subjects. This overly conservative approach to education met with a humorous jibe by the ever-critical *New Republic* magazine. In the event that some CCC enrollee should raise the subject of full employment in the Soviet Union, for instance, the magazine suggested that the instructor simply set off a few firecrackers and blame the attack on the Reds.[76] To its credit, the War Department overrode the Third Corps commander when he confiscated a paper one of the men had subscribed to called "Champion of Youth," which advocated soviets. The army's position was that anything allowed to be sent through the mail could not be prohibited by them.[77]

In the 1937 legislation making the CCC an independent agency, Congress mandated that enrollees be provided ten hours of vocational education if they so chose. Fechner appointed a commission to study the implementation of this directive, but when it recommended that Wednesday afternoons and Saturdays be devoted to education in the camps, it received no support from either him or the president. Things continued as before with the army and technical services remaining coolly aloof from supporting anything other than basic literacy and on-the-job instruction. Fechner saw the CCC as a place of "actual work," not as a school in the woods. His hopes were that as a "work-centered organization," the CCC would help young men bridge the gap between their precamp conditions of unemployment and inexperience and postcamp gainful employment.[78]

In Pennsylvania the most successful educational program offered CCC men was at the Williamsport School District Vocational School. From the beginning men from Camps S-145, S-125, and S-80 had been taking courses there, but the relationship became more formalized in 1936. Every Saturday about sixty enrollees came to the school to take certified courses in such subjects as metal working, clerical skills, electrical work, woodworking, and commercial art, courses taught by Williamsport vocational teachers or WPA personnel. At the end of a course, the graduates received certificates and assistance in job placement. By 1941, eighty-five men were participating in the program and they were reportedly having great success in landing war-related jobs.[79]

There were other positive stories in the state about education, scattered from camp to camp. Camp s-96 at Hillsgrove, home in 1935 to Company #317, had such an excellent educational program that *Happy Days* dubbed it "Hillsgrove University." In April 1935 they held a commencement ceremony wherein Captain D. D. Griffith awarded 260 certificates to men who had completed various courses of study. Another nearby camp, s-95 at Forksville, had an extensive catalogue of courses offered in 1935: American government was taught by the educational adviser, math by a teacher provided by the FERA, auto mechanics by one of the enrollees, "Company Administration" and "Social Courtesy" by the CO, first aid by the medical officer, landscaping by one of the technical staff, and religious education by the chaplain.[80]

In addition to the courses offered in camp, enrollees in Pennsylvania were given opportunities to take correspondence courses from various colleges at a cost of $.50 to $1.50 per course. Penn State invited camps located nearby to come to its campus for lectures, musical performances, and manual training in its shops. Moreover, in 1937 thirty-nine men in Pennsylvania camps received college scholarships.[81]

As time went on, the educational emphasis began shifting back to more on-the-job training, something to which the project superintendents were always more favorably inclined. The U.S. Forest Service boasted of never undertaking a CCC job without first explaining it to the men. The American Council on Education found that the technicians did a good job of explaining the nature of upcoming tasks and offered careful instruction on the use of the tools needed. But its study found that the supervisors were not as attentive in explaining the steps necessary to complete the job.[82]

From CCC to World War II

Ambitious CCC boys could acquire many more skills than those taught in camp classes. Clair "Rusty" Swarmer, who had graduated from high school in Punxsutawney in 1934, was eager to learn anything the CCC could teach him. In his three years in the Corps, as enrollee and then as a LEM, Swarmer worked at an impressive variety of jobs, including digging fire trails; keeping books as assistant company clerk and later as chief clerk; working as an assistant cook; editing the "Camp ANF-10" newsletter; leading a tree stand surveying crew; operating road graders, bulldozers, and stake-body trucks; setting dynamite charges in rocks for road building crews; and maintaining air compressors in forty-below temperatures.

But as adventurous as Swarmer's CCC days were, they paled in comparison to his service in World War II. He was a radio operator in a B-17 that was shot down over Tunisia in early 1943 and spent the rest of the war in German POW camps. With two companions he managed to escape from one but was recaptured; he was finally liberated by Patton's Third Army in April 1945. He has recounted his knight-errant tale in a privately printed and aptly titled memoir, "The Nine Lives of 27436."

As the war neared, McEntee and Congress began to require more instruction in military-related skills. By 1941, every enrollee had to take the Red Cross program in first aid, for example, and those taking formal vocational classes related to defense work were credited with up to five hours a week with work release time. Moreover, the CCC by then had established 176 schools of its own, offering instruction to some thirteen thousand enrollees in such militarily useful areas as cooking, radio operation, and mechanics.[83]

In the end, it is difficult to evaluate the worth of the elaborately organized CCC educational programs. Had the Corps continued, it is almost certain that more standardized instructional programs would have been developed along with more carefully articulated arrangements with local educational institutions. There would undoubtedly have been systematic follow-up studies on the usefulness of the skills learned by enrollees in camp, studies that the CCC never had enough time or manpower to undertake. The CCC clearly performed a useful educational service in ending the illiteracy of the approximately 3 percent of its enrollees, and many other individuals found their lifetime vocations thanks to their CCC work or instruction, but the evidence is only anecdotal.[84]

The FERA did some studies of the employment histories of former CCC men early in the program, in 1933 and 1934. The findings were not encouraging. Of the 205,200 CCC men included in the study, only 58,448 had found employment a year later.[85] The scope of these early follow-up studies was never approached again. The American Council on Education 1941 study was a much smaller one of 224 former enrollees. Only 18 percent found work in the first month after their discharge, but 77 percent were employed one year afterward. These results were more encouraging, but of course the general employment situation was much better in 1941 because of war production than it had been in 1933 and 1934.[86]

Frank Persons was one who realized that, despite the amount of education and work experience men received in the camps, not much would be gained if the CCC simply returned them to a condition of unemployment in their home communities. He hoped that camp education would improve their chances, but he realized the helplessness and ignorance of CCC authorities when it came to dealing with unemployment among former enrollees or even being aware of its extent. When 99,265 men completed their tours in May 1939, Persons could only muse to Fechner about what would become of them.[87]

In addition to supervising education in the camps, the camp commanders also were charged with providing religious services for the men. Although interest in religion, especially among the young, was down in the 1930s, Director Fechner thought it was important to counter the "scoffer boys" and teach enrollees how "to appreciate the value of religion in their self-development."[88] Army chaplains were in the camps from the beginning, and by 1939 there were 406 reserve chaplains resident in the camps. Most tried to service eight to twelve camps, some as many as twenty-five. In addition, 165 contracted clergymen were paid $30 a month to provide in-camp services. In western Pennsylvania the chaplain of District No. 1 covered over 69,000 miles in the first three years, paying 542 visits to camps.[89]

Fig. 35 Religious service at Camp s-66 in Mill Hall (Clinton County). National Archives.

Ecumenical altars that could be altered for Protestant and Catholic services were often set up in camps. "Other sects" would have occasional seasonal services. Walter Joyce, who joined Camp s-91 at Watrous at age seventeen in 1934, was assigned to help both Protestant ministers and Catholic priests set up their services. Although a Catholic himself, Joyce did not know the Latin responses at Mass. The priest coaxed him through the service, kidded him on paying more attention to the Protestant services, and then afterward played pool with him for $.25 a game. Enrollees in camps where there were no resident chaplains or who did not find the visiting ministers satisfactory had the option of being transported into local towns for services.[90]

Some of the clergy who preached in the CCC camps seem to have found it a refreshing change from their usual ministries. Chaplain Ira Freeman of Johnstown, Pennsylvania, enjoyed the homogeneous congregations. With no women present, he did not find "pussyfooting" necessary nor did he have "to camouflage a description of sinful practices." In the setting of a camp he could be direct—and brief. He felt that the men's attention to his sermons began to lag after ten minutes.[91]

DISCIPLINE IN THE CAMPS

With all the considerable attractions of the CCC—work, income, plenty of food, recreation, education, camaraderie—it is, perhaps, surprising that so many enrollees did not complete their terms of enlistment. Of course the many positives of CCC life could be offset for some boys by negatives, particularly in the early days in camp. For many it was their first time away from home. Others might find the mild hazing of rookies intolerable. Snipe hunts, guarding the flagpole, following "officers" into the woods for all-night watches—these mild and, in retrospect, amusing initiation rites could easily cross over into more bullying persecutions.[92]

Boys could leave camp on their own by requesting an end to their service and a return trip home or simply by going AWOL. Boys also could be sent home for some disciplinary infraction. In the beginning there were two ways men could be officially discharged from their CCC camps: honorable discharge or dishonorable discharge. The first was the most acceptable route and also the most common. It was given to enrollees who had served out their enlistment tour or who had been granted permission to leave because they had a written offer of employment. Dishonorable discharge was reserved for the most serious breaches of camp discipline; refusal to work or being AWOL for a week were the most common. Criminal convictions and moral turpitude also resulted in dishonorable discharges. In such cases, the individual forfeited forthcoming pay and allotments and was barred from re-enlisting in the Corps.

Shortly into the program, a third category of administrative discharges was added, somewhat more lenient in tone and penalties. Cases of AWOL and refusal to work would now usually merit this kind of dismissal and would not entail any loss of pay earned. In 1939, enrollees were allowed up to fifteen days AWOL before they were discharged.[93]

Army regulations required that before men could be dismissed, they were entitled to hearings, with the right to remain silent, call witnesses, and have representation, but there is little evidence of busy COs bothering with any of that. Enrollees were told that a dishonorable discharge would be a permanent stain on their record, barring them from government employment and possibly even from some forms of private employment.

After a man was discharged, he would, at the camp's convenience, be transported back to where he had been enrolled, either an army office or a local relief office. In the first year Fechner insisted on being the final authority on camp dismissals, but his reversal of half the appeals referred to him angered the army and he backed off in March 1934 and let them handle the whole process.[94]

In 1940, when McEntee assumed direction of the CCC, the system of discharges was altered slightly. Dishonorable discharges were reserved for only the most serious cases of felonies or moral turpitude. All lesser cases, including desertion, simply merited "dismissal." The administrative discharge category was dropped.[95]

Short of dismissal, which was occasionally overused by inexperienced commanders, the CO's power to discipline enrollees was limited to such small penalties as suspending privileges, assigning extra work, or assessing small fines up to $3 a month. If he so chose, he could establish a kind of kangaroo court of enrollees to handle these small matters. The strongest asset of a CO, however, was his ability to project authority and respect within the camp's organizational hierarchy.[96]

"Desertion" was the most troubling way by which men left camps before their tour of duty was completed. The word itself was an emotional one, with wartime connotations. In addition, with all the effort and expense involved in getting an enrollee to camp, it seemed all for naught when he simply walked out after a short period of time. Fechner first became alarmed at statistics showing that 11.6 percent of enrollees were deserting in 1936. But the problem of desertion became more serious after 1937 when fewer CCC men were coming from families on relief and therefore were lacking the pressure of sending home the monthly allotment checks to desperate families. Rates climbed to approximately 20 percent a year over the next few years.[97]

Outside critics of the CCC pointed to the high numbers of enrollees who did not complete their tours. The Communist *Daily Worker,* opposed to the CCC from the beginning, trumpeted statistics showing that about one-third of the enrollees in 1935 and 1936 did not receive honorable discharges.[98] During the fiscal year ending in June 1936, only 51 percent of the men who left camp had completed the tour they had signed up for. Of the rest, 26 percent had been allowed to leave to accept employment or for some other legitimate reason. By November 1938, about 68 percent of enrollees nationwide leaving the Corps were discharged honorably, but in Pennsylvania the figure was only 60 percent. The rest—almost 40 percent—were receiving administrative or dishonorable discharges.[99]

Critics suspected that even these disappointing numbers underestimated the problem and doubted that all those receiving honorable discharges for employment had actually obtained jobs. They suspected that COs were granting discharges to boys who just wanted to leave or who had proven themselves minor nuisances around camp. Certainly the few studies done on postcamp employment never showed the kind of success rate that these discharge figures implied. The FERA studies of 1933 and 1934 showed that for Pennsylvania enrollees who had served in the first class, only 19.6 percent were working a year after leaving the CCC.[100]

The study done by the American Council on Education in 1941 estimated that over the life of the program about 500,000 of the 2.7 million men who went through CCC camps either deserted or were dishonorably discharged.[101] The CCC's own study through 1941 showed slightly worse results. Only 38.2 percent completed their term of service; 21.7 percent had left to accept employment; 13.8 percent had deserted; and 6.9 percent had been discharged for disciplinary reasons. For the remaining 19.4 percent, mostly unspecified "miscellaneous" reasons were listed as the cause of discharge.[102]

An ongoing argument over the causes of the growing desertion rate pitted the national office people, who called for more careful selection of enrollees and better orientation programs, against state selectors like Kurtz, who tended to blame desertions on a combination of very young recruits and inexperienced officers in the camps.[103] In Pennsylvania, as in the rest of the country, the problem of desertions increased as the war approached. In the first six months of 1940, about one-third more enrollees (1,039) deserted Pennsylvania camps than had done so for the entire year of 1939 (780). In the last three months of 1940, desertions numbered 809. Boys continued to slip away for many reasons, especially because of the improving job situation. By late 1941, CCC desertions across the country were running about 6,000 a month at a time when the number of camps was dropping from 1,500 to 900. During that period in Pennsylvania, desertions numbered between 150 and 200 a month from a much-reduced camp population.[104]

Aside from desertions, other public relations headaches for CCC officials were the occasional large-scale mutinies in camp. From the very beginning of the program there had been occasions of men organizing themselves in strikes against working conditions or engaging in collective violence. Pennsylvania men, especially those from coal mining regions, were reported to engage in this kind of behavior when assigned to camps in Virginia.[105]

Instances of such behavior also occurred among Pennsylvania men in Pennsylvania camps. Robert Ward remembers a group of men at Camp S-91 who refused to work in the winter of 1934 because of the extreme cold. The CO seems to have handled it coolly, and most of the men returned to work after he talked to them. Other camps also saw occasional instances of such organized resistance to authority, which usually led to investigations into the causes. One commander at S-130 in Cameron County in 1934 was admonished for dismissing forty-one men who had rioted in camp. Investigators concluded that the problem could have been better handled by dealing with a few ringleaders instead. When the CO at Camp SCS-7, Glen Rock, discharged twenty-seven members of Company #2318 on Thanksgiving eve in 1935, a riot broke out in camp and local and state police had to be brought in. The army put the blame on "communistic agitators" led by an enrollee from Scranton, that "hot-bed of Reds," but Fechner's investigator found that the episode had been blown out of proportion and had been caused by bad management by the CO and a bad camp atmosphere caused by friction between him and the project superintendent. In another case, the commander at Camp S-120 in Clinton County dismissed twenty-five Veterans for refusing to work in the winter of 1936 in circumstances that investigators again judged could have been handled with less drastic action.[106]

Although these unpleasant episodes were relatively rare, they do form part of the rich history of the work and camp life of Pennsylvania CCC men and help to show how the state's CCC program reflected the national program in microcosm. Enrollees from Pennsylvania worked, either in state or out of state, in virtually every kind of conservation work the CCC provided, and the stories of their in-camp lives were generally consistent with what studies of the national organization found. Unfortunately, Pennsylvania's CCC story also reflected national patterns of race relations. For all its economic and environmental benefits, the CCC was mired in the social values and mores of an earlier and very different America. Nowhere is it more apparent how these historical differences served to cramp its promise and possibilities than in the Corps's treatment of African-Americans.

4

AFRICAN-AMERICANS IN PENN'S WOODS

It might almost be said of African-Americans in the CCC that they inhabited a parallel universe wherein a similar organization existed, the "Colored Civilian Conservation Corps." Approximately 250,000 of the 2,500,000 enrollees in the CCC were black, and while, of course, there was no such formal organization as the "CCCC," for most practical purposes there was. In most areas of the country there were separate Colored camps for black enrollees. Because Pennsylvania, compared to other northern states, had an above average proportion of African-Americans in its population, it presents an ideal situation for studying both how the CCC provided benefits and opportunities for young black males and how the limited imaginations of the program's administrators severely crippled those benefits and opportunities.[1]

We must remember that the Constitution, at least as interpreted by Supreme Court justices after the infamous *Plessy v. Ferguson* decision in 1896, had legitimized the doctrine of "separate but equal." Separate, as the Warren Court would rule in its 1954 *Brown v. Board of Education* decision, is inherently unequal, and the CCC's treatment of black Americans certainly illustrates the point. But the CCC was actually an organization in which the theoretical dogma of *Plessy* came close to being realized—"close" being a relative term, of course. That the inequalities produced in the CCC by segregation were not as severe as in some other areas of American life, most notably in spending on public education, must not blind us to seeing how primitive racial attitudes were in the United States of Franklin D. Roosevelt's New Deal.

De facto segregation existed everywhere in the country. De jure segregation existed primarily in southern states where the vast majority of African-Americans still resided. Within the federal government, segregation of civil servants in several departments had been imposed by the Democratic administration of the Virginia-born President Woodrow Wilson (1913–21). Black Americans working in the nation's capital for their own government were assigned separate office and shop space and separate restaurants and rest rooms. Protests halted this movement before it had affected the entire federal bureaucracy, and with the return of the Republicans in 1921, the process was reversed. The armed forces of the United States, however, formally segregated for over a century, continued the practice, and the CCC did have the army as its core model.[2]

THE NEW DEAL AND AFRICAN-AMERICANS

When the law establishing the CCC was passed in 1933, Oscar De Priest, an African-American Republican congressman from Chicago, tacked on an amendment stipulating that "no discrimination shall be made on account of race, color, or creed" in the employment of American citizens in the new program. The amendment was passed without discussion by both Houses and was one of the few legislative limits on the president's discretionary authority to set up the original ECW. What the treatment of blacks would have been like without that amendment is, of course, impossible to say, but it is also impossible to envision such a massive work relief program as the CCC became that would not have included blacks. The subsequent inclusion of veterans and American Indians, as well as the racially inclusive WPA relief projects, suggest that De Priest's amendment, though useful in its appeal to the conscience of the country, was probably redundant in affecting the practical treatment of blacks in the Corps.

The New Deal, as is well known, had no civil rights agenda. But the administration did include several prominent individuals sympathetic to the plight of African-Americans, notably Secretary of Interior Harold Ickes, a native of Altoona, Pennsylvania, and a former president of the Chicago NAACP; Aubrey Williams, director of the National Youth Administration, whose record on racial matters was far superior to that of the CCC; and, most famously, the president's wife. The combination of a few such sympathizers and a president who provided assistance and hope for the underprivileged was enough to produce the seismic shift in the political orientation of African-Americans away from the party of Abraham Lincoln to that of the Democrats, even with their still strong lily-white southern base. Roosevelt became the first Democratic presidential candidate in American history to win a majority of the black vote in his re-election campaign in 1936. He also carried about 80 percent of the black vote in Philadelphia and Pittsburgh that year.[3]

In Pennsylvania the key figure in attracting black support for the Democrats was Joseph F. Guffey, who later reflected that his role in this matter was one of the most important achievements of his career. He worked closely in 1932 with Robert L. Vann, the publisher of one of the most important black newspapers in the country, the *Pittsburgh Courier.* Vann's advice to his fellow African-Americans in 1932 has been often quoted: "My friends, go home and turn Lincoln's picture to the wall—that debt has been paid in full."[4]

Even though Roosevelt did not win the black vote in Pennsylvania in 1932, Guffey did secure Vann's appointment as assistant attorney general and began to help organize black Democratic organizations around the state. The New Deal policies of relief for the unemployed, including the CCC, were much appreciated by black Americans devastated by the Depression. Guffey conceded that Roosevelt had no racial policies, only economic ones. But he also stressed to black audiences that, because the needs of African-Americans were so great, the New Deal programs had demonstrated that Roosevelt had proven himself their best friend since Lincoln.[5]

Robert Fechner, the labor union executive from the south whose father had lost a leg fighting with the Confederate army in the Civil War, was not one of the prominent civil rights leaders in the administration. In his mind, the interests of African-Americans were always subordinate to the fundamental goal of creating a successful and harmonious work relief program, and he tended to view any matter involving race as an "irritant." He boasted that, as a southerner, he "clearly understood the Negro problem."[6] But his policies were always guided by the realities that existent conditions seemed to allow and not by other transcendent possibilities.

In 1937 correspondence with Fred Kurtz, who was always trying to find more places for young black men in the CCC, Fechner denied that there was any discrimination against blacks in the program. He claimed that, in accordance with the Advisory Council decision in 1933 to use recruitment quotas based on the 1930 census figures, he had kept the percentage of blacks in the Corps at a "reasonable" level. He explained away the limits on black numbers in the CCC as due to local community opposition to black camps and to the tendency of black men to remain in the CCC longer than whites, thus limiting the number of open slots for them. Fechner disingenuously avoided mentioning that he had, by that time, ruled against the opening of any more black camps and was limiting black enrollments to filling vacancies in existing camps. The existence of a few integrated camps in states where there were too few blacks to form separate companies was an anomaly that annoyed him.[7]

The United States Army was not about to push Fechner very far on these matters either. It would remain a segregated institution until several years after World War II. Segregation within the army was at the company level (about two hundred men), and while blacks were eligible to become officers, they could not command white companies, although some black companies were commanded by white officers. The prejudice that white soldiers would not follow the leadership of black officers carried over into the army's administration of the ccc, and no black officer ever commanded a white camp.[8]

It may be said, then, that while the treatment of black Americans in the ccc usually hovered around the "separate but equal" minimum, it often fell below that inadequate and imprecise standard. There was certainly no equal opportunity for poor blacks to get into ccc camps in proportion to what general eligibility standards would have allowed in a color-blind society. And, although the black camps in Pennsylvania were no different from white camps in matters of pay, food, and living quarters, educational opportunities outside camp classes were more limited for black enrollees because black camps were usually located in isolated parts of the state. Leadership positions for blacks were also decidedly less available to black military and technical supervisors.[9]

BLACK CCC CAMPS IN PENNSYLVANIA

When the selection of enrollees began in 1933, the Advisory Council decided that quotas be established for every state, dependent on the state's population. Moreover, it extended this quota thinking to the enrollment of blacks and ordered that the number of black recruits from each state should equal the percentage of blacks in the state's population. As it turned out, however, because of southern resistance, the percentage of black enrollees in the first class of ccc recruits was about 5 percent and did not meet the 10 percent level of black Americans in the general population until 1935. Pennsylvania had slightly higher percentages of blacks in ccc camps than strict quotas would have mandated. Blacks made up about 5 percent of Pennsylvanians in 1930 but amounted to about 10 percent of the state's ccc men over the life of the program.[10]

A second problem with using census population figures to set ccc quotas lay in the disproportionate numbers of African-Americans who were unemployed in the Depression and eking out substandard existences with the help of relief programs. In Pennsylvania, various local estimates usually put the percentage of blacks receiving relief as at least double the rate in the overall population. Limiting recruitment of African-Americans into the CCC when so many of the state's blacks were on relief deprived large numbers of needy families from the assistance the CCC was intended to provide. This became even more unfair after 1937 when it was no longer required that CCC recruits be from families on relief. As the economy picked up, more and more white boys from families not on relief but simply classified as "needy" or even "borderline" were joining the CCC, while large numbers of black boys from families still on relief rolls were prevented from signing up because of the quota system.[11]

Once Fechner and Persons decided that enough blacks would be recruited to fill 9 of the 97 camps in Pennsylvania in 1933, the question then arose as to where to put them. Sensitivity about potential community opposition to having groups of young black men placed in the midst of the largely white rural areas of Pennsylvania led to the decision to place the first black camps on federal rather than state lands.[12]

The very first African-American CCC camp in Pennsylvania was established at "Sugar Run" (briefly called Camp De Priest) in the Allegheny National Forest on April 24, 1933—Camp F-5, Company #321-C. The "C" of course, was for "Colored," the quasi-official term for African-Americans in the CCC. Another such camp, Camp F-4, Company #336-C, was set up in the same area near Kane soon afterward, on May 5. This part of the state was remote from sizable centers of population. But when another black camp, MP-1, Company #385-C, was set up on June 9 in the army's Military Park at Gettysburg, soon to be transferred to the NPS as a national park, some trouble arose. This camp was in a very different environment with a fairly dense, overwhelmingly white population, and its placement there met with protest by the area's "terribly disturbed" Democratic congressman, Harry L. Haines. Haines urged Fechner to consider moving the company back into the remoter areas of Pine Grove Furnace or Caledonia.[13] His plea was ignored, and not only did the camp remain at Gettysburg, but it was joined by another black company, MP-2, Company #1355-C, later in the year.

As the number of black companies from the state, organized at Fort Meade and Fort Hoyle in Maryland and Fort Monroe in Virginia, increased to accommodate the 1,700 blacks recruited, it became necessary to place camps on state forest lands, and by July 1933, there were six such camps: S-56, Company #314-C;

Fig. 36 One of the first CCC camps for African-Americans was Camp S-56 at Licking Creek. Here, a road crew is ready for work in May 1933. Pennsylvania State Archives

S-62, Company #361-C; S-69, Company #361-CV; S-72, Company #315-C; S-83, Company #316-C; and S-84, Company #303-C.

In the second enrollment period, the additional camp at Gettysburg put the number of black camps in the state at ten. Nonetheless, enrollment problems for blacks in the state grew tighter in May 1934 when Third Corps army officials reported that the conditioning camp at Fort Meade in Maryland was "crowded" with black enrollees, with no work camp vacancies to receive them. They informed Eric Biddle of SERB that they could not receive any more blacks for fear of creating a health crisis at the fort. When Frank Persons was informed of this, he advised Biddle to keep on sending his assigned quotas to the army, "irrespective of color." Persons thought the army was at risk of breaking the law by only accepting black recruits when vacancies arose in black work camps. When Fred Kurtz complained to Persons about these army-imposed limits on accepting

African-American recruits, he was put off with the bromide that the law forbade discrimination and "no one has the right to change that law." The result was that although Kurtz was being advised to keep on selecting black recruits, the army would accept only as many as were needed to fill vacancies in black camps. When more were sent, the army simply refused to accept them at their receiving stations and sent them back home.[14] In 1935, both Fechner and the president endorsed this practice, and the net effect was that the army determined how many black recruits could be enrolled in the CCC.[15]

Separate but Not Always Equal

Although the legislation creating the CCC outlawed discrimination and mandated equality of treatment for blacks and whites, segregation of camps, which was not considered legal discrimination in 1933, was the practice from the start. As time went by, the lack of equal opportunity for gaining admission to the Corps and attaining leadership positions proved to be a key obstacle for blacks in the program. But the practice of segregation occasionally produced inequality of conditions as well. The implicit tension in the separate but equal standard showed up early in the treatment of black enrollees in Pennsylvania.

The Philadelphia Tribune, the city's leading African-American newspaper, provided its readers with occasional reports on the start-up of the CCC in 1933, including letters from young black men about their CCC experiences that first summer. The first reports were upbeat and reflected the general excitement that greeted the CCC across the state. Louis Carter, a member of Company #336-C, wrote the paper a glowing account from Camp ANF-4 on May 25. Despite the steady rains that had been falling since they arrived at their "desolate looking place," the men early got to work setting up camp, planting trees, and arranging sports contests with local workers from nearby gas fields. "The life is grand and the fellows are happy," Carter reported.

The Tribune had a similarly positive report on June 1 about Camp S-56. An article entitled "Morale Splendid at Negro Civilian Conservation Camps" was illustrated with three handsome photos of the new camp. The paper quoted Ellen S. Britten of the Women's International League for Peace who had visited this and a white camp in south central Pennsylvania. She found morale much higher at the black camp, which she alleged was due to the men being more used to hard work than the whites. Indeed, they found it to be "fun." Despite the dreary weather and almost constant rain across the state that May, only six men had deserted S-56 and two of them had since returned.

By July 6 the Tribune *was presenting a somewhat more sober picture. They published an angry letter from George Crump, an enrollee from Philadelphia, about his experiences in the CCC thus far. His company, #303-C, had had two weeks of army drill at Fort Hoyle in Maryland, "something we are not supposed to have." He claimed that white companies at the fort were given brand-new clothing, but his company received used and paint-stained work clothes, lightly laundered. They had then been moved to Tobyhanna to prepare a camp site to be used by whites and then were sent back to Fort Hoyle for two more weeks. Here they had to make camp "in back of horse and mule stables where our sensitive nostrils were assailed by the most peculiar odors." He was writing from Benezette, where the company had spent two whole days clearing space for their tents but with no confidence that they would remain there long. "We are the utility company of the CCC," he bitterly commented. He closed his bleak account with sardonic observations: "Don't call this segregation because we are below the Mason and Dixon line and besides we were all treated alike except in privileges, the white boys received first choice in everything."*

The good news, however, was that in the years of 1934 and 1935, the selectors of recruits in Pennsylvania, receiving their quotas from Washington through Harrisburg, were working in a period of steady expansion during which the number of CCC camps in the state grew from 97 to 141 (+45 percent). The number of black camps increased at a slightly lower rate from 9 to 12 (+33 percent). By early 1935 there were about two thousand black Pennsylvanians in these camps, more than in any other state. Moreover, the new requirement in 1935 that recruits be taken only from relief rolls resulted in Pennsylvania recruiters failing to meet their targets. There was, of course, no shortage of young black men from families on relief in Pennsylvania to fill the dozen camps allocated to them, and consequently, for a short while, the percentage of blacks recruited in the state surpassed the original 9 percent figure of 1933. By the spring of 1936, when the number of camps in the state had dropped to 106, 12 were still manned by black Juniors and Veterans.[16]

When the relief requirement was waived for recruits in 1937, the state selectors had no more problems recruiting whites again and, indeed, sometimes succeeded in enrolling more men than any other state. But since the number of camps in Pennsylvania was being sharply cut, many men from the state ended up working in Eighth or Ninth Corps camps. Unfortunately for black Pennsylvanians, they could not avail themselves of this opportunity because Fechner forbade black recruits to be sent out of their home Corps. At the same time, he ordered a halt to the establishment of any new camps for them in their home areas. Only black replacements were accepted after fall 1935.

Requiring all black men to be placed in a diminishing number of camps obviously put pressure on selectors like Kurtz to find places for them. Added to his difficulties was the tendency of black enrollees to remain in the CCC for periods that were about 50 percent longer than whites, thus cutting down on turnover rates and further reducing opportunities for needy young African-Americans. Kurtz pointed out to Dean Snyder that, although there were 40,000 black families on relief in Allegheny County in 1937, he was permitted to recruit only 27 of their young men in the April enrollment. The county relief official complained to Kurtz that only one-fourteenth of the men he had signed up for the CCC were black whereas one-quarter of his caseload consisted of black families. In Philadelphia as well, because of the abundance of black applicants to the CCC, the practice continued of enrolling only those whose families were on relief, a requirement that no longer applied for whites. In late 1938 Kurtz reported that he could easily have enrolled 2,000 black applicants in the latest enrollment period, but his assigned quota had been 146.[17]

It must be pointed out, however, that even though Kurtz struggled with the problem of trying to accommodate the needs of young African-Americans and their families, he was not about to push matters too aggressively. When the army reported that there would be room for only 200 blacks in the first enrollment period in 1936 and no effort was going to be made to increase the number of black camps in Pennsylvania, Kurtz confined his complaints to Dean Snyder. He rejected the possible solution of sending the state's black men to camps in other states in the Third Corps, such as Maryland or Virginia, because his "experience," whatever that had been, was that "Northern Negroes do not mix well with Southern darkeys." He also did not take the obvious route of asking the governor to request more black camps in Pennsylvania, preferring,

Fig. 37 Life at Camp Licking Creek. Men spruce up the camp (above) and pose outside their tent (opposite). Pennsylvania State Archives

as Dean Snyder characterized Kurtz's approach, to let "sleeping dogs lie." On the other side of this story Fechner had visited the two black camps at Gettysburg and found them undermanned. To his credit, he made an issue of this, and Kurtz was soon prompted to find 55 black recruits from Philadelphia to bring the camps up to full strength.[18]

By 1938, because of the general reduction in the number of CCC camps, there were only six Colored camps open in Pennsylvania. Fewer places for young black men, the resistance to opening new camps for them, and the unwillingness

to send them out of state combined to cut into the CCC opportunities for African-American families. With a policy limit of 1,500 camps, Fechner had ruled that a Colored camp could be opened only if a white one closed and then only if it had the support of local citizens and the governor. Pennsylvania Governor Arthur James, responding to pressures from African-American civic groups, did request more camps for blacks in January 1939, but none was opened. Kurtz complained to Persons that he had three to five times more black applicants than he had openings for and pleaded in vain for the Corps to open abandoned white camps for black enrollees.[19]

As Pennsylvania camps continued to be closed, black camps were actually kept open a bit longer than the others, and by 1940 they numbered 6 of the 48 camps still open in Pennsylvania, about 12 percent of the total. Near the end, black camps represented 4 of the 17 camps open in January 1942; 2 of the 9 open in April; and 1 of the last 4 open in May 1942 was a black camp, s-158, Company #1330-c.[20]

Opportunities for African-Americans in the CCC were not just limited for the young recruits, but they were equally sparse for those men who aspired to leadership positions in the camps. While many whites had opportunities to serve as leaders in black CCC camps, opportunities for blacks were restricted to black camps. In the beginning all the military people and all the work project technicians in all the camps, both black and white, were white. In some of the earliest black camps in Pennsylvania even the enrollees who served as leaders and assistant leaders were white men. There was a widespread feeling in some areas of the state that putting a white face on the leadership of black camps would lessen the "ill feeling" of local communities about having such camps in their midst. These discriminatory policies met with early protests from the National Urban League and other organizations.[21]

General Paul Malone's original policy for the Third Corps was to appoint twelve white enrollees as leaders in certain black camps where they served in clerical and technical positions and had their own separate mess and living quarters. In May 1934, Malone assigned a newly organized black company, #1330-c, to a formerly white camp, s-76, near Renovo. But he kept all the white leaders of s-76 in this new black camp out of concern that they might lose their ratings if they were transferred with the rest of their company to an already existing camp.[22]

Malone's successor, General R. E. Callan, responding to criticism in black newspapers and complaints made to the president by Carl Murphy, publisher of the *Afro-American,* liberalized policy by limiting white positions in black camps to four leaders and two assistants and set as his goal the staffing of all leadership positions in black camps with black enrollees. By 1935 all the enrollee leadership positions in the two black camps at Gettysburg were held by blacks, and progress was being made at the other black camps as well.[23]

The first real supervisory position in black CCC camps that was made available to African-Americans was that of educational adviser, although even this small advance did not come easily. After the position was created and appointments were being made in the spring of 1934, Fechner favored giving qualified blacks opportunity to serve as educational advisers in black camps. But, as he complained to Louis Howe in the White House, although General Douglas MacArthur, the army chief of staff, had endorsed this idea on paper, he took a stance against such appointments in Advisory Council discussions. Fechner did not feel strongly enough on the matter to impose his views, and when he asked for guidance on the question, Howe replied, "I don't give a darn about this thing." Nonetheless, a door opened and by mid-May fourteen African-Americans were serving as educational advisers in black camps in the country, still under the command of all white military officers, and by 1940, 142 of the 152 black camps had African-American educational advisers.[24]

The strongest resistance to opening up opportunities for African-Americans in the ccc came from the army and its unwillingness to appoint black officers to camps, even to black camps. When the army began replacing its regular officers with reserves in 1934, it did not call up any African-Americans, who made up about 3 percent of that pool and numbered approximately 200 in the Third Corps. The army position was that black officers in black camps would add to community hostility and create friction with the technical work supervisors, who were all white at that time. One African-American reserve officer from Philadelphia, R. R. Wright, who had served in the Spanish-American War, wrote a plaintive letter to Howe, wondering why men like him were being denied the right to serve in Colored camps. Fechner was given the job of replying to Wright and he, correctly but evasively, denied any authority over military appointments.[25]

As protests like these mounted, President Roosevelt tried to nudge things a bit in 1935 when he recommended to his staff that "I think it would be a good ball" if the army appointed at least six black officers to black camps. But when his aides advised the president to "let it roll" for now, arguing that the army was very fearful of community flare-ups and was taking great pains to appoint some of their very best white officers to black camps, Roosevelt refused to push the issue.[26]

The growing criticism of these inequities achieved some results in 1936. The army agreed to appoint twenty-five African-American reserve officers as medical officers and chaplains. It looked as if an important milestone had been passed on August 10, 1936, when Captain Frederick Lyman Slade became the first black officer to command a black camp, MP-2 in Gettysburg. The milestone, however, turned out to be very close to the finish line because only one other black ccc camp in the country, near Elmira, New York, was ever commanded by a black CO. At Gettysburg, all the military officers, the medical officer, and the educational adviser were African-Americans by 1938 when the camp received a glowing report by one of Fechner's camp inspectors.[27]

There was a little more progress in 1938 when LEMs were upgraded to project assistants and blacks were deemed eligible to hold these positions in black camps. But by that time the number of black camps in Pennsylvania was down to six, limiting the available number of leadership opportunities. These camps were usually located in such remote and predominantly white areas that few black LEMs were available to serve.[28]

The limited opportunities available for African-Americans in the CCC made them protective of maintaining the modest gains they had achieved. Company #2313-c at Camp SP-13, Trexler-Lehigh, was the only black camp in Pennsylvania that had all-black technical personnel. The project superintendent, two civil engineers, a landscape architect, two foremen, two mechanics, and one clerk were African-Americans and had achieved an "outstanding record," according to officials in the Interior Department. Moreover, the conduct of the company, consisting mostly of young men from Philadelphia, had been "exemplary." In 1937, the Department of Interior proposed transferring this company to Promised Land State Park, but General Albert Browley of the Third Corps objected. Browley pointed to the harmonious relations between the white company assigned to that camp and the local residents, the high morale of the men assigned there, and the difficulty of placing black camps in areas not accustomed to them. He thought Promised Land, in particular, would be a bad location, given the large number of white camping families that came there in summers. When Interior then proposed that the company be moved to the Blue Knob Recreational Development Area in Bedford County, where several years of work were anticipated, the army approved the move as it would be to federally owned land. But community opposition to this transfer arose, and the company remained at Trexler-Lehigh. The president of the National Technical Association, Paul E. Johnson, protested to Secretary Ickes about this denial of interesting work opportunities for the African-American technicians, for whom such valuable experience was in short supply, but to no avail.[29]

Similar local opposition, combined with 1938 primary election concerns, prevented the transfer of a black company, #2312-c from SP-11 at Pymatuning State Park to Hickory Run, despite support for the move from the Department of Forests and Waters. Officials concluded that it was easier to establish new black camps than to replace a white camp with a black one. Consequently, the black camp at Pymatuning was simply closed in October.[30]

These examples of the hostile attitudes of whites from some small towns in Pennsylvania to the presence of black CCC camps nearby must be seen as part of the more complex and varied picture of community reactions in the state to black camps. At one extreme was an early negative report on the first black camp established in the state at "Sugar Run" in the Allegheny National Forest. In early May, Roosevelt received a letter from a self-described "wet" from Georgia, now living near Bradford, who complained about the men hiking into town and drinking heavily. Their behavior was "creating an air of contempt," he wrote, and he demanded that lecturers be sent to the camp to straighten them out on the meaning of "American citizenship." Roosevelt forwarded the complaint to the army and, coming so early in the the CCC's history, it potentially represented the worst kind of negative public relations for the program. The War Department sent it on to General Malone of the Third Corps, who ordered the camp commander to investigate the charges. Captain Chamberlain reported no problems with his new command and sent along a letter from the chief of police in Bradford, who reported that he was "agreeably surprised" with the "good behavior and gentlemanly deportment" of the CCC boys when they were in town and had heard "nothing but praise" about their behavior. The most serious complaint about this camp that year seems to have come from the Fish Commission, which reported that some of the men were fishing without licenses, with their officers giving tacit approval.[31]

In 1934 when the selectors in Pennsylvania had been instructed by Eric Biddle to report on local community reactions to the CCC program, the comments on black camps were generally very favorable. In Cameron, Elk, McKean, and Warren Counties, where there had been some initial resentment against having so many black camps set up in the area, including "Sugar Run," the sentiments of the local communities were now reported as "enthusiastic." Similarly, the experience of Adams County residents with black enrollees coming into Gettysburg and Chambersburg from the military park camps was very positive throughout the decade.[32]

Sometimes, however, preconceived theories trumped experience and communities tried to organize preemptive strikes against black camps. In 1935, when a group of citizens in the town of Thornhurst in Lackawanna County heard rumors about a black camp to be set up in their area, they organized a petition and sent it on to Fechner. Disavowing prejudice, the petitioners nonetheless raised frightful specters of the "probable," if unnamed, dangers that "unescorted women of various ages" and "boys and girls just attaining youth and early womanhood" would be exposed to by so many "unmarried black males" set down in their midst. How these not uncommon stereotypes coexisted in a culture that also warmed to the very different stereotypes shown in some CCC films of black men dancing in camps with silent captions reading, "Banjo says, 'Yes I'm happy!'" probably comes near to the core of the agony of race relations in the history of the United States.[33]

It is somewhat surprising to find Senator Joseph Guffey, who had done so much to move African-Americans in Pennsylvania away from their traditional support for the Republican Party, becoming so agitated on matters involving black CCC camps in the state. The record of his objections dates from 1941 when the army was taking pains not to reduce the number of black camps in the state. The improved job situation was benefiting young white men more than their black counterparts, keeping black interest in the CCC at almost constant levels while white recruitment was falling sharply. In 1941 the army proposed transferring a black Veterans' company from S-113 to S-63 in Centre County and disbanding the white company that had been there since the beginning. Guffey reported to McEntee that the people of Milheim had protested what would become the second black camp in their all-white county. Guffey urged that the Colored Veterans be transferred to an area "of their own people." He went on to argue that community use of the popular recreational sites of the area would be hurt and that the Colored Veterans would not be physically up to fighting forest fires in the heavily wooded area. The army, however, refused to change its plans. The arrangement had been recommended by the state forestry people, and it allowed them to keep the same number of black camps at a time of continuing strong black enrollments.[34]

Guffey also endorsed the protests made by white vacationers in the area of Waterville that summer when the army recommended moving a black company into Camp S-82, a long-established white camp. The army again refused to budge. They claimed the camp was nowhere near the vacation cottages in the area and that the people of Williamsport had made no complaints at all about black enrollees' conduct but, on the contrary, had stressed their good behavior while in town.[35]

The senator then moved on to second the criticisms he had received from Coudersport residents about Camp S-146 near Austin. He speculated that the young black men in this camp, which actually had been there since 1935, were "maybe dangerous to the safety of white women in that vicinity." Again, the army did Guffey the courtesy of undertaking an investigation, but it found no complaints from either townspeople or local police. Unfortunately, this excellent record of several years was marred when, in November 1941, two local white women made complaints about two of the black enrollees. The women had not been harmed, but the men were jailed in Coudersport.[36]

Although no quantitative analysis has been attempted here, from the existing CCC records it does not seem that black enrollee behavior, the good and the bad, was any different from that of white enrollees. (According to Duncan Major, across the country the army had many fewer discipline problems with its black camps than it did with the white ones.)[37] Black enrollees occasionally carried the hazing of rookies too far, as often happened in white camps. One such complaint concerning Camp S-83 near Wilcox reached Fred Kurtz in 1935. It came from two boys from Harrisburg, one of whom was from what Kurtz called "one of the highest type negro homes" in the city. The boys claimed that they were dunked in a cold creek their first night in camp, and the next day they ran away, hopping a train home. A group of Philadelphia toughs, calling themselves "the syndicate," was thought to have been responsible, and when more serious allegations involving sodomy were made, the suspected boys were transferred to another camp, SP-11. More allegations of misconduct continued to follow them.[38]

As happened in white camps occasionally, there were also a few instances of mutinies and refusals to work in black camps. Sixty men were dishonorably discharged from MP-2 at Gettysburg after a riot in 1934.[39] This incident stands out as highly incongruous in a camp that usually received high marks for the conduct of the men and the quality of their work. By 1937 it had become the only camp in the country with leadership positions completely filled by African-Americans. There were plans to include its Company #1355-C in the contingent of four CCC companies that would march in the president's inaugural parade. Fechner, however, seems to have resented some black groups insisting on this company's participation, their demands amounting to what he took as "almost a command." Two weeks before the inauguration he decided to have a black camp from the District of Columbia area march instead, citing distance and weather difficulties.[40]

As in white camps, cold weather sometimes prompted work refusals by black enrollees. When a group of men at Camp F-4 refused to work because of the cold in March 1934, the newly appointed CO discharged fifty-one of them. Apparently the previous commander had handled episodes like this in a more lenient manner, and the men were shocked to be discharged. McEntee sent Charles Kenlan to the camp to investigate, and he supported the dismissals. Kenlan reported that the temperature on the day the men refused to work was only twenty-nine degrees and the men had adequate clothing. This incident was also very unusual in a camp that regularly received high marks from inspectors.[41]

Another case involving refusal to work because of cold weather occurred at Camp s-119 in Centre County in 1940. The co had tried to persuade the men to return to work, and eight of the nineteen men who had refused orders did so. The other eleven received dishonorable discharges. Inspectors had been hearing complaints from this camp for several months before this episode but, apart from some unhealthy conditions at a side camp, had generally found no basis for criticism. The inspector who investigated this incident concluded that the commander had handled things properly.[42]

If anything, the impression given in surviving accounts is that the behavior of young men in ccc camps, white or black, was usually commendable with the few exceptions expected in dealing with large numbers of adolescent and postadolescent young men. The strongest community criticism was more often directed at the behavior of Veterans' camps, whose older men had reputations for being too fond of alcohol, both in and out of camp.

THE WORK OF BLACK CAMPS IN PENNSYLVANIA

The work done by African-Americans in ccc camps in Pennsylvania was as varied as that of their white counterparts. Most of their work was of the traditional forestry type in the Allegheny National Forest and in state forestry camps. Typical was the work record of Company #303-C, transferred from s-84 to s-119 in 1937. In its three years in the Moshannon State Forest, the company planted trees, fought fires, built roads, and improved the picnic areas with landscaping and new fireplaces, shelters, and tables.[43] Black companies also worked in two state parks—at Pymatuning and Trexler-Lehigh—doing both construction and forestry work. Trexler-Lehigh, or "Camp Buffalo," was a very unusual camp in that its work involved caring for and improving an animal preserve for elk, deer, bison, and their human visitors. It was also the first camp in Pennsylvania to have an all-black technical supervisory staff.[44]

Like their white counterparts, black ccc men did their part in fighting forest fires. The work of Company #321-C at s-147 in combating the big fire that swept over parts of McKean and Warren Counties in 1935 was especially commendable. This company also did important relief work in the aftermath of the 1936 floods, cleaning debris from streets and houses. Two African-American companies were among the first responders to that disaster in the town of Renovo. Company #1330-C and Company #2336-C provided the first assistance to the badly hurt community after the disaster.[45]

The one type of work not given to blacks in the state was soil conservation. This work, done in cooperation with mostly white farmers on their privately owned lands, was reserved for white companies. An early attempt by the SCS in 1935 to establish two black camps received no support in the proposed communities, and no more attempts were made.[46]

The two black companies assigned to Gettysburg Military Park had interesting work opportunities unique to CCC men in Pennsylvania. Very early in the initial set-up phase of the CCC, the superintendent of the Gettysburg Military Park sent a request to the army for a 200-man company. He had work projects in forestry, road building, and landscaping that would occupy that many men for seven and three-quarters months. What he got almost immediately was a company that stayed four years and, soon thereafter, a second company that remained until 1942. Company #385-C was set up in Camp MP-1 in Pritzer's

Fig. 38 Road work at Camp S-56, Licking Creek, in May 1933. Pennsylvania State Archives

Woods, about three miles from town on June 17, 1933. At the start of the second enrollment period on November 1, 1933, another black company, #1355-C, arrived at MP-2 in McMillan Woods, about two miles southwest from town on Willoughby Run.[47]

In the early days of work at Gettysburg the men were intrigued with finding relics of the Confederate army—buttons, buckles, and even some bones. When an unexploded shell was found, army ordnance experts were called in to detonate it and the men celebrated "the last shot of the Civil War."[48]

Some of the work at Gettysburg involved sprucing up the many monuments. When the NPS produced a narrative report in 1934, replete with photos, someone selected as the cover a photo of an Alabama monument reading "Alabama Used All Her Manpower from Youth to Old Age."[49] No one recorded the sentiments of the young black men, some of them possibly the grandchildren of Alabama slaves, who had done this refurbishing work on behalf of Confederate veterans.

Aside from refurbishing monuments to "the Lost Cause," the men, of course, cleaned up Union memorials, did landscaping and forestry work, and cut cord wood for local needy families. The two camps also did important restoration work under the guidance of NPS historians, including Lewis E. King, an African-American who had received a Ph.D. from Columbia University. The intent was

Fig. 39 Camp PX at MP-1, Gettysburg National Military Park. National Archives

Fig. 40 Dr. Lewis E. King Jr., National Park Service historian at Gettysburg National Military Park. National Archives

to make the park resemble more closely the battlefield of 1863. By 1935, seventy-five miles of latter-day fencing had been replaced by the type of wooden rail and stone fences that had crisscrossed the area when Lee had launched Pickett on his ill-fated charge. These black companies at Gettysburg also contributed their labor to the Eternal Light Peace Memorial, a fitting monument that overlooked the spot where the boys in Blue and Gray shook hands at the "High Water Mark" when they had their last reunion in 1938.[50]

Both these camps at Gettysburg generally received good reports from Fechner's inspectors. Charles Kenlan commended MP-1 in 1934 in glowing, if awkward, language: "I commend this camp for what might be estimated as a desirable model." He found it in equally good condition in 1936 toward the end of its existence, noting high morale among the enrollees.[51] Camp MP-2 also received high marks. When General Callan, commanding general of the Third Corps, visited the camp in March 1935, he was impressed with everything he saw and remarked on the beauty of the work done in the park and the high spirits of the men.[52]

In 1937, amidst preparations for the seventy-fifth anniversary of the battle, planned for the following year, the NPS decided that only one camp was needed at Gettysburg. Even after Fechner asked that both camps be kept open, the Park Service stuck to its judgment that only one was necessary, and MP-1 was shut down in April 1937.[53]

Company #1355-C remained in MP-2 at Gettysburg until near the end of the CCC. At the reunion ceremonies in 1938, about fifty of its enrollees served as guides for 8,000 Civil War veterans who attended. Sadly, this model camp began to deteriorate in the last years of its existence. Accusations of lax discipline on the part of officers, who were accused of allowing alcohol, gambling, and marijuana in the camp, troubled the inspectors sent there, and even the camp buildings were in a run-down condition by 1942.[54]

By that late date, the entire CCC project had lost its spark and enthusiasm. Camps were emptying and recruiting was difficult. Yet even toward the end, the interest of Pennsylvanian African-Americans in the CCC continued strong. Although Kurtz was able to enroll only about 50 percent of his white quota of 1,441 in May 1941, he had no trouble filling all 219 places for blacks, and the head of the DPA was still importuning Persons for more Colored camps.[55]

When Director McEntee wrote his eulogy-like final report on the CCC, he included many self-criticisms and some recommendations for restoring an even better Corps after the war. But he was strangely silent on how some future CCC might better accommodate the needs of some of its most loyal supporters, Americans whose skin color had denied them the equal opportunities to contribute their labor and intelligence to help conserve the land that was equally theirs.

In Pennsylvania, many young African-American men and their families benefited from the income and the work opportunities the CCC provided, but the prevailing prejudices of the era limited the geographical scope of those experiences and the number of leadership positions to which they could aspire. In addition, the unwillingness of too many New Dealers to transcend those prejudices resulted in many more blacks not being granted entrée to the Corps at all.

5

FAREWELL TO THE WOODS

Congress shut down the CCC in the summer of 1942. But it was really the catastrophe of World War II, with its attendant economic boom, that had doomed the program. With the military soaking up any labor not needed by the war economy, the relief mission of the CCC was no longer necessary, and its reform and conservation missions were not sufficiently supported to prevent conservative opponents of the New Deal from canceling it and other government employment programs.

Although it was not until December 1943 that President Roosevelt announced in a press conference that "Dr. New Deal" must step aside for "Dr. Win the War," in fact that pas de deux had taken place much earlier. Not only had the New Deal seemed to have run out of new and bold ideas after 1938, but the international crises, especially after the outbreak of the European war in September 1939, had increasingly occupied the attention of the president.

Moreover, the impact of the military buildup had finally provided sufficient stimulus for economic recovery. Previously, timidity and politics had kept government spending at relatively low levels when that spending had been aimed at relief and reform measures.[1] Now that public spending was creating an abundance of war-related jobs in the private sector, the necessity for public work relief programs like the CCC and WPA was questioned. New openings were provided for attacks on them by people who had never liked the idea of government employment in the first place.

Not for the first time, nor the last, would war suppress the impetus for social reform. Dixon Wecter's epitaph for the New Deal was the concluding sentence of his pioneering study of the 1930s: "Once more the quest for social justice had been engulfed in the urgency of another great war."[2] Although this is a complex and debated subject, with some historians pointing to the G.I. Bill, Roosevelt's call for an "economic bill of rights," and the Employment Act of 1946 as signs that the spirit of reform was not part of the collateral damage caused by World War II, nonetheless the cold war, following close upon its heels, effectively dampened what New Deal embers were still aglow.[3]

Democrats continued to control Congress during Roosevelt's last years, albeit not with the dominant majorities they had enjoyed in his early years. But party labels were proving less significant after 1938 as a working coalition of Republicans and conservative Democrats, mainly from the south, began cozying up in a foreshadowing of the historic realignment that the opposition to the civil rights movement would create a generation later.[4]

The Civilian Conservation Corps became a casualty, in a curious way, of the preparations for a war whose gathering storm clouds had brought a swelling chorus of voices for militarizing the ccc. The administration, especially Robert Fechner, had always been sensitive to criticisms of militarism in the program. Despite the quasi-military appearance of ccc camps, there were no drills, no saluting, no weapons, no guardhouses. But as early as December 1938, the Gallup poll had found 75 percent of the public supporting the idea of military training in ccc camps. A year later, after the fall of Poland to the Nazis in September 1939, the same poll found 90 percent of the public endorsing some form of military training in the ccc.[5]

Fechner's death in December 1939, followed by the shocking collapse of France to Hitler's armies in June 1940, weakened the few obstacles to militarizing the ccc and prompted Congress to authorize a stepped-up program of noncombat defense preparations in the camps. More stress was now placed in the educational program on training men in skills the army would need in case of war, such as cooking, first aid, radio operation, road and bridge construction, auto mechanics, and the like.[6]

Fred Kurtz, about to run into serious recruiting problems in Pennsylvania, thought that the men would not mind having such training available to them, but he claimed that parents were usually opposed to any hint that the ccc was going to increase their sons' vulnerability to being chosen for combat. Once Selective Service was introduced in August 1940, Kurtz and others connected with the ccc tried to stress that involvement with the Corps did not increase one's chances of being drafted.[7]

Faced with declining enrollments and increasing desertions from camps, Director McEntee tried to fend off criticism that his organization was no longer necessary by stressing the importance of the ccc to the nation's new problems of defense. After Pearl Harbor, he announced in early 1942 that the ccc was now on a "victory war" footing, and he began placing more CCC camps at the disposal of the military for preparing their training bases. (Pennsylvania added an army camp, AF-1 at New Cumberland in February 1942, for example.) Fifteen minutes of infantry drilling was also introduced into the camps.[8]

McEntee also responded to fears that the Japanese might set off forest fires in the West by sending more eastern companies of men out there. Enrollees would now be sent where the need was, with no permission needed from either them or their parents. All CCC camps had to be able to justify their continuance by either aiding in war work construction or helping in the conservation of resources needed for the war.[9]

McEntee seems to have grown disheartened at his changing and dwindling program and at one point actually recommended to the Advisory Council that they shut down the entire program. He argued, against the strong objections of Conrad Wirth of the NPS, that the high overhead costs of the CCC could not justify a program with only 350 camps still open in 1942. His ordering of approximately half of those remaining camps onto military bases met with bitter objections from the council itself, some of whom argued that that kind of work was not authorized by the legislation setting up the CCC.[10]

The last six months of the Corps's existence witnessed a dramatic decline in the numbers of enrollees and camps from 190,000 to 60,000 and from 1,235 to 350, respectively. In Pennsylvania the drop was proportional, from 17 camps in January to 9 in late April to 4 in late May—one of which, s-158, was manned by Company #1330-C, the last black camp in operation in the state. There were only 3,238 enrollees from the state left in early 1942, 929 of whom were in Ninth Corps camps. By April 1, all Pennsylvania men were back in the state, but that month, of the 2,257 left in camps, 183 left because their enlistment period was over, 157 left to take jobs, 131 were dishonorably discharged, and 110 deserted.[11]

Those last months must have been demoralizing for the Corps. Men who did not desert were finding jobs after an average of five months in camp. A Gallup poll reported that 54 percent of the public was in favor of shutting down the program, a result surprising even to the pollsters. Camp SCS-12, near Homer City, which had always received high marks from inspectors, was reported to be in a "disorganized" state of affairs in April, having had five different COs in the last nine months. Camp s-88 near Galeton, which had, as recently as December 1941, been reported as an "excellent" camp, was now found in bad shape, even in a state of "unrest." The CO was preparing for army duty and had lost interest, the educational adviser was looking for a job, and notes from parents, not employers, were enough now to receive honorable discharges. Inspecting Camp s-51 at Pine Grove Furnace was a "depressing experience," Patrick King reported on New Year's Eve 1941, the camp suffering from having had four cos in the past year. Fred Kurtz was reportedly telling young men that they would be better off looking into the National Youth Administration for opportunities, and he requested a cancellation of the June enrollment even before Congress voted to end the whole program.[12]

SHUTTING DOWN THE CCC

By now the president was, of course, busy with war matters, but he did recommend to Congress in June 1942 that the ccc be continued. He tried to portray the ccc as not only necessary to the war effort, especially in its work on military bases and in its forestry protection work in the Pacific Northwest, but economically thrifty as well. The work had to be done by someone, and the ccc could do it more cheaply than anybody else.[13]

Congress was not listening. ccc supporters tried to keep its 350 camps open for another year, but the attempt failed. Although a determined effort on the part of Senator Kenneth McKellar of Tennessee to abolish the ccc also failed, Congress simply did not appropriate any money for the organization for the 1942 fiscal year. (The wpa and the nya were funded for another year, being terminated in 1943.) The ccc officially went out of business on June 30, 1942, but McEntee was allotted $8 million to wrap up its affairs. He did that efficiently and expeditiously and returned about $1.5 million to Congress a year later. Although some held out the hope that the end of the war might bring back a new and improved Corps, no serious efforts were ever made.[14]

When the shut-down commenced on June 30, 1942, there were only 350 camps still open, including 4 in Pennsylvania. But there were also 1,367 camp sites around the country that contained ccc property, including buildings and work equipment, and 45 central automotive repair shops established by Fechner in 1939 for major overhauls on the 35,000 motor vehicles the ccc owned. The disposal of all these materials would take a few years and was a sad and dreary end to the noble dream of the ccc.[15]

Congress stipulated that the military would have first claim on any ccc assets it deemed useful to the war effort. The army claimed cots and uniforms and most of the buildings and equipment. It usually dismantled the post-1936 portable camp buildings and moved them to its swelling training bases. By the end of 1942, the Bureau of the Budget reported to the president that 90 percent of CCC equipment had been assigned to the armed forces and about 90 percent of that had gone to the army. Some of the heavy construction equipment was being used by army engineers to construct the Alcan Highway to Alaska. McEntee, overseeing these disposals, was critical of what he thought was the army's cavalier and wasteful appropriation of materials, and by late summer he was able to assert his control over materials that the War Department did not need.[16]

Across the country abandoned CCC sites were used for a wide variety of purposes. The Manhattan Project in New Mexico commandeered the portable buildings of several sites. Some camps in the West were used for the internment of Japanese-Americans. Conscientious objectors to the draft and to the war were also sometimes kept in former CCC camps. Other sites were used to quarantine women who had been identified with venereal diseases and who had lived near the quarters of military personnel.[17]

In Pennsylvania, a variety of uses was found for CCC materials. At Gettysburg, because the army needed only one of the barracks buildings, the other structures were turned over to the Pennsylvania State Extension Service.[18] The military kept buildings at some camp sites to be used for POW camps. There were several of these in Pennsylvania, including three in the Allegheny National Forest, F-1, F-3, and F-13. Others were located in some of the more isolated "S" camp sites, including one at S-146, Barshanty, one at S-88, Lyman Run, and one at S-52 near Wells Tannery. Some of the prisoners at these camps were hired by lumber companies to produce wood products. One of the RDA sites, SP-7 at Hopewell, was used as a rest and relaxation center for British sailors.[19]

Another particularly interesting prisoner camp was S-51 at Pine Grove Furnace in the Michaux State Forest. This camp was one of the first to be established in Pennsylvania in 1933, and it was staffed by its original Company #329 until it was shut down in February 1942, giving it the distinction of being one of the longest-lived CCC camps in the state. (Camps S-54 and S-88, also established in 1933, continued up to the end with their original companies.) In February 1943, S-51 reopened under army intelligence auspices, filling up with German naval prisoners, soldiers from Rommel's North Africa Corps, and a few Japanese officers as well. For a while, Jewish-American intelligence personnel were brought in to interrogate the German officers. It seems to have been a closely guarded and secretive camp during the war and had the advantage of being close to both the Carlisle Army Barracks and Washington, D.C.[20]

Even before the termination of the CCC, there was a nasty little episode involving this S-51 camp. In March 1942, just after the camp had been shut down, the *Philadelphia Inquirer,* never a friend to Roosevelt or the CCC, sent a reporter to the camp to check out reports that equipment, potentially valuable to the army, was being stolen or destroyed. The reporter, Gerson H. McLush, was accompanied on his visit to the camp by G. Albert Stewart, then secretary of the Department of Forests and Waters and reputedly a staunch Republican. The *Inquirer* reported, in page-one headlines on Sunday, March 8, 1942, on the alleged destruction of valuable clothing and the careless abandonment of two hundred motor vehicles. This was a sensitive time for CCC officials in Washington who were facing congressional criticisms of their program. This troubling story led to calls in Washington and Harrisburg for explanations.[21]

McEntee sent his chief investigator, Charles Kenlan, to the camp. After interviewing the caretaker and inspecting the site for signs of the alleged destruction of equipment, Kenlan concluded that the newspaper story was "entirely without foundation." But he did caution the director about the serious problem of unused equipment lying about closed camps. McEntee reported to Congress that only about thirty cents' worth of old rags had been burned at the camp and defended the storage of trucks and tires there as a simple administrative measure of collecting and concentrating unneeded equipment until some disposition of it could be made. But later, after making further inquiries, McEntee found that the camp custodian had been pilfering some of the materials as the *Inquirer* had reported, and he requested J. Edgar Hoover to involve the FBI in the case.[22]

At about the same time as this S-51 crisis was being aired, similar allegations were made about Camps S-71 and S-119. Again, Investigator Kenlan found the charges "absurd." The adjutant-general's inspection similarly labeled these charges "false and misleading."[23] These kinds of reports, however, were embarrassing and undoubtedly motivated McEntee to expedite the transfer of CCC properties to other agencies once Congress ended the program.

The other armed services fared less handsomely than the army in claiming CCC assets, but the Coast Guard did succeed in taking possession of the buildings of two RDA sites in Pennsylvania, NP-6, Hickory Run, and NP-7, Blue Knob, as well as most of the equipment from Camps S-67 and S-125 near Williamsport. The site at NP-4, French Creek, was taken over by the Air Transport Command, and later in 1946 the Methodist Conference of Philadelphia was given some of the buildings. In early 1943, the Department of Forests and Waters transferred to the DuPont Corporation thirty-one CCC buildings and assorted equipment from Camp s-86, Sinnamahoning, valued at $16,500, for unspecified but presumably war-related purposes. Generally when private groups received permission to take ccc buildings, they had to dismantle them and restore the grounds.[24]

After the War Department had made its claims, the various states were allowed to claim remaining ccc properties. In Pennsylvania there were rich pickings as the state had maintained an average of 74 camps a year, second only to California's 98. Many of these camp sites had not lasted very long and had been shut down and disposed of in previous years. In 1942 there were 59 sites in the state still possessing ccc assets. All told, Pennsylvania was able to claim $342,250 worth of ccc property, more than any other state. The Department of Forests and Waters was able to take possession of the rigid buildings in sixteen "s" camps, which were of no use to the army. The ccc tools and equipment were valuable additions to the department's supplies, and, indeed, some of the old ccc buildings are still in use today as equipment sheds and museums.[25]

Another beneficiary, albeit short-lived, of the closing of ccc camps was the National Youth Administration. The nya had been created by Executive Order of the president, no. 7086, on June 26, 1935. Roosevelt had allocated $50 million of wpa funds to set it up and appointed Aubrey Williams, a close friend of Harry Hopkins and Mrs. Roosevelt, to run it. Like the ccc, the nya was aimed at helping needy young people and also developing intelligent conservation policies for youth. Unlike the ccc, however, it included women in its programs, and its record of equal treatment for blacks marked it as the most progressive of all New Deal agencies.[26]

The nya was initially designed to provide assistance to young people who wanted to remain in school but needed financial assistance or part-time work to do that. Soon, however, hundreds of resident centers, some on former ccc sites, were being set up in rural areas to provide vocational education for young men. nya also took over some of the FERA "She-She-She" camps for women.[27]

The nya began utilizing closed ccc camps in Pennsylvania in 1940. They took over some of the buildings at Caledonia State Park and some at another camp near Shippensburg where 180 young men were housed in old ccc barracks while getting trade instruction, particularly in auto mechanics. There was a companion school nearby, set up in a normal school, where sewing and cooking classes were given to about 40 young women.[28]

Although it was always a much smaller program than the ccc, the nya's budget rose steadily from $6.3 millions in 1935 to $119.2 millions in 1941, a period when the ccc budget was dropping from $332.9 millions to $155.6 millions.

Beginning in 1940, proposals were made to merge the two organizations, but these were stiffly resisted by CCC officials. Roosevelt gave tentative approval to such a merger in October 1941, but the demise of the CCC aborted what would have become "the National Youth Service Administration." The NYA, like its parent organization, WPA, lived on borrowed time for a year after the CCC ended.[29]

The philosophical premises of the NYA implied some telling criticisms of the CCC ideal. Eleanor Roosevelt, for example, had always been a friendly critic of her husband's forestry program. She certainly approved of its noble intent, but she was critical of its inconsistent educational program as well as its practice of isolating young men from the larger community in military-run settings. She envisioned a program of national service and rehabilitation for young people that would more directly engage them in projects needed by their home communities while affording them opportunities "for self-sacrifice for an ideal" that she thought young people craved. The NYA approach was much more to her liking. Her criticisms of the CCC should be studied by anyone who tries to propose national service programs for the young, and they have been heeded, on a small scale, by such post–New Deal programs as the Job Corps and AmeriCorps.[30]

One other item of business had to be taken care of before the CCC could terminate its relationship with the state of Pennsylvania. When Roosevelt organized the CCC in 1933, he accepted the advice of Forester Stuart and stipulated that the states bear the expenses of maintaining whatever improvements were made to state parks and forests and share with the federal government any profits gained from these improvements. Such profits could come from the sale of forest products or the rental of cabins. In Pennsylvania, the Department of Forests and Waters bragged about the usefulness of CCC-built forest roads in facilitating its sales of timber to loggers.[31]

These reimbursement requirements created accounting nightmares and political friction. Determining precisely the amount of money the states reaped from CCC improvements proved to be an unattainable and almost metaphysical number and produced unprofitable wrangles with governors. From the beginning, Governor Pinchot told Fechner that the policy was "impossible of application" in trying to calculate "direct profits" garnered from improvements to Pennsylvania's two million acres.[32]

Fechner began pressing Governor Earle to assume maintenance expenses in 1935, and the governor gave a pro forma assent. But two years later, Fechner was still complaining that the CCC was bearing 90 percent of the maintenance costs for its recreational improvements in Pennsylvania parks and forests, and he asked Earle to allocate $500,000 a year for such work, with a veiled threat of shutting down CCC projects in the state. Earle replied that he would include $300,000 in the Department of Forests and Waters budget for this kind of maintenance work. Fechner was not appeased and continued to charge Pennsylvania with "poor" cooperation and murky accounting.[33]

Roosevelt added his own pressures in a circular letter to all governors in early 1937, urging them to appropriate enough funds to maintain CCC improvements or face the loss of camps in their states.[34] These prickly issues continued to abrade relations between the CCC and the states until the final disposal of CCC assets. In the final accounting, Pennsylvania was one of only twenty states that reimbursed the federal government for such sums owed. It repaid the grand and impressively precise total of $2,973.67, a number that conjures up visions of green-eyeshaded accountants calculating columns of numbers on labor costs, value-added estimates, and depreciation schedules.[35]

CCC MEN MOVE ON

In addition to disposing of CCC equipment, McEntee also had to deal with the approximately 60,000 enrollees still in camps in 1942. This, too, was a rather squalid operation. McEntee argued that the CCC could avoid paying the men still in camps after July 1, justifying the penny-pinching by citing "the convenience of the government." The dismissal of the men was speedily completed, with some of the Veterans' camps the last to be dismantled. By the end of July, only 136 enrollees were still in the Corps, and on August 11, 1942, the last CCC enrollees, 82 members of Veterans' Company #3822, had been dismissed in Texas.[36]

It has been more than sixty years since the last CCC boys were sent home. In the nine years of the program, 2,876,638 Junior, Veteran, and Indian enrollees served in approximately 4,500 work camps nationwide. In Pennsylvania, 184,916 Juniors and Veterans served in the state's 152 camps as well as in many other camps in other states. The state enrolled the second highest number of young men for the CCC (after New York), was home to an average of 74 camps per year, second to California's 98, and received $126,435,951.40 in CCC money spent, ranking it third behind California and New York.[37]

It is much easier to trace what happened to CCC sites and equipment after 1942 than to determine what became of the CCC boys. Many, of course, went on to serve in the armed forces in World War II and added another chapter of service to their country. Although the attractions of military service had never been strong to CCC men in the 1930s, the 1940s were a different world. But because no attempt was made to track the career paths of CCC men in later years, it is unknown how many CCC men were in the war.[38]

Vale Atque Ave

We shall cherish the memory of this brief adventure. We shall be proud to have been pioneers, as we are proud of our forefathers. We say farewell with regret, but face the future with enthusiasm, feeling that we have proven ourselves men.
—from an essay written by an unnamed Pennsylvania man, included in Hoyt's *We Can Take It*

As of this writing there are uncounted tens of thousands of CCC alumni still alive and still proudly attending their reunions and exchanging stories and memorabilia of their days in camp. Some of these members of Tom Brokaw's "Greatest Generation" resent his having left out their CCC service in his *chanson de geste* homage to their World War II heroics. Although that war had a much stronger impact on American society than did the CCC, the memories of it are mingled with more tragedy for that generation than are the "happy days" many of them spent in the woods. The most common sentiment expressed by the CCC men today is what a positive and formative experience was their brief time in the work camps. Indeed, some refer to those months as the best times of their lives.

Adding a bit of credibility to these nostalgic recollections are the contemporary comments on the CCC experience that can be found in the "benefit letters" section of the CCC records in the National Archives. This was part of an early project organized by the Education Division in 1935. The newly appointed camp educational advisers were instructed to solicit written comments about the ccc from enrollees and to send them on to the national office. These letters are almost entirely positive and written, one can imagine, in a kind of booster atmosphere. The boys write glowingly about their new lives of work, recreation, and food and about their monetary contributions to their families.

The comments of Pennsylvania boys were typical of the project. "I never knew what life was like until I joined the ccc" (Richard Smedley, s-112, Company #1381). "I now look like a man" (Charles Kuzniak, s-112, Company #1381). "The first thing I received was self-respect" (Clell Miller, s-53, Company #353). The ccc was compared by one enrollee to a "finishing school" for young men who "come in boys and go out as men" (Charles Gala, s-53, Company #353). Many boys expressed particular satisfaction in being able to send the allotment money home (James R. Lowe, s-53, Company #353; William Blakely, s-56, Company #314-c; Jock Banjack, s-64, Milroy; Albert Yakimovicz, s-101, Company #1358; George Lesher, s-112, Company #1381; Anthony Sackarnoski, s-122, Company #2327).

Some, perhaps too obviously, showed the influence of writing classes. "The deep mystic beauty of the forest and the witch-like enchantment of the noisy little brook made their impression on me" (Joseph Mulhell, s-112, Company #1381). "To be out in the wild where nature presents its bare form is grand" (Morelee Frazier, s-56, Company #314-c).[39]

The popularity of President Roosevelt was a given in ccc camps, and some expressed their appreciation in these "benefit letters" and in letters home. John E. Miller of s-87, Company #346, dismissed contemptuously those critics of the president who complained about the national debt being run up and trumpeted his own willingness to shoulder it in the future. Gratitude to "our grand President" and to "my good Government" were commonly expressed sentiments by ccc boys (Henry Grohoskey, s-122, and "Anonymous Letter to a Mother by Enrollee").[40]

Roosevelt also personally received many letters from ccc men in Pennsylvania, some of whom extended him invitations to attend dinners or dances in their camps. First Sergeant George Rommel of Camp s-58 at Mt. Union wrote on behalf of 185 men at his camp, requesting an autographed photo of the president for their brand-new recreation hall. Joseph R. Rue of Company #1358 also requested one for the hall at Camp s-101. Even those who had had bad experiences in the ccc did not take it out on Roosevelt. An early, unsigned complaint from a boy at Camp s-117, Penfield, found everything wrong with his camp—bad food, with worms in the peaches and lead pellets in the chow, a "horse-doctor" physician, and a martinet CO. But still, "you are the best President we ever had . . . you done us all that you could. you [sic] did more than Hoover because Hoover starved us and you went in and fead all of us."[41]

But perhaps the more interesting comments about the CCC were the negative ones, which occasionally enlighten those aspects of CCC life its organizers were not inclined to publicize. Most of the complaints Kurtz heard from Pennsylvania boys involved food.[42] Although incompetent mess sergeants and cooks undoubtedly existed, it is difficult to take food complaints seriously, given the reported weight gains made by CCC men as well as the abundance of positive comments on camp food. Walter Joyce, for one, remembers the food at Camp S-91 at Watrous as being much better than his mother's watery soup. Robert Ward, who served at the same camp, remembers the CCC food as better than he got later in the army, despite the presence of maggots in his farina cereal one morning. He simply picked them out and ate "the good part." Edwin Smith, coming from a Pittsburgh family on relief, remembers that "any food was good," because there was rarely enough at home.[43]

More serious complaints about CCC camps centered on the camp commanders. These officers, usually relatively young captains or lieutenants in the reserves, varied widely in their personalities and approaches to discipline. The arrival of a new commander with new ideas often disrupted customs felt by the men to be established rights. The poor rating given Camp SP-18 at Scotland was due to its having had five COs in eighteen months.[44] Many complaints about such men reached the ears of Fred Kurtz in Harrisburg and were the cause of most of the ongoing friction he had with the military in the Third Corps.

A few of the complaints involved extreme cases of criminal behavior. The CO at Camp S-138, Morris, received a court-martial for cutting the men's food orders and pocketing $600. Another embezzled $1,442 from Camp S-155, Darling Run, and walked off. There was one serious charge from a woman in Williamsport who taught clerical skills at Camp S-125 who claimed she had been assaulted by a lieutenant in his office. Other, less serious complaints included allegations against officers reportedly too fond of drink or loose women. The CO at Promised Land, Camp S-139, was accused of spending too much time in the "beer garden" and allowing women in the barracks at night.[45]

It must be said, however, that these cases of malfeasance or incompetence among the military officers serving in the CCC were exceptional in the generally admirable record they made. The American Council on Education study of

1941 surveyed ccc men on their camp officers and found 68 percent of ccc men having favorable opinions and only 22 percent with unfavorable opinions.[46]

Most of the ccc officers not only served honorably in their positions of trust and responsibility, but they did so under almost microscopic surveillance, risking criticism from many directions. It is impressive to read in the ccc records the diligence with which almost every complaint reported by enrollees or others was looked into by investigators from Fechner's office. In Pennsylvania this work was usually done by Charles Kenlan or Patrick King. Almost invariably these investigations found more ambiguous circumstances than the complainants alleged and usually resulted in no actions or, at most, mild reprimands.[47]

Moreover, it is rare to hear ccc alumni saying anything but good words about their former cos. Edmond Dochod, who served in Camp s-80, Masten, from 1937 to 1939, is typical of most in his memories of camp officers as "strict but very fair and solicitous of the men's welfare." Indeed, alumni recollections and reunion gatherings are replete with positive comments about the entire ccc experience. One can also sample some typical alumni comments in the National Association of Civilian Conservation Corps Alumni publication of hundreds of capsule life histories and reminiscences. The collection includes selections from about fifty Pennsylvanians, and the comments of the men usually refer to their ccc days in such terms as "the greatest experience in my life."[48]

THE CCC MODEL OF NATIONAL SERVICE

The men who attend ccc reunions, in addition to recalling pleasant memories, often comment about the applicability of a ccc-type program for today's youth. Indeed, one of the purposes in founding the National Association of Civilian Conservation Corps Alumni in 1977 was to promote the establishment of similar youth service programs.[49] Some alums think such a program would benefit young people by instilling some discipline and a work ethic in them. Others seem to think today's youth are too soft, spoiled, and materialistic to "take it" as they proudly remember what they went through in the ccc.

Leaving aside the alleged "softness" of today's youth, which the men and women in the Special Forces would find risible, it seems obvious that the ccc could never be revived in its 1930s form. Racially segregated camps, for men only and run with a military ethos, could never seriously be proposed. Any program of national service in the contemporary world would have to be in accord with the different mores and the more enlightened social consciousness. But in many ways, the basic problem tackled by the CCC, one of trying to ensure a smooth integration of young people into the larger community of work and responsibility, continues to exist. Some recent meditations on "Lost Boys" that have received public attention would seem to indicate that American society does not handle the transition from adolescence to adulthood with complete success and that critical reflections on other tactics that have been tried, such as the CCC, may be helpful.[50]

There have been several other models of youth service organizations, both at federal and state levels, since the days of the CCC. President Kennedy's Peace Corps, President Johnson's Job Corps, President Clinton's AmeriCorps, and Pennsylvania's own Conservation Corps are just a few of the organizations that have tried to tap into the CCC combination of providing financial assistance and community service opportunities for the young. These, however, have been small and meagerly funded programs. If we want to imagine or propose something on the scale of the CCC for today's youth, a ruthless and unsentimental critique of the original may provide cautionary warnings about some of its missteps. We may begin by asking just how well the CCC actually worked in its own day.

The original purpose of the Emergency Conservation Work program was very clear—conserve the forests and conserve the young men. But once the program got under way, various people within and outside the organization realized the serious deficiencies in education that existed among many of the recruits. Years of ad hoc, make-it-up-on-the-fly educational offerings to occupy the men's abundant free time followed. Although this kind of instruction often provided valuable benefits to CCC boys, it was not part of the original mission and lacked strong administrative support or guidance. As the war approached, the program's original relief and conservation purposes, now with education and job training added, became jumbled together with military preparations.

Over the years, the CCC had shifted from a conservation and relief project, to one emphasizing education and job training, to one touting its usefulness to national defense after 1940. Its jerry-built administrative apparatus reflected and affected its lack of clarity of purpose and clouded perceptions of its mission.[51] At the end, none of these purposes was strong enough or considered necessary enough to prevent its abolition.

The CCC had a kind of oxymoronic quality in its very name. "Civilian" and "Corps" are almost antonyms, and the organization always struggled for balance between the two, tipping strongly toward the military side near the end. Most of the left in the 1930s, acutely aware of the dangers of Fascism, was opposed to the CCC at its start and, apart from organized labor, remained critical of it throughout.[52] What a leftist political philosophy would think of such a program in less threatening times is, of course, debatable. But certainly the CCC's stress on community service was not, per se, an exclusively rightist philosophy, especially when it promised, in the phrase of William James, a "moral equivalent to war." Only a philosophy of extreme libertarian individualism, which in recent history has been associated with some of the most conservative tendencies in American society, could object to the principle of community responsibilities that the CCC promoted in its conservationist ethic.

The idea of military conscription also shows, then and now, how the principle of obligations to the community does not seem to divide right and left; only specific applications of the principle do. The chief opponents of FDR's Selective Service Act in 1940 were of the isolationist right whereas during the Vietnam War, opposition to the draft was led by leftist opponents of that war. But times and views change. Congressman Charles B. Rangel of New York, a liberal critic of the invasion of Iraq in 2003, made telling arguments for restoring the draft and equalizing the burdens of sacrifice among all classes of society.[53]

If the name "Civilian Conservation Corps" betrayed semantic confusion, the original official name, Emergency Conservation Work, revealed other problems. As many have pointed out, the CCC was never able to shake that early "emergency" characteristic as a *relief* agency, cobbled together quickly to alleviate the effects of the Depression. It was never able to achieve permanent status and lurched from year to year, expanding and contracting, trying to evolve a long-range mission when its meager staff was overtaxed in simply running the day-to-day operations. At the end, Director McEntee had to acknowledge that the CCC had never been able to develop any long-range plan.[54]

Considered purely as a relief measure, the CCC could not justify its existence on economic grounds. The estimated cost of maintaining a CCC enrollee for a year varied, depending on who was doing the cost accounting, but usually ranged in the $1,000 to $1,200 range.[55] Distributing direct public relief to individuals in the 1930s was much less expensive, never exceeding $700 per person per year. If, as Roosevelt and Hopkins thought, people on relief also needed the dignity of performing useful work, again the CCC, considered purely in the light of cost efficiency, was a hard sell. By way of contrast, NYA and WPA spent between $400 and $800 a year per person on their work relief projects.[56]

Even more telling, the short-lived Civil Works Administration experiment in work relief in the winter of 1933–34 supplied much more cost-effective forestry labor to the Pennsylvania Department of Forests and Waters than did the CCC. Furthermore, those 6,631 CWA laborers in Pennsylvania were usually more experienced and efficient woodsmen than most of the young men of the CCC, who were often from urban backgrounds and had never been in the woods before. Some CWA men even brought their own tools with them.[57]

To put in perspective the costs of CCC relief, it is helpful to recall that the goal of Fair Labor Standards Act of 1938 was a minimum wage of $.40 an hour. If we take the low estimate of CCC labor costs at $1,000 a year, and if we calculate the workday at 6 hours (the CCC 8-hour workday included travel time and lunch), we arrive at a 30-hour workweek. Assuming 50 weeks of work a year, the 1,500 hours of work for $1,000 amounts to $.67 an hour, about 67 percent above the minimum wage. Of course, if $1,200 is taken as the yearly cost for each CCC worker, the real labor costs would rise to double the minimum wage figure. Without denying the importance of the relief benefits to the men and their families, the CCC cannot be justified in economic terms as an efficient deliverer of either relief or work relief.

Was the CCC, then, an effective organization in terms of instilling a disciplined work ethic among the young men it received in camp? According to the many proud alumni who went through the camp experience and emerged as better men, it certainly was. But, on the other hand, we have never heard much from the tens of thousands of CCC boys who were dishonorably discharged or who deserted. For whatever reasons, the CCC was a failure for them. The uneven quality of camp commanders was one of the chief reasons for unhappy enrollees, and the emergency nature of the program precluded any type of specific training in how to run a CCC camp.[58] With all due respect to the many fine military officers whose leadership skills were honed in their CCC service, too many of them could not manage men outside the rigid hierarchical command system of which they themselves were part. That sort of military discipline, requiring unquestioning obedience, did not suit the needs or temperaments of many young men.

So, if the relief measures of the CCC were not cost effective and if the militarism of the camps was not the ideal approach for preparing men for work, we still have the conservation work to consider in evaluating the CCC. Here, the judgment on the work done by the CCC has been almost universally favorable. The Department of Agriculture's eulogy for the Corps should be sufficient praise: "The Civilian Conservation Corps was the greatest blessing ever to come to the forests, soils and waters of this country."[59] Without drowning in the immense sea of statistics on trees planted, diseases fought, fires prevented, soil conserved, and dams, cabins and trails constructed, it is enough to say that the daily labor of more than 2.5 million men over a nine-year period was of immense value to the parks, forests, and farms they worked on. Today virtually every state forester or park manager in the country would drool at the prospect of having the labor of 200 men available to them for their ever-behind work needs.[60]

Not only has the conservation work done by the CCC been appreciated by the public, but the Corps also owed much of its popularity to its "back to nature" image. One of the few things Franklin Roosevelt and Herbert Hoover had in common was an antiurban prejudice that has often been traced back to Thomas Jefferson's promotion of the agrarian ideal. Both men saw nature as providing some kind of virtuous uplift. Hoover, in addressing the White House Conference on Child Health and Protection in 1930, expressed the kind of ideas that, in part, would make the CCC so popular: "Some of the natural advantages of the country child must somehow be given back to the city child—more space in which to play, contact with nature and natural processes. Of them the thoughtless city cheats the children."[61] And Roosevelt, in his message to Congress in 1933 requesting authorization for Emergency Conservation Work, stressed that the "moral and spiritual value of such work" in "healthful surroundings" was more important than any material improvements made.[62]

At a time when more and more Americans were becoming urbanized, they worried about the corrupting effects the mean streets of the cities were having on the virtue of their young. Some of the founding fathers of the CCC, like Horace M. Albright of the NPS, saw "an opportunity to play a leading part in the development of a wholesome and patriotic mental attitude in this younger generation."[63] Albright's superior in the Department of Interior, Harold Ickes, praised the almost puritan character of the CCC in contrast to the "fool's paradise" of the decadent 1920s, when the country was "spiritually drunk" on the sounds of "blaring jazz" while pursuing get-rich-quick schemes and "gross, false gods."[64] The familiar pictures of tanned, muscular, and smiling young men, taking time off from their woodsmen chores to pose for photographers, provided reassurance to many Americans that the boys were all right. Photos of boys in town, in pool halls, in bars or brothels, if they exist at all, were not part of the idealized image of the CCC.[65]

Images and antiurban prejudices aside, there is no gainsaying the valuable conservation work done by the CCC, and yet that valuable work was not enough to keep attracting young men to the camps when other, more profitable work opportunities returned with the war buildup. Men then spurned the Corps or deserted it in favor of better-paying work and career opportunities. Although most former CCC men today look back with pride in what they accomplished and in their youthful ability to "take it," the reality is that if they had had other alternatives for work in their home communities, few would have chosen the barracks life of the CCC.[66]

As the war approached, CCC administrators like McEntee began downgrading the conservationist purpose of the agency with arguments and work programs based on its importance to national defense.[67] The congressmen who administered the final coup de grâce clearly did not value the conservation work enough to continue funding it, even at reduced levels, once it no longer seemed necessary as a relief measure. Even the public seemed to view conservation as a kind of fringe benefit of the CCC, not its raison d'être. The Society of American Foresters, always sympathetic to the CCC, thought that its conservation mission should have been more clearly focused and not diluted by its ancillary activities, such as education or job training.[68] And the president, whose passion for conservation had driven him to almost will the CCC into existence, became more and more of a shadowy background figure as other demands commanded his time.

Was the CCC, then, a wasteful diversion of scarce relief and conservation funds into an expensive experiment in romantic rural nostalgia? Here, the realities of 1933 have to be remembered. The land and the poor young men in the land both needed assistance. The kind of work relief that CWA and WPA would later provide, although more economical than the CCC, was not targeted at the young and proved to be much more politically contentious programs. The CCC, with its quasi-military and nature-friendly traits, had a political appeal that transcended its emergency rescue mission.

There is no doubt either about the excitement that such a massive and imaginative program created. Hundreds of thousands of young men leaving home, taking train rides, seeing the country, living like Boy Scouts, and earning money while they did it clearly provided a colorful narrative in a drab and dismal season of Depression. No other New Deal program started with such flair—certainly not its other major youth program, the NYA.

With more time to plan and think things through, a better CCC might have emerged. But in 1933, the young men were idle and hungry, the land needed tending, and the country was ready for bold action. The emergency existed and the CCC was an imaginative and speedy response to it that also helped fuel a revival of hope, a contribution not to be lightly dismissed in importance. It is regrettable that it was not allowed to evolve through war and postwar prosperity, to adjust its mission appropriately in less dire times.

Would a CCC work today? Not, of course, in its original form, but the smaller federal and state jobs programs for youth created in the post–New Deal periods have shown us other possibilities of organization. Although Eleanor Roosevelt and others in the 1930s were critical of the exclusive use of CCC labor in isolated and woodsy settings, this was not an altogether true picture.[69] The work done in county and city parks near Pittsburgh, Johnstown, and Reading showed a wider range of possibilities, as did the occasional emergency use of CCC labor in such disasters as the 1936 Pennsylvania floods. Disasters like that are, thankfully, relatively rare, but the daily disasters of squalid environs in the towns and cities of today's America seem to present as many work opportunities as the neglected forests of 1933 did.

Indulging in flights of the open imagination, it seems that the United States could occupy the unskilled and too-idle energies of millions of its youth for many years in forest, field, and town. And, when we consider how unevenly American society manages the transition from youth to adulthood in the areas of education and socialization, the idea of demanding, or at least strongly tempting, all young people to put in time at public service has much to recommend it. Providing them with a more varied choice of work opportunities than the CCC offered and adding the promise of further educational assistance when they completed their service would seem to be salutary improvements on the CCC model.

Residential work camps would appeal to some, not to others. Gender-segregated camps or college coed dormitory models could be options. Governance of such camps would involve yet more choice and experimentation. Vocational instruction could be more elaborate and structured than the CCC ever envisioned. Some of these modifications have been tried in the small programs that have followed the CCC, but no one has been bold enough to suggest them on the scale of the original.

The possibilities are many and invite utopian dreaming. As we try to imagine ideal educational and socialization programs for youth, the history of the ccc cautions us how not to do some things. It was, after all, an experiment, the first federal program in history concerned with the problems of saving and guiding youth through the transition to the adult world of work. But with all its limitations, its history also continues to inspire us with the memory that, once upon a time, a man dreamed big dreams and made them come true.

Appendix 1

CCC CAMPS IN PENNSYLVANIA, 1933–1942

The following list of CCC camps in Pennsylvania is based on strength and station reports, camp inspection reports, and various other sources, including available camp histories. The existence of the camps listed below is firmly based on sources, but the dates and companies assigned to them, while also based on sources, are undoubtedly incomplete.

CAMPS IN ALLEGHENY NATIONAL FOREST

Camps	Companies	Dates
F-1, Marienville	318	1933–42
F-2, Heart's Content	319, 5453	1933–36
F-3, Red Bridge	320, 3339	1933–41
F-4, Highlands	336-C	1933–35
F-5, Sugar Run	321-C	1933–35
F-6, Seldom Seen	1323	1933–36
F-7, Hoffman Farms	1319, 2327	1933–39
F-8, Endeavor	2320	1935–36
F-9, Rock Spring	2329	1935–38
F-10, Ridgway	2334, 1358, 5439	1935–37
F-11, Kane	2322	1935–36
F-12, Camp Kane	2314-C	1935–37
F-13, Bull Hill	2319	1935–41
F-14, Corydon	2315-C	1935–36

CAMPS RUN BY THE NATIONAL PARK SERVICE

Camps	Companies	Dates
Military Parks		
MP-1, Gettysburg	385-C	1933–37
MP-2, Gettysburg	1355-C	1933–42
Recreational Development Area Parks		
NP-3, Raccoon Creek		
(SP-6)	2332, 3305-V	1935–42
(SP-16)	1328-V	1935–37
NP-4, French Creek		
(SP-7) Hopewell	2313, 3304-V	1934–42
(SP-17)	3301-V	1935–37
NP-5, Laurel Hill		
(SP-8)	2332	1935–41
(SP-15)	2330	1935–37
NP-6, Hickory Run		
(SP-19)	1324	1939–41
NP-7, Blue Knob		
(SP-14)	3304, 2327	1937–42
State Parks		
SP-1, Wildwood	1312, 1383	1933–35
SP-2, Cooksburg (S-100)	360	1933–37
SP-3, South Park	1301	1933–34
SP-4, Mt. Penn	250, 1366	1934–35
SP-5, Johnstown	1397-V	1934–37
SP-11, Pymatuning	2312-C	1935–37
SP-12, Fort Necessity	1329, 2326, 2330, 5462	1935–37
SP-13, Trexler-Lehigh	2313-C, 2312-C	1935–39
(SP-18, Caledonia, see S-107)	1324	1936–39

CAMPS ON ARMY BASES

Camps	Companies	Dates
A-1, Carlisle Military Reservation	3314	1935–37
A-2, Tobyhanna	3315	1935–37
AF-1, New Cumberland	329	1942

SOIL CONSERVATION SERVICE CAMPS

Camps	Companies	Dates
SCS-1, Homer	1301	1935–38
SCS-2, Punxsutawney	1383	1935–39
SCS-3, Slickville	308, 5440, 2321	1935–41
SCS-4, Glen Furney	1356, 5460, 2335	1935–40
SCS-5, Sligo	2323, 2347	1935–42
SCS-6, Crooked Creek	2328	1935–38
SCS-7, Glen Rock	2318, 5457, 367	1935–42
SCS-8, Lancaster	1327-V	1935–42
SCS-9, Todd	308	1935–38
SCS-12, Homer City	2328	1939–42
SCS-13, Sunbury	1383	1940–41

CAMPS ON STATE FORESTRY LANDS OR IN PRIVATE FORESTS

Camps	Companies	Dates
S-51, Pine Grove Furnace	329	1933–42
S-52, Well's Tannery	381, 5442	1933–38
S-53, Hays Lot	353	1933–37
S-54, Richmond Furnace	305	1933–42
S-55, Big Spring	1307, 1378, 5454	1933–37
S-56, East Licking Creek	314-C	1933–35
S-57, Paradise Furnace	1331, 5448, 3302-V, 3306-V	1933–41
S-58, Bell Furnace	382, 2335	1933–37
S-59, Greenwood Furnace	308	1933–35
S-60, Whipple Place	399, 1381, 1355-C, 3306-V	1933–42
S-61, Diamond Valley	1305, 1376	1933–37
S-62, Stone Creek Kettle	361-C	1933–35
S-63, Poe Valley	1333, 3308-CV	1933–41
S-64, Treaster Valley	1314, 1385, 3312, 5458	1933–36
S-65, Treaster Kettle	388, 3306-V	1933–37
S-66, Loganton	306	1933–41
S-67, Livonia	340, 3338-V	1933–42
S-68, Weikert	1394-V	1933–41
S-69, Beaver Springs	361-CV, 1326-CV	1933–36
S-70, Old Forge	307	1933–41
S-71, Beaver Meadows	359	1933–36
S-72, Clearfield	315-C	1933–36
S-73, Tyler	309	1933–35
S-74, Bucks Camp	330, 5452	1933–37

CAMPS ON STATE FORESTRY LANDS OR IN PRIVATE FORESTS (*continued*)

Camps	Companies	Dates
S-75, Hyner	310, 1394-V	1933–42
S-76, State Camp	1330, 1330-C	1933–41
S-77, North Bend	311	1933–35
S-78, Keating	345, 5450, 2327, 2312-C	1933–37
S-79, Kato	347, 1353, 5459	1933–37
S-80, Masten	301, 1381	1933–42
S-81, Pump Station (Slate Run)	364	1933–37
S-82, Waterville	312, 1357, 5456, 321-C	1933–41
S-83, Straight	316-C	1933–36
S-84, Dent's Run	303-C	1933–38
S-85, Sizerville	313, 385	1933–35
S-86, Sinnamahoning	1328-V, 3302-V	1933–41
S-87, Cross Fork (Ole Bull)	346, 2359, 5444	1933–41
S-88, Lyman Run	342	1933–42
S-89, Conrad	327	1933–36
S-90, Leetonia	328, 3308-CV	1933–42
S-91, Watrous	313, 1384	1933–36
S-92, Asaph	1354	1933–34
S-93, Laurel Run	302	1933–36
S-94, Edgemere	1399	1933–37
S-95, Forksville	383	1933–41
S-96, Hillsgrove	317	1933–36
S-97, Salisbury	1329	1933–37
S-98, Blue Hole	344, 5461	1933–36
S-99, Summit	308, 2330, 1379, 5481	1933–40
(S-100, Cooksburg, see SP-2)	360	1933–35
S-101, Ridgway	1358, 5446, 321-C	1933–41
S-102, Mehoopany	1306, 1377	1933–38
S-103, Laquin	387, 5464, 1377	1933–41
S-104, Elkgrove	341	1933–38
S-105, Port Allegheny	1328-V	1933–35
S-106, Strattonville	378	1933–34
S-107, Caledonia (see SP-18)	1324	1933–36
S-108, Big Pond	1332	1933–37
S-109, Bear Valley	1325	1933–36
S-110, Kansas Valley	1303, 1365	1933–36
S-111, New Germantown	1311, 1382	1933–41
S-112, Martin's Gap	1310, 1381	1933–37
S-113, Purvis	388, 5458, 3308-CV	1933–41
S-114, Tea Springs	368	1933–35
S-115, Woodward	1355	1933–34
S-116, Clearfield	331, 303-C	1933–42
S-117, Penfield	1361	1933–37
S-118, Medix Run	1309, 1380, 5470, 2340	1933–41

CAMPS ON STATE FORESTRY LANDS OR IN PRIVATE FORESTS (*continued*)

Camps	Companies	Dates
S-119, Wolf Rock	373, 5471, 303-C	1933–41
S-120, Farrandsville	1396-V	1933–41
S-121, Monument	1356	1933–35
S-122, Westport	347, 2327	1933–37
S-123, Armstrong Valley	278, 1326-V	1933–36
S-124, Cammal	365	1933–35
S-125, Elimsport	366	1933–41
S-126, Bodine	367, 1317	1933–36
S-127, Pine Camp	1317	1933–37
S-128, Hillsgrove	1327-V	1933–35
S-129, Waterville	386, 5456, 1357, 3301-V	1933–38
S-130, Sinnemahoning	369	1933–37
S-131, Hicks Run	370	1933–35
S-132, Cameron	1321, 3330-V, 3302-V	1933–42
S-133, Renovo	348	1933–36
S-134, Moore's Run	380	1933–37
S-135, North Bend	357	1933–38
S-136, Cherry Springs	343, 5437	1933–38
S-137, Cross Forks	1322	1933–35
S-138, Morris	384	1933–37
S-139, Promised Land	337, 5463, 1399	1933–41
S-140, Thornhurst	279, 382	1933–36
S-141, Indiantown Gap	1304, 1366, 5472	1933–37
S-142, Martin's Hill	1397-V	1933–34
S-143, Karthaus	2331, 5469	1935–37
S-144, Emporium	2325, 5453	1935–37
S-145, Montoursville	367, 3303	1935–38
S-146, Bark Shanty	2336-C	1935–41
S-147, North Creek	321-C	1935–37
S-148, Joyce Kilmer	2324	1935–37
S-149, Bear Creek	3309-CV	1935
S-150, Moosic	3309-CV	1935–37
S-151, Mifflin	2333	1935–37
S-152, Columbia	3323-C	1935
S-153, Nesquehoning	3308-CV	1935–38
S-154, Chaneyville	2317-C	1935–37
S-155, Darling Run	1354	1935–41
S-157, Ligonier[a]		1935
S-158, Dry Hollow	2336-C, 1330-C	1941–42

[a] This camp was listed in the camp directory for the fifth enrollment period in 1935 but with no company listed. There is no information on it at the Ligonier Historical Society. It may have been simply a proposed camp that was never actually established.

Appendix 2

CCC WORK PROJECTS IN PENNSYLVANIA

The CCC collected abundant statistics on the work performed by the men in the camps, but unfortunately most of the information compiled on miles of trails cleared or blazed, fences built, mosquito ponds drained, and the like have little or no interest to the contemporary student of the organization. What would be valuable for understanding the work of the CCC in Pennsylvania would be a systematic inventory of all its major and enduring accomplishments. The organization best equipped to undertake such a comprehensive cataloguing, the Pennsylvania Department of Conservation and Natural Resources (DCNR), has never undertaken such a project, although recently, as of this writing, Charlie Miller has initiated a Web site—www.dcnr.state.pa.us/stateparks/ccc/index.aspx—which intends to provide information on the CCC in Pennsylvania, including information on camps, a list of CCC buildings on the National Register of Historic Places, companies, and enrollees. The site also has a brief history of the work of the three camps involved in the building of Parker Dam State Park. Until this Web site is completed, one is left with only fragmentary and anecdotal evidence of the existence of CCC improvements throughout the state.

Michael Schultz is also presently at work, in cooperation with the DCNR, on an ambitious project of mapping the precise locations of CCC camp sites, which, when completed, will be an invaluable aid for scholars and all other interested parties.

From my correspondence with state park managers, state foresters, and interested students of the CCC in Pennsylvania, as well as from my own extensive, though incomplete, travels throughout the state, I offer here a partial listing of some of the more important CCC projects and artifacts still extant. Books that have been helpful include: Thorpe, *The Crown Jewel of Pennsylvania;* Cupper, *Our Priceless Heritage;* De Coster, *The Legacy of Penn's Woods.*

STATE PARKS

Black Moshannon State Park	Cabins, pavilions, recreational dam; small display in park office; plaques marking sites of Camps s-71 and s-119
Blue Knob State Park	Some group camp buildings; incinerator at camp site
Caledonia State Park	CCC built park office, pool building, Dock Memorial latrine, a maintenance building, and two picnic pavilions
Cherry Springs State Park	Large picnic pavilion; annual Woodsmen's Festival takes place on site of a CCC camp
Clear Creek State Park	Park buildings, including cabins of supervisors, picnic pavilions, and stone fireplaces; a dam with stone marker of s-53, Company #353 next to it; box of photos and documents in park office; nature center with a small CCC display
Colonel Denning State Park	A dam, spillway, nature center cabin, pavilion, and two exhibit houses featuring CCC pictures, clothing, and tools
Cook Forest State Park	Cabins, small bridges, a dam, a dynamite shack, chimney from a CCC recreation hall; CCC built environmental center; two kiosks at campsite of SP-2 along Clarion River; photographs and written and taped recollections of CCC men
Cowan's Gap State Park	Ten rustic cabins, four picnic shelters, forty-two-acre lake created by CCC earth and stone dam; visitor center displays; documents and photos in files
French Creek State Park	Two group camps; two stone dams; several camp buildings of SP-17 still in use across from park office

STATE PARKS (*continued*)

Greenwood Furnace State Park	Picnic pavilions and a stone dam, built by Camp s-59; tree nursery remnants; stone and earthen dam and picnic pavilions built by Camp s-60 at Whipple Dam State Park; documents and photos in files
Hickory Run State Park	Two dams; work order documents in files
Hyner Run State Park	On site of former ccc camp
Kettle Creek State Park	Pavilion, wooden dam (recently rebuilt), cabins
Kooser State Park	ccc built cabins and stone foundations of Camp s-99; a plaque in honor of the camp is in the main office
Laurel Hill State Park	Two group camps, including original buildings, barracks and mess hall of sp-8 and sp-15; plaques marking sites of sp-8 and sp-15; recreational dam built by Company #2332, now used as backup to modern dam and spillway; smaller dam and stone spillway, once used as source of water for sp-8 at Jones Mill Run; more ccc buildings than any other site in Pennsylvania; visitor center with ccc memorabilia, including uniforms, tools, and photographs
Leonard Harrison State Park	ccc building, incinerator, and modern statue of a ccc worker near park office
Mt. Penn State Park	Picnic facilities, shelters, foot bridge, water lines
Old Forge State Forest	Near complete buildings of Camp s-70, including mess hall, educational building, barracks; maintained by church group today for summer camps

STATE PARKS (*continued*)

Ole Bull State Park	Lodge building, pavilions, stone fireplace, a dam, and remnants of footbridge; box of photos and documents pertaining to Camp s-87 in park office, including a copy of Charles E. Gregg's "CCC Life at Ole Bull": rows of CCC planted hemlocks along Route 144 approaches to park
Parker Dam State Park	Park built on CCC site; recreational dam built by three CCC companies; flagpole site and a CCC education building at the site of Camp s-73; CCC interpretative center in a CCC building alongside Parker Dam, maintained by Lou and Helen Adams, containing many photos and explanatory placards and memorabilia; buildings, cabins, pavilions, and a museum in a CCC cabin at S. B. Elliott State Park, overseen by Parker Dam
Penn Roosevelt State Park	Log crib dam (now stone); two stone fireplaces, one marked with Company #361-C, and stone oven; ruins of Camp s-62
Pine Grove Furnace State Park	Building foundations in Michaux State Forest, including decorative fountain and swimming hole; some files
Poe Valley State Park	A dam, a plaque commemorating Camp s-63, and a stone monument in memory of an enrollee killed in the line of duty
Promised Land State Park	Several buildings; stone dam; footbridge; museum of CCC artifacts; two trunks of CCC artifacts and publications
Raccoon Creek State Park	Many buildings still in use, including more than one hundred cabins built by the CCC; two CCC-built dams; incinerator of SP-6; some documents and photos in files

Ravensburg State Park	Camp s-127 built a dam, picnic pavilions, and infrastructure for the park
R. B. Winter State Park	First stone-and-cement dam built by CCC in the country; stone picnic tables; at nearby site of s-68 there is an officers' quarters building on the grounds of a sportsmen club; in Bald Eagle State Forest the site of s-148 is being used as a junkyard—one CCC shed remains and some stonework lining the nearby creek
Sizerville State Park	Pavilions, stone fireplace, old CCC-built shower building, plaque to s-85; file in park office with photos
World's End State Park	Many structures, including a dam and family cabins; park files contain photos and newsletters and some correspondence dealing with s-95 and s-96

Dan Cupper's book on the state parks includes a partial list of parks where the CCC worked: Bendigo, Big Spring, Black Moshannon, Blue Knob, Caledonia, Clear Creek, Colonel Denning, Colton Point, Cook Forest, Cowan's Gap, Doubling Gap, Dry Run, Greenwood Furnace, Elk, Hyner Run, Hyner View, Kettle Creek, Kooser, Leonard Harrison, Linn Run, Little Pine, Lyman Run, Ole Bull, Parker Dam, Poe Valley, Ravensburg, R. B. Winter, Reed's Gap, S. B. Elliott, Sizerville, Trough Creek, Upper Pine Bottom, Whipple Dam, World's End.

STATE FORESTS

Bald Eagle State Forest	Four CCC camps in Union County
Buchanan State Forest	Remnants of CCC camps used for POWs and conscientious objectors in World War II; Oregon Ranger Station on site of Camp s-52

STATE FORESTS (*continued*)

Delaware State Forest	Trails, roads, dams; Camps s-139, s-94
Elk State Forest	Camp buildings on Dents Run Road; two buildings on Brooks Run Road; camp buildings on Hunts Run Road; several signs indicating ccc building sites; camps, s-83, s-84, s-85, s-101, s-130, s-131, s-132, s-144, s-147
Forbes State Forest	Cabins in Blue Hole and Negro Mountain Divisions; three ccc camps in this forest built Kooser State Park and improved Fort Necessity
Lackawanna State Forest	Bear Lake Camp, s-140
Michaux State Forest	Ruins of s-51, Pine Grove Furnace; documents from s-107, Scotland; a virtually intact ccc camp of s-70, Old Forge, now used by Methodists; ruins of scs camp
Moshannon State Forest	Ten ccc camps
Rothrock State Forest	Remnants of six ccc camps
Sproul State Forest	Ten ccc camps: Farrandsville, Hyner Run, Shingle Branch, Two Mile Run, Cook's Run, Hammersley Fork, State Camp, Coon Camp, Monument, Kato
Susquehannock State Forest	Several buildings; camp sites; ccc building from here was sent to Lumberman's Museum
Tiadaghton State Forest	Nine ccc camps: s-80, s-81, s-82, s-124, s-125, s-126, s-127, s-129, s-145
Tioga State Forest	Building foundations; shed at Watrous; signs for four camp sites, Darling Run, Elk Run, Leetonia, Dixie Run
Tuscarora State Forest	Five camp sites; s-111 buildings at Blain; foundations at Wynn Gap and West Licking Creek

STATE FORESTS (*continued*)

Weiser State Forest	s-123 near Elizabethville
Wyoming State Forest	Remnants of three camps: s-95 of La Porte; s-96 of Hillsgrove—one officer cabin; s-128 of Mill Creek—barracks used as two leased cabins; third building also used as a leased cabin; Hillsgrove Ranger Station on site of s-96, with some artifacts

OTHER SITES

Allegheny National Forest	Twin Lakes and Loleta recreational areas built by CCC; Farnsworth Fish Hatchery
Fort Necessity National Battlefield Site	Two picnic pavilions and fireplaces; stone bridges and culverts; files of documents and photos
Hopewell Furnace National Historic Site	Remnants of picnic grounds, including a concession stand; two stone springhouses
Pennsylvania Lumber Museum	On Route 6 in Potter County; one wing of the museum is devoted to the CCC: photos, memorabilia, lists of camps in Pennsylvania with particular emphasis on the camps in the area—s-63, s-66, s-81, s-85, s-88, s-89, s-126, s-133, s-134, s-135, s-136, s-138, s-146

Notes

ABBREVIATIONS

ACM	Advisory Council Minutes
A-G	Adjutant-General
CIR	Camp Inspection Reports
CWSSA	Correspondence with State Selecting Agents
DPA	Department of Public Assistance (Pennsylvania)
DS	Division of Selection
FDRL	Franklin D. Roosevelt Library, Hyde Park, N.Y.
POF	President's Official File
PPF	President's Personal File
PSF	President's Secretary's File
PVF	President's Vertical File
FWS	Fish and Wildlife Service
GAF	General Administrative Files
GFSP	Greenwood Furnace State Park
HFC	Harper's Ferry Center
HRSP	Hickory Run State Park
LC	Library of Congress
MSF	Michaux State Forest
NA	National Archives
NACCCA	National Association of Civilian Conservation Corps Alumni
NPS	National Park Service
PCHS	Potter County Historical Society
PDFW	Pennsylvania Department of Forests and Waters
PGFSP	Pine Grove Furnace State Park
PLSP	Promised Land State Park
PMHB	*Pennsylvania Magazine of History and Biography*
PP	Pinchot Papers
PSA	Pennsylvania State Archives
RDA	Recreational Development Area
RF	Reference File
RFSP	Richmond Furnace State Park
SSR	Strength and Station Reports

INTRODUCTION

1. "Study of the CCC by the American Youth Commission, 1939," Records of the CCC Educational Program, CCC Records, NA; Dixon Wecter, *The Age of the Great Depression, 1929–1941* (New York: Macmillan, 1948), 294–95.

2. Quoted in William E. Leuchtenburg, *The New Deal: A Documentary History* (New York: Harper and Row, 1968), 143.

3. Wayland F. Dunaway, *A History of Pennsylvania,* 2nd ed. (New York: Prentice-Hall, 1948), 26–27. Although many in the state mispronounce its name, omitting the "l" in the middle, most seem to find it a satisfying place to live. In 1990 about 85 percent of the state's inhabitants were born in the state, the highest such figure in the United States. E. Willard Miller, ed., *A Geography of Pennsylvania* (University Park: The Pennsylvania State University Press, 1995), 4.

4. Richard D. Schein and E. Willard Miller, "Forest Resources," in Miller, *Geography of Pennsylvania,* 76–79.

5. Dunaway, *History of Pennsylvania,* 4; Schein and Miller, "Forest Resources," 75–80; Lester A. De Coster, *The Legacy of Penn's Woods: A History of the Pennsylvania Bureau of Forestry* (Harrisburg: Commonwealth of Pennsylvania, Pennsylvania Historical and Museum Commission for the Department of Conservation and Natural Resources, 1995), 49.

6. Dunaway, *History of Pennsylvania,* 4; Thomas Cox et al., *This Well-Wooded Land: Americans and Their Forests from Colonial Times to the Present* (Lincoln: University of Nebraska Press, 1985), 93; Wilbur Zelinsky, "Geography," in Randall M. Miller and William Pencak, eds., *Pennsylvania: A History of the Commonwealth* (University Park: The Pennsylvania State University Press and Pennsylvania Historical and Museum Commission, 2002), 391. A small portion of the state in the south central region, including the Michaux State Forest, is in the Potomac River watershed.

7. Cox, *This Well-Wooded Land,* 64; a succinct and useful discussion of this era is in De Coster, *Legacy of Penn's Woods,* 18–19.

8. Cox, *This Well-Wooded Land,* 169; De Coster, *Legacy of Penn's Woods,* 24.

9. Cox, *This Well-Wooded Land,* 169; De Coster, *Legacy of Penn's Woods,* 13. In recent years, forest fires have consumed 8,424 acres in 1999, 4,800 in 2000, and 7,135 in 2001. Pennsylvania Bureau of Forestry, www.dcnr.state.pa.us/forestry. It is telling that the chief threat to Bambi in the 1929 book set in Austrian forests came from poachers, not from the great forest fire that is the climax in the 1942 Disney film. Stephen J. Pyne, *Fire in America: A Cultural History of Wildland and Rural Fire* (Seattle: University of Washington Press, 1982), 196.

10. A fondly written tribute to Rothrock was written by George H. Wirt, the first trained forester hired by Rothrock and also head of the Mont Alto School for several years. See "Joseph Trimble Rothrock: Father of Forestry in Pennsylvania" in *American-German Review* 8 (February 1942): 5–8. See also De Coster, *Legacy of Penn's Woods,* 4–10; Harold Pinkett, *Gifford Pinchot: Private and Public Forester* (Urbana: University of Illinois Press, 1970), 17. Today, Rothrock State Forest, centered in Huntingdon County, honors his memory. See the Pennsylvania Bureau of Forestry Web site at www.dcnr.state.pa.us/forestry.

11. Gifford Pinchot, *Breaking New Ground* (New York: Harcourt, Brace, 1947), 1. Gifford had been named after an artist friend of his father, Sanford Gifford.

12. See the Web site www.pinchot.org for information about the house and activities available for the public. Today most of the estate is public property managed by the United States Forestry Service. On September 24, 1963, President John F. Kennedy came to Grey Towers to dedicate the Pinchot Institute for Conservation Studies. Ralph R. Widner, ed., *Forests and Forestry in the American States* (National Association of State Foresters, 1967), 252. Kennedy praised Pinchot as "the father of American conservation." For the family background of the Pinchots,

see Char Miller, *Gifford Pinchot and the Making of Modern Environmentalism* (Washington, D.C.: Island Press, 2001), pt. 1, "Family Tree."

13. Pinchot, *Breaking New Ground*, 1.

14. M. Nelson McGeary, *Gifford Pinchot, Forester and Politician* (Princeton: Princeton University Press, 1960), 23, 31.

15. McGeary, *Gifford Pinchot*, 87; Pinchot, *Breaking New Ground*, 27. Samuel P. Hays explores this theme in chap. 3, "Woodman, Spare That Tree," pp. 27–48, in *Conservation and the Gospel of Efficiency: The Progressive Conservation Movement, 1890–1920* (New York: Atheneum, 1972 [1959]); *Woodsmanship*, 12. A copy of this 1937 booklet is in Circular Letters, DS, CCC Records, NA.

16. McGeary, *Gifford Pinchot*, 46, 49–50. Pinchot's title was "forester," not "chief," a title not used officially by the service until 1935.

17. William S. Greeley, *Forests and Men* (Garden City, N.Y.: Doubleday, 1951), 82. This praise is more impressive when one takes into account the bitter disagreements between the two men and Pinchot's dismissal of Greeley's tenure as "pitiful." McGeary, *Gifford Pinchot*, 291.

18. Pinchot, *Breaking New Ground*, 392. Many years later Pinchot would admit that Taft had been "perfectly justified" in firing him on procedural grounds but that he had been right on all the substantive issues (p. 450).

19. Pinkett, *Gifford Pinchot*, 132.

20. Ibid., 138–41.

21. De Coster, *Legacy of Penn's Woods*, 57–61.

22. R. R. Thorpe, *The Crown Jewel of Pennsylvania: The State Forest System* (Harrisburg: Bureau of Forestry, 1997), 12.

23. Cox, *This Well-Wooded Land*, 211; De Coster, *Legacy of Penn's Woods*, 91.

24. Edward Robb Ellis, *A Nation in Torment: The Great American Depression, 1929–1939* (New York: Capricorn Books, 1970), 288. Thomas Minehan, *Boy and Girl Tramps of America* (New York: Farrar and Rinehart, 1934), 256.

25. Jonathan Norton Leonard, *Three Years Down* (New York: Carrick and Evans, 1939), 7. Perhaps the popular song of 1932, "Brother, Can You Spare a Dime?" best sums up this mix of emotions. In December 1930, Mayor Mackey of Philadelphia reported the sale of 132,000 apples a day by the unemployed on street corners in that short-lived experiment that swept the country. James A. Kehl and Samuel J. Astorino, "A Bull Moose Responds to the New Deal: Pennsylvania's Gifford Pinchot," *PMHB* 88 (January 1964): 40.

26. *Historical Statistics of the United States, 1933* (Washington, D.C., 1933), 7. The population of Pennsylvania in 1930 was 9,631,350, up 10.5 percent since 1920, lower than the national increase of 16.1 percent. The state would continue to grow slowly in the 1930s, up only 2.8 percent by 1940, compared to the national increase of 7.2 percent. United States Department of Commerce, Bureau of the Census, *Fifteenth Census of the United States, 1930, I, Population* (Washington, D.C.: GPO, 1931), 12, 15; *Sixteenth Census of the United States, 1940, I, Population* (Washington, D.C.: GPO, 1942), 14, 16.

27. Philip S. Klein and Ari Hoogenboom, *A History of Pennsylvania* (New York: McGraw-Hill, 1973), 397; Bonnie Fox Schwartz, "Unemployment Relief in Philadelphia, 1930–1932: A Study of the Depression's Impact on Voluntarism," in Bernard Sternsher, ed., *Hitting Home: The Great Depression in Town and Country* (Chicago: Quadrangle Books, 1970), 64; "Stephen Raushenbush Testimony before the United States Senate Committee on Manufacturers, February 2, 1933," in GP 2556, PP, LC; Richard M. Ketchum, *The Borrowed Years, 1938–1941* (New York: Random House, 1989), 15.

28. "No One Has Starved," *Fortune* 6 (September 1932): 21–24, in William Leuchtenburg, ed., *The New Deal* (New York: Harper and Row, 1963), 8.

29. Gifford Pinchot, "The Case for Federal Relief," *Survey Graphic* 67 (January 1, 1932): 349.

30. Broadus Mitchell, *Depression Decade* (New York: Holt, Rinehart and Winston, 1947), 93, 94, 451.

31. Thomas H. Coode and John F. Bauman, eds., *People, Poverty, and Politics: Pennsylvania During the Great Depression* (Lewisburg: Bucknell University Press, 1981), 14; Frances Perkins, *The Roosevelt I Knew* (New York: Viking Press, 1947), 183; Thomas C. Cochran, *Pennsylvania: A Bicentennial History* (New York: W. W. Norton, 1978), 294.

32. Mitchell, *Depression Decade,* 99; Bruce M. Stave, "Pittsburgh and the New Deal," in Robert H. Bremner, David Brody, and John Braeman, eds., *The New Deal: The State Level,* 2 vols. (Columbus: Ohio State University Press, 1975), II, 390; Anthony Badger, *The New Deal: The Depression Years, 1933–1940* (Chicago: Ivan R. Dee, 1989), 22; Klein and Hoogenboom, *History of Pennsylvania,* 407. African-Americans were 4.5 percent of Pennsylvania's people in 1930, about half the national percentage of 9 percent. U.S. Department of Commerce, Bureau of the Census, *Fifteenth Census of the U.S., 1930, I, Population,* 1229. He had been instrumental in getting Pennsylvania's first professional school of forestry established at Mont Alto.

33. Josephine Chapin Brown, *Public Relief, 1929–1939* (New York: Henry Holt, 1940), 15; see also the "Report by Henry Francis to Harry Hopkins, March 28, 1933," in Thomas H. Coode and John F. Bauman, eds., *In the Eye of the Great Depression: New Deal Reporters and the Agony of the American People* (DeKalb: Northern Illinois University Press, 1988), 109.

34. Kingsley to Pinchot, July 23, 1932, GP 2556, PP, LC.

35. Bonnie Fox Schwartz, "Unemployment Relief in Philadelphia, 1930–1932"; Leonard, *Three Years Down,* 98.

36. Pinchot to FDR, July 25, 1933, PPF, 289, FDRL; Coode and Bauman, eds., *People, Poverty, and Politics,* 15, 55, 134; Richard C. Keller, "Pennsylvania's Little New Deal," in John Braeman, Robert H. Bremner, and David Brody, eds., *The New Deal,* 2 vols.(Columbus: Ohio State University Press, 1975), I, 52; Bruce Stave, *The Last Hurrah: Pittsburgh Machine Politics* (Pittsburgh: University of Pittsburgh Press, 1970), 110; Wecter, *The Age of the Great Depression,* 39.

37. Frederick Lewis Allen, *Since Yesterday, 1929–39* (New York: Bantam Books, 1965), 50; Leonard, *Three Years Down,* 185–86; James Gray Pope, "The Western Pennsylvania Coal Strike of 1933: Part One: Lawmaking from Below and the Revival of the United Mine Workers," and "Part Two: Lawmaking from Above and the Demise of Democracy in the United Mine Workers," *Labor History* 44 (February 2003): 15–48 and (May 2003): 235–64.

38. Lorena Hickock, "Report from Pennsylvania, August 7–12, 1933," in Richard Lowitt and Maurine Beasley, eds., *One-Third of a Nation: Lorena Hickock Reports on the Great Depression* (Urbana: University of Illinois Press, 1981), 11. Coode and Bauman, eds., *In the Eye of the Great Depression,* 109. Beginning in 1933, the State Emergency Relief Board, created by Pinchot, authorized the distribution of shoes, medical assistance, clothing, and housing assistance and helped in establishing "thrift gardens." Money payments, much preferred by relief recipients tired of the paternalism of the boards of assistance and the cheating by grocers, were authorized by SERB for Philadelphia and Allegheny Counties in December 1934 and extended to the rest of the state in 1936. Karl de Schweinitz, *Fourth Annual Report of the Executive Director of SERB: Unemployment Relief in Pennsylvania, 1936* (Harrisburg: SERB, 1937), 111; George R. Leighton and Richard Hellman, "Half Slave, Half Free: Unemployment, the Depression and American Young People," *Harper's Magazine* 171 (August 1935): 342.

39. Brown, *Public Relief,* 91–92; Arthur M. Schlesinger, Jr., *The Coming of the New Deal* (Boston: Houghton Mifflin, 1958), 337.

40. Pinchot to his secretary, Katherine Lindsay, December 9, 1931, GP 2556, PP, LC. Pinchot had asked for a larger appropriation and, in protest, allowed the bill to become law without his signature; Brown, *Public Relief,* 95; Donald D. Housley, "The Rural Dimension: Welfare and Relief in Snyder County," in Coode and Bauman, eds., *People, Poverty, and Politics,* 76; Stave, *Last*

Hurrah, 110. Pinchot was critical of the lack of adequate state supervision over these local boards. Arthur Durham, "Pennsylvania and Unemployment Relief, 1929–1934," *Social Service Review* 8 (June 1934): 251.

41. "Emergency Labor Camps in Pennsylvania," *Monthly Labor Review* 34 (June 1932): 1289–91.

42. John W. Keller, "Forestry and the Depression," PDFW, *Service Letter,* January 19, 1933, 1–2.

43. Pinchot to Hoover, August 18, 1931, GP 2556, PP, LC; even some of the heretofore conservative business types who had firsthand experiences with relief questions came to support federal relief assistance. Horatio Gates Lloyd of Drexel and Company, who ran Philadelphia's Committee on Unemployment Relief in 1932, ended his tenure with calls for federal help. Schwartz, "Unemployment Relief in Philadelphia," 79.

44. While the state supreme court of Pennsylvania had allowed the legislature to borrow $10 million under the Talbot Act for relief, it ruled that that sum be cut from other items in the budget to conform to the state constitution. This ruling created severe limits on Pinchot's ability to take advantage of RFC loans. Pinchot to Senator James J. Davis, June 7, 1932, GP 2556, PP, LC.

45. Brown, *Public Relief,* 465; Keller, "Pennsylvania's Little New Deal," 53.

46. Keller, "Pennsylvania's Little New Deal," 54; Stave, *Last Hurrah,* 32.

47. See, e.g., Barton J. Bernstein, "The New Deal: The Conservative Achievements of Liberal Reform," in Barton J. Bernstein, ed., *Towards a New Past: Dissenting Essays in American History* (New York: Pantheon, 1967), 263–88.

48. Joseph F. Guffey, *Seventy Years on the Red-Fire Wagon: From Tilden to Truman Through New Freedom and New Deal* (privately printed, 1952), 121, 127.

49. McCallum (Pinchot's secretary) to Secretary Zimmerman of Democratic State Committee, August 3, 1933, and August 7, 1933, GP 2560, PP, LC.

50. Pinchot to FDR, May 13, 1933, PPF 289, FDRL; Pinchot to FDR, October 29, 1934, PPF 289, FDRL, where Pinchot describes both Guffey and Earle as "unfit" for office. Pinchot's attempts to explain his behavior in 1934 met with little sympathy from Roosevelt, who gave him a lecture on the necessity of fighting for principles even when it involved working with people we dislike. FDR to Pinchot, November 9, 1934, GP 2104, PP, LC.

51. McGeary, *Gifford Pinchot,* 434.

CHAPTER 1

1. "Philipsburg Remembrances," by Catherine Wrye, clipping dated February 2, 1983, in Black Moshannon State Park Records.

2. See, e.g., Clarence J. McMaster's recollections of Camp S-101 in M. Chester Nolte, ed., *The Civilian Conservation Corps: The Way We Remember It, 1933–1942* (Paducah, Ky.: Turner Publishing, 1990), 151–52, and "History of Promised Land State Park," PLSP Records.

3. Pinchot memo to the White House, July 25, 1933, PPF 289, FDRL.

4. Dorothy Kahn to W. Frank Persons, April 14, 1933. CWSSA, CCC Records, NA.

5. The budget for state parks had been cut 45 percent. *Four Year Summary Report of the Department of Forests and Waters, 1935–1938,* 2, PSA, Harrisburg.; "The CWA in Pennsylvania's State Parks," typescript report in PDFW Records, PSA. Conrad L. Wirth of the National Park Service wrote that Pennsylvania proved "fertile ground" for conservation work. *Parks, Politics and the People* (Norman: University of Oklahoma Press, 1980), 16.

6. Robert Y. Stuart to Louis Howe, April 15, 1933, OF, Agriculture, FDRL; Pinchot to Robert Fechner, December 29, 1933, Correspondence with Governors, CCC Records, NA. Pinchot told Fechner that Pennsylvania had no need of adding to its state-owned holdings. Copy in GP 2560, PP, LC.

7. "Big Crowds Here Seek Forest Jobs," *Evening Bulletin,* April 3, 1933, 1; Philadelphia *Public Ledger,* April 3, 1933, 1.

8. Malone to Adjutant-General, April 21, 1933, GAF, A-G Records, NA; Pinchot to Howe, April 17, 1933, OF 268, FDRL.

9. Persons to State Selectors, May 6, 1933, Documents Relating to the Organization and Operation of the CCC, CCC Records, NA; *Annual Report of the Director of* ECW, *1933,* 19.

10. Ermentrout, *Forgotten Men,* 18; *Happy Days,* March 30, 1940, 4; Adjutant-General to Third Corps Commander, April 2, 1935, Camp S-107 Records, MSF, Fayetteville, Pa. Charges of drunkenness at Camp SCS-8 near Lancaster in 1942 led to an investigation, which concluded that the charges were exaggerated by some local Women's Christian Temperance Union people. Kenlan to McEntee, May 15, 1942, CIR, CCC Records, NA;

11. Circular Letters, DS, CCC Records, NA; Weston M. Kelsey to Fred Kurtz, State Procedural Records, DS, CCC Records, NA. For information on work camps for women run by the Federal Emergency Relief Administration and the National Youth Administration, see Richard A. Reiman, *The New Deal and American Youth: Ideas and Ideals in a Depression Decade* (Athens: University of Georgia Press, 1992), 145–46, and *Happy Days,* May 22, 1937, 20.

12. Persons to *Time* magazine, April 17, 1933, DS, CCC Records, NA.

13. Persons to All Directors of Selection, May 26, 1933, CWSSA, CCC Records, NA; General Paul Malone to Adjutant-General, June 13, 1933, GAF, A-G Records, NA.

14. There is some confusion about early allotment requirements. When the original policy decisions of April 5 were made public, Fechner announced that preference would be given to young men who were willing to allot "a substantial portion" of their pay to dependents. *New York Times,* April 6, 1933, 6. Originally Stilwell had told the county relief boards that recruits "must voluntarily" [*sic*] contribute $25 as an allotment. Persons objected to this language, and some flexibility was then allowed in the amounts promised. Stilwell to County Emergency Relief Boards, April 20, 1933, CWSSA, CCC Records, NA. By November, Dorothy Kahn was reporting to Persons that in her area about 25 percent of the boys were sending less than $20 home. She thought preference should be given to applicants who promised more generous allotments, but Persons gave her no clear guidance. Hahn to Persons, November 22, 1933, CWSSA, CCC Records, NA. Later, in March 1934, Biddle was informed by Persons's office that the *minimum* allotment that recruits must promise was $22 a month. Thelma B. Dade (Persons's secretary) to Eric Biddle, March 17, 1934, CWSSA, CCC Records, NA. Stilwell to County ERB Agents, April 20, 1933, CWSSA, CCC Records, NA.

15. Interview with Robert Ward, August 26, 2003. Ward had been earning $.50 a day doing some occasional farm work. The $25 he was able to send home from Camp Watrous was greatly appreciated by his family. Nor was the family of Walter Joyce, also a member of S-91 in 1934, on relief. Although his father was unemployed, an older sister was earning $18 a week in Ambridge. Interview, August 11, 2003. Tom Frantz, with ambitions to be a forester, persistently begged the local welfare office to sign him up, even though his family was not on relief. Communication to author, September 20, 2003.

16. *Evening Bulletin,* April 7, 1933, 1; Dorothy Kahn to Persons, April 11, 1933, CWSSA, CCC Records, NA; *Pittsburgh Press,* April 6, 1933, 21.

17. "The CCC and Our National Plan for American Forestry," typescript of a radio address, September 7, 1933, CCC Records, NA. Enrollee Joseph Gorman of Company #1378, S-55, reported that before entering the CCC, he "had never seen a mountain or forest." Benefit Letters, 1935, CCC Records, NA; Tom Frantz, who came from the anthracite region around Jim Thorpe, saw black people for the first time in his life when he passed through Richmond on his way to a Virginia work camp. Interview, September 20, 2003.

18. *Annual Report of the Director of the Civilian Conservation Corps for 1940,* 5.

19. See the lists in Howe Papers 69, FDRL.

20. *Sentinel* (Lewistown, Pa.), June 11, 1971, 11, clipping in GFSP Records.

21. The shots did not prevent an outbreak of diphtheria in a camp near Bloomsburg in December 1933, which hospitalized four enrollees and resulted in the camp's being quarantined and immunity shots given. *New York Times*, December 8, 1933, 5. Camp S-109 at Beaver Valley was quarantined for German measles in 1934 and spinal meningitis in 1935. James E. Potts, "Civilian Conservation Corps, Bear Valley, 1933–36" (privately printed, 1979), NPS Records, HFC.

22. The lists are in Howe 69, FDRL; *First Report of the Director of ECW, April 5, 1933–September 30, 1933* (Washington, D.C.: 1933), 25; Colonel E. M. Shinkle to Commanding General, Third Corps, April 19, 1933, GAF, A-G Records, NA.

23. See a biographical sketch of Malone in *Happy Days*, March 16, 1935, 12.

24. "A Chance to Work in the Forests," *Bulletin*, no. 1, U.S. Department of Labor, April 12, 1933. This was a pamphlet of questions and answers designed to let a new recruit know what the likely steps would be before he was sent to a work camp. GP 2560, PP, LC.

25. Persons to State Selectors, May 26, 1933, DS, CCC Records, NA. Pennsylvania had fifty-four of its first ninety-seven camps approved by May 12. "List of ECW Camps to May 12," NPS Records, HFC.

26. John J. Graham remembered being at Fort Meade for three weeks before being sent out to Camp ANF-1. "Memoir" in *Civilian Conservation Corps: 50th Anniversary, 1933–1983, June 4, 1983* (Harrisburg, 1983), 19.

27. *Evening Bulletin*, April 27, 1933, 1; May 9, 1933, 1.

28. Persons to State Selectors, May 1, 1933, Circular Letters, DS, CCC Records, NA.

29. *Galeton Leader-Dispatch* on April 27, 1933, reported the first teams of officials from the three organizations inspecting sites for the first twenty-one camps. Clipping in PCHS Records.

30. *Civilian Conservation Corps Annual, 1936, District No. 1, Third Corps Area*, 21. After 1936 the Eastern District was divided into four subdistricts and the Western District into six subdistricts. *Happy Days*, April 25, 1936, 11.

31. Staley to Hendrix, June 2, 1933, GP 2560, PP, LC.

32. Florence Hackenbush to Persons, June 19, 1933, CWSSA, CCC Records, NA.

33. *New York Times*, April 12, 1933, 2.

34. The system was outlined in a War Department memo to all Corps commanding generals on June 28, 1933, RF, CCC Records, NA.

35. *Happy Days*, April 8, 1939, 7.

36. War Department list of first ECW camps for Third Corps Area, Howe Papers 69, FDRL. *Happy Days*, April 9, 1938, 21. This article also lists ten early Pennsylvania companies, located in May 1933 on state-owned lands, that were still in operation at their original sites five years later: #301 at Matson, S-80; #305 at Richmond Furnace, S-54; #306 at Loganton or Mill Hall, S-66; #307 at Old Forge or Waynesboro, S-70; #310 at Hyner, S-75; #328 at Cedar Run or Leetonia, S-90; #329 at Pine Grove Furnace, S-51; #331 at Clearfield, S-116; #366 at Elimsport, S-125; and #383 at La Porte or Forksville, S-95.

37. Fechner memo, April 18, 1933, OF, FDRL. The U.S. Forestry Service regional forester assigned to Third Corps work was Joseph C. Kircher.

38. *New York Times*, April 5, 1933, 6. Duncan McCallum (Pinchot's secretary) to Staley, April 7, 1933; Staley to McCallum, April 21, 1933, GP 2560, PP, LC. Staley's letter reads like a basic primer on CCC procedures, as if Pinchot's office knew nothing about what had been decided in the previous two weeks. See Guy McKinney to Howe, May 12, 1933, for a list of those first fifty-four camps to be approved. Howe Papers 69, FDRL. Adjutant-General McKinney to General Malone, June 2, 1933, GAF, A-G Records, NA. Only ninety of the ninety-seven camp sites on the list given to Louis Howe were occupied on July 1. Seven Veterans' camps were set up by

mid-July, completing the total of ninety-seven for this first enrollment period. See the list given to Howe in Howe Papers 69 FDRL. As a result of ongoing discussions between the Forest Service and the NPS over the nature of work projects, Camp S-100 was transferred to NPS jurisdiction as SP-2. Camps S-101 through S-106 were on state game lands. PDFW, *Service Letter,* July 5, 1933, PDFW Records, PSA.

39. "With the Civilian Conservation Corps," *American Forests* 39 (July 1933): 302, 334; *First Report of the Director of ECW, 1933,* 26; Malone to Adjutant-General, June 13, 1933, GAF, A-G Records, NA; ACM, June 30, 1933, CCC Records, NA.

40. *First Report of the Director of ECW,* 26.

41. General Malone to Adjutant-General, May 8, 1933, GAF, A-G Records, NA. Persons wrote to the Pennsylvania selectors on May 19 warning about the possibility of more of their enrollees being sent west. Persons to State Selectors, May 19, 1933, DS, CCC Records, NA.

42. SSR, Ninth Corps, August 1933, CCC Records, NA. This company returned to Pennsylvania in October to man SP-3, and in 1935 they established a tent camp at SCS-1, the state's first Soil Conservation camp.

43. Adjutant-General to Malone, May 24, 1933, GAF, A-G Records, NA. Apparently more had been sent in early and mid-May, as Persons reported 1,200 Pennsylvania men working out of state on June 30. Persons to Stilwell, June 30, 1933, CWSSA, CCC Records, NA. ACM, June 30, 1933, CCC Records, NA. *Forestry News Digest* (October 1933): 1.

44. Pinchot to Malone, June 16, 1933, Malone to Pinchot, June 5, 1933, GP 2560, PP, LC; PDFW *Service Letter,* July 6, 1933, PDFW Records, PSA.

45. Fechner to Pinchot, May 24, 1933; Fechner to Pinchot, June 5, 1933, GP 2560, PP, LC.

46. Duncan Major memo to Fechner, June 30, 1933, RF, CCC Records,

47. Pinchot telegram to FDR, May 26, 1933, Fechner to Pinchot, June 9, 1933, PPF 289, FDRL; Howe to Pinchot, June 24, 1933, with a copy of the quartermaster's report of June 15, 1933, OF 25, FDRL.

48. Charles W. Johnson, "The Civilian Conservation Corps: The Role of the Army" (Ph.D. diss., University of Michigan, 1968), 194–95.

49. Nolte, ed., *Civilian Conservation Corps,* 151–52; "History of Promised Land State Park," PLSP Records; M. S. Reifsnyder, "A History of Camp Michaux," PGFSP Records; *Happy Days.* June 24, 1933, 7.

50. Wirth, *Parks, Politics and the People,* 92. These early camps required eighty different kinds of tools, more as time went by. "The CCC in Our State Forests," PDFW, *Service Letter,* January 18, 1934, PDFW Records, PSA.

51. "ECW Work in Forbes State Forest," *Service Letter,* September 13, 1934, PDFW Records, PSA.

52. Fechner to Pinchot, May 11, 1933. Pinchot told him that the state could only supply twenty-five trucks at the time. Pinchot to Fechner, May 17, 1933, GP 2560, PP, LC.

53. Stuart to Fechner, July 6, 1933; McEntee to Stuart, July 21, 1933, GAF, A-G Records, NA.

54. "Consolidated Instructions, CCC, Prepared as a Matter of Assistance to All Concerned with the CCC," Third Corps Area, 1935, 1-A. PLSP Records. This is a relatively rare but very useful 200-page booklet of detailed regulations on the conduct of CCC camps.

55. For example, Camp S-119 at Philipsburg had a captain, one lieutenant, four enlisted men, including two noncommissioned officers, and a contract surgeon in camp in August 1933, SSR, CCC Records, NA.

56. Adjutant-General James McKinley to Corps Commanding Generals, November 16, 1933, RF, CCC Records, NA. General Malone of the Third Corps sent a memo to all his COs reminding them that the enrollees were civilians. Camp S-107 Records, MSF Records.

57. Thomas Brannan to Superintendent Book, January 10, 1934, Camp S-107 Records, MSF Records.

58. Charles P. Harper, *The Administration of the Civilian Conservation Corps* (Clarksburg, W.Va.: Clarksburg Publishing, 1937), 44; Ermentrout, *Forgotten Men,* 78–79. Ermentrout is particularly good in explaining how things *really* worked at the camp level, outside the formal regulations.

59. PDFW, *Service Letter,* July 5, 1934, PSA; Harper, *Administration of the* CCC, 67; salary lists in PLSP Records. Comparable salaries were being paid at Camp S-107, Caledonia, in 1935. John R. Williams, district forester, to Superintendent Book, May 24, 1935, S-107 Records, MSF Records.

60. Report of Carl Deen to McEntee, September 29, 1933, CIR, S-108, CCC Records, NA.

61. Emma Guffey Miller to FDR, June 30, 1933, OF 268, FDRL.

62. Charles H. Rhodes to Pinchot, July 19, 1933; Pinchot to Rhodes, July 31, 1933, GP 2560, PP, LC.

63. Guffey to "Dear Louie," February 5, 1935, Howe 70, FDRL. Guffey reminded Howe how important these CCC jobs would be to Pennsylvania Democrats in 1936 and was aghast at rumors he had heard that these positions were to be put on a civil service basis.

64. See, e.g., Congressman Benjamin Focht to Fred Kurtz, March 31, 1935, complaining that when he voted for the CCC he "had no idea it would be administered that a Republican Congressman would not get a single job." CWSSA, CCC Records, NA. The deputy secretary of forests and waters sent out word to his district foresters in July that henceforth political affiliations should be disregarded in the appointment of LEMS to CCC camps, but it is impossible to say how effective that directive was. J. F. Bogardus to District Foresters, July 19, 1935, PDFW Records, PSA.

65. Elmo R. Richardson, "Was There Politics in the Civilian Conservation Corps?" *Forest History* 16 (July 1972): 14–17; Johnson, "CCC: The Role of the Army," 205; *New York Times,* July 21, 1936, 1, has a story on the politics of these appointments. Keller to J. R. Williams, December 6, 1935, Camp S-107 Records, MSF Records.

66. Guy McKinney (Fechner's assistant) to Stephen Early, March 1936, OF 268, FDRL. McKinney was upset that the newspaper had "dug up" this obscurely published report, which he had hoped "would remain buried." The *New York Times* picked up on this theme in July 1936 when it reported the charges by the Republican national chairman of political favoritism in the CCC. An anonymous source even alleged that enrollees from Pittsburgh needed approval from Democratic ward leaders before being allowed to enlist. July 21, 1936, 1 and 11.

67. Kenneth Holland and Frank Ernest Hill, *Youth in the* CCC (Washington, D.C.: American Council on Education, 1942), 118.

68. *Happy Days,* May 27, 1933, 8, and June 3, 1933, 6; Henry Clepper, "20,000 Men in Penn's Woods," *American Forests* 39 (September 19, 1933): 427.

69. Leo Ruvolis remembers the men at his camp in Virginia being allowed a "$.15 quota" for their lunches. Bread and makings were given "prices" and the men could fill up their bags to that limit. Communication to author, February 21, 2004.

70. The enrollees' days have been described in many places. See Salmond, *Civilian Conservation Corps,* 137–41, and Ermentrout, *Forgotten Men,* passim.

71. Camp Inspection Report, S-71, October 20, 1934, CCC Records, NA.

72. Colonel Duncan Major in ACM, June 20, 1933, CCC Records, NA; "Singing in the Rain," *Happy Days,* May 20, 1933, 1. In the CCC video collection of the Pennsylvania State Archives, there is a silent film about the early setting up of Pine Grove Furnace Camp, S-51. *Happy Days* was a privately published but quasi-official booster-type weekly newspaper that contained information about the activities of the CCC, including material sent in to it by camps all around the country. Although *Happy Days* was clearly looked on with approval by CCC officials, Fechner insisted that no public funds be used to pay for it but that it should be subscribed to by the enrollees in camp or by the camp exchanges on a voluntary basis. C. H. Granger, "Forest Service Memo," August 4, 1933, Fish and Wildlife Service Records, RG-22, Entry File 188, NA. The

paper supported itself through subscriptions and advertising. Most of the advertising seems to have involved cigarettes and the sale of various CCC souvenirs, but Fechner also authorized some CCC ads as well "rather than have the paper go to the wall." Advisory Council Minutes, July 6, 1933, CCC Records, Entry File 10, NA. *Happy Days*, May 20, 1933 (vol. 1, no. 1). Robert Allen Ermentrout claimed that, as camp commander, he was pressured to subscribe to fifteen copies for his camp library. *Forgotten Men*, 44.

73. John J. Graham remembered catching flu because of his leaky tent. *Civilian Conservation Corps: 50th Anniversary*, 19; Fechner to FDR, May 17, 1933, OF 268, FDRL; *Happy Days*, August 26, 1933. One year later, Fechner's assistant wrote to the family denying any financial compensation because the death was ruled not to have occurred in the line of duty. Charles Taylor to F. J. Connell, September 6, 1934, World's End State Park Records.

74. Hill, *School in the Camps*, 1.

75. At the time of this writing, Michael Schultz is working on a project with the Pennsylvania Department of Conservation and Natural Resources to locate GPS locations for CCC camps.

76. Kenneth E. Hendrickson, Jr., "The Civilian Conservation Corps in Pennsylvania: A Case Study of a New Deal Relief Agency in Operation," *PMHB* 100 (January 1976): 69. Hendrickson's sampling of twenty newspapers throughout the state found that all but one (the intensely Republican *Philadelphia Inquirer*) applauded the establishment of the CCC.

77. Jere C. West of Bedford to Pinchot, June 5, 1933, GP 2560, Ernest E. Harwood (Pinchot's secretary) to business leaders in Clarion, April 14, 1934, GP 2560, PP, LC; Major John A. Porter, "The Enchanted Forest," *Quartermaster Review* (March–April 1934), 5; Camp S-107 records at MSF office are filled with such local business dealings. By early June, a baseball team from Company #305 at Camp S-54 had defeated a team from the town of Richmond Furnace. *Happy Days*, June 3, 1933, 11.

78. The town of Emporium provided dances for Company #313 at Camp S-85, Sizerville, and transportation to Sunday church services. *Happy Days*, May 27, 1933, 5. Clair "Rusty" Swarmer, who served in camps near Ridgway, reports that town attractions included "girls, movies, girls, visit friends, girls, drink beer, girls." Communication to author, June 26, 2004. Persons to Stilwell, June 30, 1933, CWSSA, CCC Records, NA.

79. *Happy Days* reports on Company #1354 at S-92, Asaph, August 19, 1933, 6; Company #1333 at Coburn, S-63, August 5, 1933, 9; Company #328, S-90, at Leetonia, August 5, 1933, 10. The popularity of minstrel shows was such that even the black men of Camp Penn-Roosevelt, S-62, put one on at the community hall in Milroy in June 1933. *Sentinel* (Lewistown, Pa.), June 17, 1933, clipping in GFSP files; *Happy Days*, May 27, 1933, 1.

80. The editors sent some early issues to President Roosevelt, containing some sports and education news as well as an article on "Uncle Frankie's CCC," OF 218, FDRL. Roosevelt was sent many such materials from CCC camps, as well as birthday greetings, invitations to dances, dinners, etc. Affection for the president is just about universal in these papers.

81. Alfred Emile Cornebise, "Heralds in New Deal America: Camp Newspapers of the Civilian Conservation Corps," www.scripps.ohiou.edu/mediahistory/mhmjour2-1htm.

82. Graham, "Memoir," *Civilian Conservation Corps: 50th Anniversary*, 20; Staley to District Foresters, November 27, 1933, S-107 Records, MSF.

83. Memo for Camp Superintendents, July 1, 1933, Entry File 188, FWS Records, NA; "Instructions to Regional Foresters from the Forest Service, April 24, 1933," Documents Relating to the Organization and Operation of the CCC, CCC Records, NA; Pinchot to Malone, May 3, 1933, Malone to Pinchot, May 8, 1933, GP 2560, PP, LC.

84. C. C. Marsh to Howe, February 3, 1934, Howe 70, FDRL. The camp educational adviser would select one of the enrollees to serve as assistant educational adviser, and he would receive an extra $6 a month in pay.

85. Extensive correspondence on this matter is in the Howe Papers 70, FDRL.

86. Report by Special Investigator Charles Kenlan, June 19, 1934, in PLSP Records. There was also some resentment among forestry personnel that their own educational services, both on and off the job, had not been appreciated. Hill, *School in the Camps*, 15.

87. Hill, *School in the Camps*, 14.

88. "Report of the Adjutant-General, October 27, 1938," in RF, CCC Records, NA.

89. *Forestry News Digest* (October 1933): 1; PDFW *Service Letter*, November 23, 1933, 2, PDFW Records, PSA; see "Fact Sheet" on white pine blister rust on currants and gooseberries, by Ohio State University, http://ohioline.osu.edu/hyg-fact/3000/3205.html.

90. Fechner to Howe, October 5, 1933, OF 268, FDRL.

91. *Forestry News Digest* (October 1933): 1–2. The War Department informed its Third Corps commander on February 11, 1936, that this had been the average cost. RF, CCC Records, NA. In 1933, the cost of camp construction in Pennsylvania was about $25,000. Tony Shively, *The CCC Camps of Union County* (Lewisburg: Union County Historical Society, 2002), 42, 45. The construction of buildings at Camp S-127, Pine Camp, began on October 16, 1933, and cost $24,198.74. CIR, CCC Records, NA; *Annual Report of the Director of ECW, 1936*, 8;

92. McEntee to Carl Deen, n.d. OF 268, FDRL; McEntee to VFW commander, August 16, 1935, P-150, November 27, 1935, CIR, CCC Records, NA. By 1935, Fechner compromised with the army on these building contracts. If the army could not get commitments from local building trade unions within forty-eight hours, they were free to contact local employment agencies. Johnson, "Civilian Conservation Corps," 187; *Civilian Conservation Corps Annual, 1936*, Third Corps Area, District No. 1, 35.

93. Michael W. Sherraden, "Administrative Lessons from the Civilian Conservation Corps (1933–42)," *Administration in Social Work* 9 (summer 1985): 235.

94. Fechner to Pinchot, August 22 and August 25, 1933, GP 2560; Pinchot to Fechner, August 28, 1933, GP 2560, PP, LC.

95. Harper, *Administration of the CCC*, 26–27; *Annual Report of the Director of ECW, 1933–1935*, 59–61.

96. PDFW, *Service Letter*, November 23, 1933, 1; *Civilian Conservation Corps Annual, 1936*, District No. 1, 21; Records of Project Applications, All Service Camp Directories, 1933 Directory, NPS Records, NA. Two camps of small enrollments, S-123 and S-140, were manned by companies from New York, SSR, October 1933, CCC Records, NA.

97. "It is a dreadful loss." Pinchot to Mrs. Stuart, October 23, 1933, GP 2560, PP, LC; *New York Times*, October 24, 1933, 22; Steen, *U.S. Forestry Service*, 196–97. "Robert Y. Stuart, Forester: An Appreciation," *American Forests* 39 (December 1933): 535. *Happy Days*, May 20, 1933, had provided a brief biographical sketch of Stuart's background. He was a graduate of Dickinson College and Yale University and had served with distinction in France during World War I.

98. Porter, "Enchanted Forest," 6; Adjutant-General to Corps Commanding Generals, November 14, 1933, RF, CCC Records, NA. Paul Slovan, who served in Camp ANF-13 in 1938, was one who had never eaten turkey until he joined the CCC. "My CCC Life," NACCCA *Journal* (June 2002).

99. Fechner to Pinchot, December 19, 1933. This continued to be a problem in the mountains of Pennsylvania. An investigation of Camp S-139 in the Poconos in November 1938 reported that the Highway Department sometimes neglected to plow the three-mile road to town. Report of Patrick J. King, Special Investigator, to Fechner, November 26, 1938, in PLSP Records.

100. Persons to Biddle, November 8, 1933, CWSSA, CCC Records, NA.

101. Interview with Robert B. Ward of Wellsboro, August 26, 2003. Walter Joyce, at the same camp that winter, has a similar recollection. Interview, August 11, 2003.

102. See, e.g., the investigative report to General Malone, December 22, 1933, concerning Camp S-99 at Bakersville, GAF, A-G Records, NA. A new regular army captain had recently

assumed command and his "hard-boiled" approach had created friction with just about everyone in the camp. A complaint had been made by 123 of the men from Company #1379, but the army investigator simply counseled the officer on more tact and patience.

CHAPTER 2

1. Kurtz to Ruth Blakeslee, regional social worker, ECW, December 11, 1935, CWSSA, CCC Records, NA.

2. Biddle was receiving criticism from some Democrats, especially Congressman J. Buell Snyder of Fayette County. It is unclear if this had anything to do with Kurtz assuming more authority over the Pennsylvania selection process. A.I.M. to Persons, May 24, 1934 (reporting on an angry phone call from Snyder about Biddle), CWSSA, CCC Records, NA.

3. Kurtz provided a biographical sketch of his background to Persons, August 30, 1935, CWSSA, CCC Records, NA.

4. Although the Social Security Act of 1935 required civil service status for state personnel distributing its relief benefits, the CCC was allowed to appoint one state selector outside that requirement. "Plan of Operations, 1941–42," DS, CCC Records, NA.

5. Kurtz to Persons, October 5, 1935, Kurtz to Dean Snyder (Persons's assistant), December 7, 1935, CWSSA, CCC Records, NA. At least two state selection agents did receive appointments with the national offices—Neal Guy from Texas and Dean Snyder from Ohio.

6. After spending two days with Kurtz in Harrisburg in 1938, Snyder reported to Persons that he "lacks imagination and tact at times." Snyder to Persons, February 15, 1938, CWSSA, CCC Records, NA.

7. This Pennsylvania story was part of a larger pattern of ongoing friction between the army and the CCC civilian officials. Adjutant-General E. T. Conley complained to Fechner that his camp inspectors afforded COs fewer procedural courtesies than enrollees accused of camp offenses. "The War Department is as much interested as your office," he wrote, "in the maintenance of high standards in the conduct of the Civilian Conservation Corps camps." Conley to Fechner, May 25, 1935, GAF, A-G Records, NA.

8. The relevant correspondence on the S-71 matter is in CIR, S-71, CCC Records, NA. Another instance of Kurtz's referring complaints about camp COs is CIR, S-112, July 15, 1935. Kurtz's complaints about the Veterans' camps at NP-4 and S-123 is in Kurtz to Persons, July 11, 1935, CWSSA, CCC Records, NA.

9. Snyder memo of phone call to Kurtz, October 16, 1935; Kurtz to Snyder, agreeing to go to Baltimore to visit with Third Corps officials at his suggestion; Kurtz to Persons October 24, 1935, telling him of his visit and the agreement he worked out to forward any complaints of camp COs to Third Corps officials, CWSSA CCC Records, NA. This visit, however, did not end Kurtz's troubles with Pennsylvania COs. Acting on complaints he heard from Pennsylvania boys, Kurtz wrote to a CO of a Maryland camp, implying that he was responsible for so many boys deserting, Kurtz to Persons, November 17, 1937; Snyder was still complaining to Persons about Kurtz's tactless dealings with army personnel in 1938, Snyder to Persons, February 8, 1938, CWSSA CCC Records, NA.

10. Persons to Fechner, August, 8, 1936, CWSSA, CCC Records, NA; see also one of several letters of recommendation that Persons wrote, including this one to Kurtz's new superior, Karl de Schweinitz, in 1936: "Mr. Kurtz has an outstanding grasp of the program as a whole . . . one of the most thorough and sincere individuals with whom we have contact." Persons to de Schweinitz, June 23, 1936, CWSSA, CCC Records, NA.

11. FDR to Fechner, January 25, 1934, Nixon, *FDR and Conservation*, I, 246.

12. Persons to Fred Kurtz, June 15, 1934, CWSSA, CCC Records, NA. LEMS continued to be selected by district foresters from lists sent to them by the Emergency Relief Boards. Biddle to Persons, October 23, 1933, CWSSA, CCC Records, NA. The *Potter Enterprise* for June 1, 1933, reported that twenty troublemakers from Philadelphia had already been sent home and had been replaced by local boys at S-89. Clipping in PCHS.

13. Kurtz had another 800 men he could just as easily have sent forward but Persons kept him within his limits. Kurtz telegram to Persons, July 10, 1934; Persons reply July 10, 1934, CWSSA, CCC Records, NA.

14. Persons to DPA Director Russell, September 25, 1940, CWSSA, CCC Records, NA; "Plan of Operation of State Selecting Agency for CCC, 1939–1940," States' Plans of Cooperation for CCC Selection, DS, CCC Records, NA.

15. An instance of how this worked was in 1938 when Senator Guffey and Congressman Gray complained to Fechner about insufficient CCC positions in Cambria County, an area of high unemployment. Kurtz was immediately authorized to recruit fifty additional young men from there. Fechner to Persons, October 3, 1938, Snyder to Kurtz, October 6, 1938, CWSSA, CCC Records, NA.

16. Persons, Circular Letter, May 21, 1934, DS, CCC Records, NA.

17. These reports from SERB were sent to Persons by Biddle in a booklet, "Social Benefits Derived from the Civilian Conservation Corps," on July 25, 1934, and August 3, 1934, Procedural Records, DS, CCC Records, NA.

18. Kurtz to Persons, January 17, 1935, CWSSA, CCC Records, NA.

19. In Pennsylvania the trend began by Governor Pinchot of involving the state government in relief, heretofore the business of local governments, continued through the decade, and by 1941 its budget provided a higher percentage of relief payments to its needy citizens than any other state. "Public Assistance," *Social Security Bulletin* (October 1941): 1–2, in Publications of State Selection Agencies, CCC Records, NA.

20. *Annual Report of the Director of ECW, 1936,* 22. Roosevelt had pledged to Congress when the CCC law was passed in 1935 that the program would be now reserved for men on relief. M. H. McIntyre, assistant to the president, to Congressman Alfred Beiter, June 2, 1935, OF 268, FDRL; Kurtz, "CCC Guide for Selection Agents," December 21, 1936, in State Procedural Records, DS, CCC Records, NA.

21. Kurtz to Persons, March 7, 1935, CWSSA, CCC Records, NA.

22. *Happy Days,* April 27, 1935. Pennsylvania was projected to have 48,700 enrollees, second to New York.

23. Salmond, *Civilian Conservation Corps,* 61; Rosenman, *Public Papers,* III, 425; Fechner reported peak enrollments in August 1935 with 505,000 in camps. *Annual Report of the Director of ECW, 1933–1935,* 15.

24. Navy and marine officers were to head about 10 percent of the camps. The Third Corps now received sixty-three of them. War Department to Corps Commanders, May 3, 1935, RF, CCC Records, NA.

25. Frank Hines, "Rules on Selection," October 17, 1935, RF, CCC Records, NA. The seventeen-year-olds were a boon to selectors, but they never got much interest from men over twenty-five. Kurtz to Persons, November 21, 1935, CWSSA, CCC Records, NA.

26. Fifth Enrollment Period Report, All Service Camp Directories, Records of Project Application Section, NPS Records, NA.

27. Snyder reported Kurtz as "conscientious" but "overly cautious and meticulous." Snyder Memo, June 13, 1935, Circular Letters, DS, CCC Records, NA.

28. Kurtz to Persons, July 22, 1935; Persons to Robert Johnson, July 26, 1935, denying the request. CWSSA, CCC Records, NA.

29. Kurtz to Persons, July 30, 1935; also clips from *Norristown Times-Herald*, July 6, 1935, in file, CWSSA, CCC Records, NA.

30. Malone to Adjutant-General, June 15, 1935, GAF, A-G Records, NA; Larry N. Sypolt, "Fort Necessity: Civilian Conservation Corps, Camp S-12" (Morgantown, W. Va.: privately printed, 1988), reports interviews with several such men.

31. Johnson to Persons, September 6, 1935, Robert L Johnson, Circular Letter #26, September 11, 1935, CWSSA, CCC Records, NA.

32. Kurtz, Circular Letter #6, October 23, 1935, Kurtz, Circular Letter #1, September 23, 1935, CWSSA, CCC Records, NA.

33. *Annual Report of the Director of ECW, 1936*, 27; Kurtz, Circular Letter #35, March 1, 1937, DPA Records, PSA. Seventeen-year-olds made up 45 percent of November 1936 recruits; Kurtz, Circular Letter #30, November 16, 1936, DPA Records, PSA.

34. FDR to Fechner, March 23, 1936, in Rosenman, *Public Papers*, V, 151; Salmond, *Civilian Conservation Corps*, 66–67.

35. *Annual Report of the Director of ECW, 1936*, 23; Kurtz to Persons, May 1, 1936; Persons to Fechner, November 5, 1936, reporting on Pennsylvania falling far short of its fall goals. CWSSA, CCC Records, NA. Kurtz blamed the relatively poor showing of his selectors on competition from the WPA, which paid better. An example of out-of-state companies in 1936 was the movement of Company #5463 from Alabama into Camp S-139 in Promised Land State Park, replacing a disbanded Company #337. "History of Promised Land State Park" in PLSP files. Every member of Company #5462 from Mississippi, which came to Fort Necessity in 1936, had hookworm. Sypolt, "Fort Necessity," 66.

36. Kurtz to Persons, April 8, 1936; Persons to Kurtz, April 18, 1936; Department of Labor Directive to State Selectors, August 15, 1936, CWSSA, CCC Records, NA.

37. Kurtz to Persons, December 15, 1936, Kurtz to Persons, September 3, 1936, CWSSA, CCC Records, NA; Adjutant-General to Corps Commanding Generals, May 23, 1934, RF, CCC, NA; Persons to Kurtz, September 17, 1938 State Procedural Records, CCC Records, NA; *Happy Days*, November 19, 1938, 1.

38. Kurtz, Circular Letter #35, March 1, 1937, DPA Records, PSA; *Annual Report of the Director of CCC, 1936*, 53, 56; Alfred C. Oliver and Harold M. Dudley, *This New America: The Spirit of the CCC* (London: Longmans, Green, 1937), 186.

39. Fechner to FDR October 24, 1936, in Nixon, *FDR and Conservation*, I, 591–93. *Annual Report of the Director of ECW, 1936*, 6.

40. Rosenman, *Public Papers*, VII, 144–45.

41. Ibid., 144–45. Nixon, *FDR and Conservation*, II, 343. See this 1937 law in Paige, *CCC and the NPS*, app. A. The Budget Office, ever obsessed with spending, later forced some cuts, leaving funds for only 250,000 men in 1,200 camps. In the fall, part of the president's response to the "Roosevelt Recession" resulted in rescinding those cuts. Salmond, *Civilian Conservation Corps*, 170. Three Pennsylvania congressmen spoke against giving the CCC permanent status—two Democrats, Guy Moser and Joseph Grey, and a Republican, Robert Rich. *Congressional Record*, 75th Cong., 1st sess., 1937, vol. 81, 4363, 4383, 4385.

42. Salmond, *Civilian Conservation Corps*, 157–58; *Happy Days*, February 19, 1938, 1.

43. Snyder to Kurtz, September 16, 1939, CWSSA, CCC Records, NA.

44. Kurtz explained the Pennsylvania organization of CCC work and his own peculiar position in it to Dean Snyder on November 15, and December 17, 1937, CWSSA, CCC Records, NA; Kurtz, Circular Letter #15, March 1, 1938, DPA Records, PSA. Kurtz's DPA half-time salary was $2,100, his clerical help received a total of $4,950, and the miscellaneous expenses of his department, including his travel for the CCC, came to $1,700, for a total cost to the state of Pennsylvania of

$8,750. "Pennsylvania Plan of Operation for CCC Selection, 1938–1939," States' Plans of Cooperation, DS, CCC Records, NA.

45. Kurtz, Circular Letter #44, June 24, 1937, DPA Records, PSA.

46. Ketchum, *Borrowed Years*, 618.

47. "My CCC Life," NACCCA *Journal* (June 2003).

48. Kurtz to Persons, February 23, 1937, CWSSA, CCC Records, NA; on August 30, 1937, the DPA sent to the Labor Department a copy of its revised procedures. States' Plans of Cooperation for CCC Selection, DS, CCC Records, NA. The conditioning camp for enrollees to be sent west was moved from Tobyhanna to New Cumberland in fall 1938. *Happy Days*, October 1, 1938, 4.

49. For example, he calculated that Pennsylvania had enrolled 92,440 men by May 1937 and the federal government had spent $80 million on the CCC in the state. Kurtz, Circular Letters #43 and #6, May 4 and September 10, 1937, DPA Records, PSA. Still, he was getting pressure from the Labor Department to keep even more detailed records. R. Miles, "memo" of visit to Kurtz, June 25, 1937, DS, CCC Records, NA.

50. Kurtz to Snyder, July 15, 1937, CWSSA, CCC Records, NA; "Pennsylvania Plan of Operation for CCC Selection, 1938–1939," States' Plans of Cooperation for CCC Selection, DS, CCC Records, NA. With all this effort, nonetheless, come enrollment day, some boys who had signed up failed to show up. Report by Weston M. Kelsey, executive director, Lehigh Unit, Northampton County, to Kurtz, January 27, 1937, Circular Letter file, DPA Records, PSA. Kurtz encouraged selectors to line up alternates for instances like this.

51. From January 1938 to January 1939 the number of applicants in the country steadily soared from 143,129 to 259,953. General Headquarters Letters, Quarterly Selection Reports, January 1939, DS, CCC Records, NA.

52. Karl de Schweinitz to Governor Earle, January 3, 1938, DPA Reports and Manuals, DPA Records, PSA.

53. Kurtz to Snyder, January 8, 1938, CWSSA, CCC Records, NA.

54. A Gallup poll in July 1936 had reported 82 percent in favor of keeping the CCC, including 79 percent of Socialists and 67 percent of Republicans. Of those polled in Philadelphia, 89 percent were in favor of the CCC, and in Pittsburgh the figure was 88 percent. Governor Earle reported to Fechner that the people of Pennsylvania were "enthusiastic" about the CCC. Earle to Fechner, February 18, 1937, Correspondence with Governors, CCC Records, NA. The Roosevelt Papers has a small collection of dozens of favorable editorials from Pennsylvania newspapers, dating from a bit later, in 1939, commending the CCC's "splendid" (*Pittsburgh Press*, August 8, 1939) and "impressive" (*York Dispatch*, August 7, 1939) record. OF 268, FDRL.

55. De Lyle Davis to Secretary Bogardus, October 9, 1936, DPA Records, PSA.

56. General Headquarters Letters, January 1939, DS, Division of Selecting Agencies Publications, Quarterly Selection Reports, January 1939, DS, CCC Records, NA.

57. Kurtz, Circular Letter #17, March 18, 1938, DPA Records, PSA. In 1937, 1,224 Pennsylvania men had deserted and another 168 had been discharged for refusing to work.

58. "Letter to Enrollees," April 1937, State Procedural Records, DS, CCC Records, NA; Kurtz to Selectors, May 11, 1938, States' Plans of Cooperation for CCC Selection, CCC Records, NA.

59. Kurtz, Circular Letter #22, June 28, 1938, DPA Records, PSA.

60. Snyder to Kurtz, May 12, 1939, CWSSA, CCC Records, NA.

61. Kurtz, Circular Letter #29, December 12, 1938, DPA Records, PSA; Kurtz, Circular Letter #43, June 28, 1939, DPA Records, PSA.

62. Kurtz, Circular Letter #21, June 20, 1938, DPA Records, PSA; Kurtz to Persons, April 30, 1937 State Procedural Records, DS, CCC Records, NA; General Headquarters Letters, December 23, 1938, DS, CCC Records, NA.

63. *Annual Report of the Director of* CCC, 1938, 86–87. In July, 4,680 were transferred. Kurtz,

Circular Letter #21, June 20, 1938, DPA Records, PSA; *Happy Days* reported that most of the men were being housed in tents at Tobyhanna. June 18, 1938, 3.

64. DPA press release, September 21, 1938, CWSSA, CCC Records, NA.

65. Kurtz, Circular Letter #27, November 10, 1938, DPA Records, PSA.

66. *Annual Report of the Director of* CCC, *1939*, 2.

67. Some of the relevant correspondence is in OF 268, FDRL; see also Fechner to FDR, April 14, 1939, in Nixon, *FDR and Conservation*, II, 321–22. For background on this 1939 reorganization, see Richard Polenberg, *Reorganizing Roosevelt's Government: The Controversy over Executive Reorganization 1936–1939* (Cambridge: Harvard University Press, 1966).

68. File of Publications, Quarterly Enrollment Report, July 1939, DS, CCC Records, NA.

69. Memo to Harold Ickes from Conrad Wirth, November 5, 1940, in OF 218 FDRL; see also Salmond, *Civilian Conservation Corps*, 175–80; *Happy Days*, May 20, 1939, 1.

70. Adjutant-General to Corps Commanders May 28, 1937, and May 29, 1937, in RF, CCC Records, NA.

71. Unsigned memo, January 6, 1940, OF 268, FDRL; *Annual Report of the Director of* CCC, *1943*, 28. *New York Times*, June 16, 1939, 27; *Happy Days* June 17, 1939, 1. A picture of the new CO uniforms is in *Happy Days*, July 19, 1939; Holland and Hill, *Youth in the* CCC, 94; Adjutant-General to Corps Commanders, June 16, 1939, Documents Relating to the Organization and Operation of the CCC, CCC Records, NA; McEntee, *Now They Are Men*, 36.

72. *Annual Report of the Director of* CCC, *1939*, 112. This report is the first to list Kurtz as supervisor of CCC selection, under Howard L. Russell of the DPA. Persons to Howard Russell, March 23, 1939, CWSSA, CCC Records, NA.

73. "DPA Statistics," 4–5, May 1939, in Publications of State Selecting Agencies, DS, CCC Records, NA. An American Youth Commission bulletin in December 1938 reported these numbers. This private group had set up some short-term work camps of its own in New York. Records of Educational Program, CCC Records, NA. *Happy Days* was reporting the highest ratio of applicants per opening ever on December 10, 1938, 1.

74. Kurtz, Circular Letter #29, December 12, 1938, DPA Records, PSA; Plans for Cooperation for CCC Selection, "Plan of Operation of Selection Agencies for CCC, July 1, 1939 to June 30, 1940," DS, CCC Records, NA; Kurtz, Circular Letter #42, June 20, 1939, DPA Records, PSA. On the other hand, a study done on seventeen-year-olds by the national office in 1939 concluded, somewhat counterintuitively, that seventeen-year-old recruits were proving to be the most stable of all! Memo from Bill Phillips to Snyder, October 2, 1939, File on Publications, DS, CCC Records, NA. Unfortunately, Kurtz never reported on the ages of those Pennsylvanians who deserted camp.

75. Kurtz, Circular Letter #49, September 28, 1939, DPA Records, PSA. Not all the work was interesting. A company of boys from Philadelphia and Pittsburgh found sifting dirt at an archaeological mound on University of Arizona land hot and "sissy" work. The discovery of some pottery shards produced some occasional excitement. *Happy Days*, June 22, 1940, 7.

76. See Richard Melzer, *Coming of Age in the Great Depression: The Civilian Conservation Corps Experience in New Mexico, 1933–1942* (Las Cruces, N.M.: Yucca Tree Press, 2000), 206, 220, 233, 238, 239, 242, 248, and passim for accounts of Pennsylvania boys in New Mexico.

77. Kurtz to Snyder, September 14, and September 28, 1939, CWSSA, CCC Records, NA.

78. Kurtz, Circular Letter #41, June 12, 1939, DPA Records, PSA.

79. Persons to Kurtz, June 12, 1939, CWSSA, CCC Records, NA; Kurtz, Circular Letter #47, September 14, 1939, Circular Letter #55, December 21, 1939, DPA Records, PSA; Persons to Selectors, July 25, 1940, RF, CCC Records, NA; Persons to Kurtz, June 6, 1940, CCC Educational Programs, CCC Records, NA; Kurtz, Circular Letter #94, June 20, 1941, DPA Records, PSA. Holland and Hill, *Youth in the* CCC, 55.

80. Russell had succeeded Arthur Howe in January. Russell to Persons, January 26, 1939, CWSSA, CCC Records, NA.

81. Booklet in CWSSA, CCC Records, NA. For example, a study by the American Youth Commission in 1942 described the average CCC enrollee as seventeen or eighteen, weighing 145 pounds, and being 5 feet 8 inches tall. His family was on relief and lived in a house with no running water or telephone. American Council on Education, *The Civilian Conservation Corps* (Washington, D.C., 1940), 5.

82. Communication to author, May 5, 2004, May 19, 2004; Ermentrout, *Forgotten Men*, 81.

83. Kurtz, Circular Letter #51, November 20, 1939, DPA Records, PSA.

84. Fechner's obituary appeared in *New York Times*, January 1, 1940, 23.

85. Wirth, *Parks, Politics and the People*, 137–41.

86. State Plans for Cooperation, "Summary and Analysis of Plan of Operation, May 29, 1940," DS, CCC Records, NA; Persons to Kurtz, February 14, 1940, Publications File, DS, CCC Records, NA.

87. Persons to Kurtz, October 1, 1940, CWSSA, CCC Records, NA; *Annual Report of the Director of CCC, 1940*, 73, 77; *New York Times*, August 25, 1940, 10; Kurtz, Circular Letters #59, March 13, 1940, and #70, September 18, 1940, DPA Records, PSA.

88. Persons to Selectors, Circular Letters, July 25, 1940; Persons to Selectors, November 4, 1940, CWSSA, CCC Records, NA. Leaders would be allowed to keep $23 of their $45 pay and assistant leaders $14 of their $36 as spending money.

89. Russell to Persons August 14, 1940, Records Relating to the Proposed Merger of NYA and CCC, CCC, Records, NA; Kurtz, Circular Letter #72, November 18, 1940, DPA Records, PSA.

90. *Annual Report of the Director of CCC, 1940*, 15. "The CCC has been transformed from a monetary relief and job-giving agency into a work-training agency." Circular Letters, February 24, 1940, DS, CCC Records, NA.

91. This apt phrase is the title of a book by John Lukacs in 1976.

92. *Happy Days*, June 29, 1940, 1.

93. Kurtz, Circular Letter #100, December 19, 1941, DPA Records, PSA; *Annual Report of the Director of CCC, 1941*, 9.

94. Leslie Alexander Lacy, *The Soil Soldiers: The Civilian Conservation Corps in the Great Depression* (Radnor, Pa.: Chilton Book, 1976), 203; Ermentrout, *Forgotten Men*, 65; Circular Letters, transcript of McEntee radio interview, November 30, 1941, DS, CCC Records, NA. Cooks were being trained at forty-four different CCC camps, and McEntee ordered fifteen minutes of compulsory calisthenics before breakfast for Junior enrollees. *Happy Days*, July 6, 1940, 1; *Annual Report of the Director of CCC, 1940*, 2, 5–7. *New York Times*, February 9, 1941, IV, 6.

95. "Improvement of Artillery Ranges, January 2, 1941," Memo from A. P. Burgley, NPS, to Field Inspector Heinrich, HRSP Records; *Annual Report of the Director of CCC, 1941*, 5.

96. Kurtz, Circular Letter #83, March 20, 1941, DPA Records, PSA. In the good years, recruiters stressed the potential harmful effects of a dishonorable discharge on enrollees' future job prospects. Now the message was that such discharges would not be assets, a subtle but telling change.

97. The *Harrisburg Patriot* thought it "little short of scandalous" that, with industry booming and money needed for defense, the CCC, which had outlived its usefulness, was still going strong. Clipping, June 23, 1941, in Publicity File, DS, CCC Records, NA.

98. Pennsylvania was credited with enrolling 26,397 men for the fiscal year 1941, almost 10,000 more than New York. There were, however, only sixteen camps still open in the state by then and only 11,775 of its men in those and other camps, indicating the high turnover rate that was eroding the program. *Annual Report of the Director of CCC, 1941*, 61, 65.

99. Kurtz, Circular Letter #65, July 2, 1940, #79, February 21, 1941, DPA Records, PSA.

100. Pennsylvania men leaving ccc camps, honorably or otherwise, were now far outnumbering the new men recruited—9,583 vs. 2,776 in the second quarter of 1941. Kurtz, Circular Letter #97, September 10, 1941, DPA Records, PSA. This was the national story as well. McEntee reported the highest number of recruits since 1937, but not enough to keep up with those leaving camp. He mused on the idea of requiring *all* seventeen- and eighteen-year-olds to spend six months in a ccc camp. *Annual Report of the Director of* ccc, *1941*, 2, 6; Kurtz to Persons, March 27, 1941, CWSSA, CCC Records, NA.

101. Circular Letter, March 24, 1941, DS, CCC Records, NA.

102. Kurtz to Persons, March 27, 1941, Persons to Russell, June 28, 1941, CWSSA, CCC Records, NA. Kurtz, Circular Letter #85, April 14, 1941, DPA Records, PSA.

103. McEntee to Persons, April 12, 1941, Kurtz, Circular Letter #92, June 17, 1941, DPA Records, PSA.

104. Kurtz, Circular Letter #86, May 1, 1941, DPA Records, PSA; Claude R. Wicker, secretary of agriculture, to FDR April 5, 1941, Nixon, *FDR and Conservation,* II, 497; Kurtz to Persons, January 27, 1942, CWSSA, CCC Records, NA. The parents had each brought eight children from first marriages and then had eight more between them. Kurtz, Circular Letters #86, May 1, 1941, and #90, June 6, 1941, DPA Records, PSA. Some camps in the state were down to 124 enrollees, and the April class drew 71 percent from nonrelief families. Kurtz, Circular Letters #83, March 20, 1941, #87, May 8, 1941, #88, May 14, 1941, DPA Records, PSA.

105. Kurtz, Circular Letter #93, June 20, 1941, DPA Records, PSA.

106. McEntee, August 5, 1941, Circular Letters, CCC Records, NA; Kurtz, Circular Letter #96, August 15, 1941, DPA Records, PSA. Selection returned to its quarterly system in September. ACM, August 26, 1941, CCC Records, NA.; Kurtz, Circular Letter #100, December 19, 1941, DPA Records, PSA.

107. Russell to McEntee, October 2, 1941; Kurtz to Persons, September 25, 1941, CWSSA, CCC Records, NA.

108. Neal Guy, assistant director of selection, Minutes of Conference of the Office of the Director and Field Representatives, March 30–April 2, 1942, 116, CCC Records, NA.

CHAPTER 3

1. Communication to author, February 21, 2004.

2. "Final Report of the Director of the CCC, 1933–1942," 108, CCC Records, NA.

3. See Appendix 1 for a list of camps and companies in Pennsylvania. Uncertainty about Camp S-157 may result in an altered total of 151 camps.

4. There was another "SP" camp, SP-18, Caledonia, which started as S-107, and whose company, #1324, was moved to Hickory Run RDA in 1939. SP-18 has been counted in the "S" totals. SP-2 was briefly S-100 in the summer of 1933, but Conrad Wirth argued that, on the nature of the work planned there, it should be a SP camp. It has been counted here in the SP totals.

5. *Four Year Summary Report of the Department of Forests and Waters, 1935–1938,* 29–30.

6. These totals are from Division of Planning and Public Relations, CCC Records, NA.

7. *Happy Days,* July 7, 1934, 1; "Porcupine Damage in Northern Pennsylvania's Forests," PDFW *Service Letter* (October 24, 1932), PDFW Records, PSA; *Civilian Conservation Corps Annual, 1936,* Third Corps, District No. 1, 29; Trexler-Lehigh Game Preserve Report, February 10, 1936, Entry File 41, NPS Records, NA; Charles Kenlan to McEntee, May 24, 1937, CIR, S-145, CCC Records, NA.

8. Perhaps that is why the nickname for ccc men that *Happy Days* tried to popularize,

"Peavey," after a common tool of loggers, never took. None of the CCC men interviewed for this study had ever heard of it being used that way.

9. Roosevelt thought it "common sense" that the work should be in the Department of Agriculture. FDR to Ickes, March 22, 1935, Nixon, *FDR and Conservation*, I, 364; "Soil Conservation," March 1938 publication, General Headquarters Letters, DS, CCC Records, NA. Harper, *Administration of the Civilian Conservation Corps,* 74.

10. "Soil Erosion Control" in Documents Relating to the Organization and Operation of the CCC, CCC Records, NA; there are three boxes of work orders and cost estimates on Pennsylvania farms in RG-114, Soil Conservation Service Records, NA.

11. "Hands to Save the Soil," 1939 CCC publication, DS, CCC Records, NA.

12. By 1937, 350 new state parks had been added in 37 states, thanks to CCC labor. "The CCC and Its Contribution to a Nation-Wide State Park Recreation Program," 4, Circular Letters, DS, CCC Records, NA; Dan Cupper, *Our Priceless Heritage: Pennsylvania State Parks, 1893–1993* (Harrisburg: Department of Environmental Resources, Bureau of State Parks, 1993), 7–8. See also William C. Forrey, *History of Pennsylvania's State Parks* (Harrisburg: Department of Environmental Resources, 1984), especially chap. 6, "Depression and the Civilian Conservation Corps."

13. Cupper, *Our Priceless Heritage,* 23, 28; the budget of the Department of Forests and Waters was cut from $3 million in 1929–31 to $1.4 million in 1933–35. Thorpe, *Crown Jewel of Pennsylvania,* 17, 18. Pennsylvania increased its spending on parks from $114,000 in 1934 to $161,000 in 1937. *1937 Yearbook, Parks and Recreation Programs, NPS* (1938), NPS Records, HFC. Between December 1933 and March 1934, CWA workers worked in a number of park areas in Pennsylvania, including Valley Forge and Fort Necessity. W. E. Montgomery, "The CWA in Pennsylvania State Parks," typescript report, May 1934, PDFW Records, PSA. See also the typed recollections of S. Herbert Evison, an NPS administrator under Conrad Wirth in NPS Records, HFC; "Report of the Bureau of Parks, 1935–37," PDFW Records, PSA.

14. *Happy Days,* January 22, 1938, 5.

15. The NPS kept 848 acres of the French Creek RDA for its own Hopewell Village when it turned over the area to Pennsylvania in 1946. Wirth, *Parks, Politics and the People,* 185. There is extensive documentation on the RDA at Hickory Run, Laurel Hill, and Blue Knob in the NPS Records at HFC. These records include studies on the need and expected benefits of these parks and the purchase prices on the tracts of land acquired.

16. Most of the work done in establishing the group camps at Camp Shehequa and Camp Daddy Allen at Hickory Run seems to have been done by the WPA. Work Order Files, HRSP Records. Similarly there are work orders at Promised Land State Park showing WPA construction of eighteen tourist cabins. On the other hand, the Department of Forests and Waters in 1938 credited the CCC with improving 2,325 acres of park lands, including the construction of 352 park buildings and 83 tourist cabins. *Four Year Summary Report of the Department of Forests and Waters, 1935–38,* 35.

17. Harold Ickes to Governor Earle, September 30, 1937, Records of Project Application, NPS Records, NA; W. E. Montgomery to Col. Earl Areford, August 26, 1935, Bureau of Parks Correspondence, PDFW Records, PSA; Records of Project Application, October 1, 1937, CCC Camps, NPS Records, NA. This project was apparently pushed by Judge Michael Musmanno of Pittsburgh. Sypolt, "Fort Necessity," 10.

18. Wirth, *Parks, Politics and the People,* 185.

19. James F. Bogardus to State Foresters, March 1, 1937, PDFW Records, PSA; Eric von Hausswolff, chief of parks, to District Foresters, July 26, 1935, PDFW Records, PSA. Of course, in addition to managing CCC work, the usual business went on. Hausswolff had to take time to warn off a New York City man from even thinking about establishing a nudist colony on state

lands because of Pennsylvania's laws against "indecent exposure." Hausswolff to W. H. Fowley, October 15, 1936, PDFW Records, PSA.

20. John C. Diggs to H. E. Klugh, Jr., project manager, September 17, 1937, in HRSP Records.

21. A. F. Perkins, acting assistant regional director, NPS, to Inspector Heinrich, September 5, 1939, HRSP Records.

22. *Happy Days*, February 22, 1936, 1, 23, March 14, 1936, 10, February 1, 1936, 5–6, January 11, 1936, 21, January 18, 1936, 12; *Happy Days*, January 11, 1936, 12, 17, on work done by Company #2324 at S-148, Mifflinburg, and Company #1329 at S-97, Somerset. Tom Frantz, who served both as an enrollee and a foreman at S-139 at Promised Land, remembers cutting saplings as common winter forestry work. Communication, September 20, 2003. Robert Ermentrout, an army officer who commanded camps in Wisconsin, claimed that in one bitterly cold stretch of four days, his camp burned 400 cords of wood. Ermentrout, *Forgotten Men*, 93.

23. *Pittsburgh Press*, March 17, 1936, 9, March 19, 1936, 5, March 20, 1936, 1; *Evening Bulletin*, March 18, 1936, 1, March 21, 1936, 1.

24. Fechner to Commanding General, Third Corps, March 25, 1936, War Department to Third Corps, March 26, 1936, RF, CCC Records, NA.

25. Materials on Camp SP-5, Johnstown, Branch of Recreation, Land Planning and State Cooperation, NPS Records, NA; *Civilian Conservation Corps Annual, 1936*, Third Corps, District No. 1, 121. These four companies—numbers 2326, 1379, 1329, and 344—were organized into a "flood relief expeditionary force" and published a series of "flood relief bulletins" while engaged in their relief work. Copies are in the files at Fort Necessity National Battlefield.

26. Quoted in *Four Year Summary Report of the Department of Forests and Waters*, 31–32; press release, April 27, 1936, CCC Records, NA. P. A. Kinsley of the town council wrote more than a year later, expressing the gratitude of the people of Renovo for the assistance given during the flood. *Happy Days*, June 19, 1937.

27. *Four Year Summary Report*, 28.

28. Work Report, November 1938, Delaware State Forest, PLSP Records. The nurseries were at Mont Alto, Clearfield, Greenwood Furnace, and Potters Mills.

29. Communication from Tom Frantz, enrollee and foreman at Camp S-139, Promised Land, September 20, 2003. "Co. 305," the newsletter of S-54, reported that the men had killed 144 snakes in 1940, including 48 copperheads and 10 rattlers. Sometimes men would shake the rattles of the snakes they killed as they trucked back to camp, to the cheers of people they passed. "Outline on the Planting of Forest Trees," PDFW, *Service Letter* (January–February 1942), 29–32, PDFW Records, PSA; H. R. Kylie, G. H. Hieronymous, and A. G. Hall, CCC *Forestry* (Washington, D.C.: GPO, 1937), 122; "Biography of John D. Chepetz, Company 2323, SCS-5, Sligo," 2, accessed at www.geocities.com/oral/bio/chepetzdjdbio.html. Tree planting was both hard work and boring to the men, who sometimes found ways to "plant" their quotas whenever the foreman wasn't looking. Ermentrout, *Forgotten Men*, 95; when the men had to carry the seedlings deep into the woods where trucks could not go, an individual would be able to plant only 150–200 trees a day. Paul Slovan, "My CCC Life," NACCCA *Journal* (June 2002).

30. Kylie et al., CCC *Forestry*, 92; De Coster, *Legacy of Penn's Woods*, 49–50. This description of the work owes much to an interview with Walter Joyce of Camp S-91 at Watrous, Pennsylvania, conducted August 11, 2003.

31. *Four Year Summary Report*, 3.

32. Leonard B. Wing, "Naturalizing the Forests for Wildlife," *American Forests* 42 (January 1936): 14; "Letter" by C.A.B., Lancaster, Pa., *New York Times*, September 1, 1936, IV, 9; May 19, 1934, GP 2560, PP, LC; "CCC Needs a Clearer Policy on Conservation," *American Forests* 44 (May 1938): 224; see comments by Professor Merritt L. Fernald of Harvard University at the Franklin Institute in Philadelphia in *New York Times*, May 21, 1938, 1 and 13, and a retort by a landscape

architect, *New York Times*, June 5, 1938, IV, 9. When Roosevelt received a complaint from a Swarthmore, Pennsylvania, man about CCC work being done in the Okefinokee area, he referred it to Secretary Wallace and added his own lament: "Why, oh why, can't we let original nature remain original nature!" Nixon, *FDR and Conservation*, II, 66–67. If applied literally, of course, it would have put the CCC out of business.

33. *Annual Report of the Director of* ECW, *1933–35*, 2; *Annual Report of the Director of* CCC, *1939*, 43; "Final Report of the Director of CCC, 1942," 43. During the CCC years the annual acreage destroyed by fires dropped 27 percent. Major John Guthrie, "The CCC and American Conservation," *Scientific Monthly* 57 (October 1943): 407.

34. Chad Pysher, "The Crafting of a Treasure Chest: The Legacy of the Civilian Conservation Corps," www.allegheny-online.com/ccccorp.html. Pysher interviewed Michael Schultz, a widely recognized authority on the camps in the Allegheny National Forest and producer of a video, "The CCC: Its Time and Legacy." Fechner first authorized the mobilization of CCC companies to help fight large fires in Montana in August 1933. Salmond, *Civilian Conservation Corps*, 46.

35. *Happy Days*, August 28, 1937, 1. The paper also reported a mess hall fire at A-2, Tobyhanna, that destroyed the building. January 2, 1937, 4.

36. *Happy Days*, October 22, 1938, 1. A moving and detailed account of this fire is by Michael Schultz, "'Puny' Fire at Pepper Hill Claimed Lives of Seven CCCers," NACCCA *Journal*, June 2001, 1, 6–8.

37. "Information on Fires," GAF, A-G Records, NA. *Happy Days*, October 22, 1938, 1. See the story on the fire, highlighting the story of May, in "Hopewell Howl," the newsletter of SP-7, October 1938, Furnace Creek State Park Records; testimony of enrollee Andrew Kiliney, "Army Hearing at Camp S-132, October 20–24, 1938," GAF, A-G Records, NA; see also the "Memorial Issue" of the "Hunt's Run Echo" of S-132 for October 19, 1939, in the PCHS.

38. "Report of Dr. J. D. Johnston, Cameron County Coroner, at Emporium, Pennsylvania, October 31, 1938," in GAF, A-G Records, NA.

39. "Army Hearing at Camp S-132"; Secretary of War George Tyner to Army Chief of Staff Malin Craig, November 14, 1938; General J. K. Parsons, commanding general, Third Corps to Adjutant-General, December 6, 1938, GAF, A-G Records, NA.

40. Fechner to Adjutant-General, November 11, 1938, GAF, A-G Records, NA.

41. Parsons to Adjutant-General, December 6, 1938, Craig to Parsons, January 11, 1939, Fechner to Tyner, January 3, 1939, GAF, A-G Records, NA; Fechner to FDR, January 6, 1939, OF 268, FDRL. Camp S-132 later became a Veterans' camp, and in a 1942 inspection report was cited as one of the "most attractive" camps in the state. April 9, 1942, inspection, CIR, CCC Records, NA; Harper, *Administration of the Civilian Conservation Corps*, 144; Johnson, "Army and the Civilian Conservation Corps," 144.

42. ACM, November 29, 1938, CCC Records, NA.

43. Fechner to FDR, May 31, 1935, OF 268, FDRL.

44. *Happy Days*, October 21, 1939, July 29, 1939; De Coster, *Legacy of Penn's Woods*, 73–74. Some forty camps contributed to the costs involved in building the site. "Hunt's Run Camp History," in PCHS, which also has a copy of the "Hunt's Run Echo" newsletter for October 19, 1939, a memorial issue; Ermentrout, *Forgotten Men*, 97,

45. Enrollees were not the only camp members at risk. The CO of Camp S-155 was drowned trying to rescue a man from a flooding creek. *Wellsboro Gazette*, September 2, 1937; Circular Letter, October 31, 1941, DS, CCC Records, NA.

46. Division of Safety, "Safety Regulations, 1938," Documents Relating to the Organization and Operation of the CCC, CCC Records, NA; Harper, *Administration of the Civilian Conservation Corps*, 95.

47. John Williams to All Camp Superintendents, March 9, 1934, Camp s-107 Records, MSF Records.

48. *Annual Report of the Director of* CCC, *1941,* 21, and *Annual Report of the Director of* CCC, *1942,* 19.

49. *Annual Report of the Director of* CCC, *1940,* 24. Other leading causes of accidental deaths that year were drowning, 42; suicides, 9; and homicides, 8.

50. Glenn Cordell, "The Cowan's Gap CCC Camp of Fulton County, Pa." (Fulton County Historical Society, 2004), 8, copy in RFSP Records; CIR, SP-16, CCC Records, NA. *New York Times,* November 12, 1936, 4, reported four killed in this accident. Veterans' camps usually had more lenient policies on alcohol and received more community complaints about its abuse by the men, especially on paydays. See, e.g., the camp inspection report on s-105, housing Veterans' Company #1328 in Potter County, October 27, 1935, CIR, CCC Records, NA.

51. *Annual Report of the Director of* CCC, *1940,* 21, 23. In the earlier years CCC sickness rates were below those of army men. *Annual Report of the Director of* ECW, *1936,* 13. There were only 9 deaths from pneumonia in 1940, compared to 1,145 deaths from it in the previous six years. Although no breakdown of categories was kept, it seems likely that the heart-related deaths would have occurred among the veterans.

52. *Annual Report of the Director of* CCC, *1941,* 19; communication from Dochod to author, April 20, 2004.

53. *New York Times,* December 8, 1933, 5; Progress Reports on State and Local Parks, December 4, 1934, NPS Records, NA; Hetfield to Book, September 11, 1935, Camp s-107 Records, MSF Records.

54. *Civilian Conservation Corps Annual, 1936,* Third Corps, District No. 1, 107; Philip M. Conti, *The* CCC: *Salvaging Boys and Other Treasures* (privately printed, 1998), 11; James E. Potts, "CCC: Bear Valley"; communication from Leo Ruvolis, February 21, 2004.

55. *Annual Report of the Director of* CCC, *1939,* 32, and *Annual Report of the Director of* CCC, *1940,* 22; McEntee, *Now They Are Men,* 59; Eric Gorham, "The Ambiguous Practices of the CCC," *Social History* 17 (May 1992): 242.

56. Kenneth Holland and Frank Ernest Hill, *Youth in the* CCC (Washington, D.C.: American Council on Education, 1942), 194; Salmond, *Civilian Conservation Corps,* 144. At the end McEntee reported a venereal disease rate of 20 per 1,000, with 23 percent of the cases involving syphilis. *Annual Report of the Director of* CCC, *1942,* 20. Charles Taylor, one of Fechner's investigators, reported to Senator Royal S. Copeland, on the measures taken against bedbugs at NP-4, near Reading, after members of Company #3304 had complained. Taylor to Copeland, June 2, 1937, in CIR, CCC Records, NA.

57. Communication of Leo Ruvolis to author, February 21, 2004; communication of Edwin Smith to author, September 8, 2003. James Potts, who wrote a memoir of his days at Camp "Bear Valley," s-109 in south central Pennsylvania, claims that fifteen men from his camp, including himself, married local girls.

58. John D. Chepetz reports having to break up with his first girlfriend in Sligo because of her father's objections to CCC men. "Biography of John D. Chepetz," 6. Joseph De Cenzo, also of Camp SCS-5, reports that young women invited to dances at SCS-5 usually were chaperoned, three girls to a parent. Interview by author, June 26, 2004.

59. Holland and Hill, *Youth in the* CCC, 215–17. Kinsey found much lower rates of intercourse among adolescents. Alfred C. Kinsey, Wardell B. Pomeroy, and Clyde E. Martin, *Sexual Behavior in the Human Male* (Philadelphia: W. B. Saunders, 1948), 316.

60. "The Adviser," July 6–22, 1936; Wecter, *Age of the Great Depression,* 263. Walter Joyce remembers a troupe of unemployed New York City actors performing at Camp s-91 in 1934, interview, August 11, 2003.

61. "Study of the C.C.C. by the American Youth Commission, Fall 1939," in Records of CCC Educational Program, CCC Records, NA. In an era just entering the age of mass media entertainment, maybe the number of pianos is not surprising. Besides, Robert Ermentrout reported that, while he paid $75 for pool tables for his recreational halls, he could purchase used pianos for $5. *Forgotten Men*, 85.

62. The best known was Red Schoendist who went from a CCC camp in Illinois to star for the St. Louis Cardinals. Donald Dale Jackson, "They Were Poor, Hungry and They Built to Last," *Smithsonian* 25 (December 1900): 72. In October 1936 about fifty men from Camp S-51 at Pine Grove Furnace were taken to see Gettysburg College play Drexel. "Bunker Hill Bunk," mimeographed newsletter, October 1936, in PGFSP Records.

63. Frank Persons later boasted of his early advocacy of camp education. "Remarks" at Educational Conference of the Third Corps, Williamsport, July 10, 1939, Records of CCC Educational Program, CCC Records, NA; *Happy Days*, April 25, 1936, 7. Early educational advisers sometimes had to service more than one camp. In the summer of 1935 there were only 1,087 of them for the 1,468 camps. Harper, *Administration of the Civilian Conservation Corps*, 48.

64. "Report of the Special Committee on Education," Records of CCC Educational Program, CCC Records, NA; "History of Promised Land State Park," in PLSP Records.

65. Memo from Neal Guy to Snyder, December 28, 1938, Records of Educational Division, CCC Records, NA.

66. "Report of the Special Committee on Education, 1938," Records of Educational Division, CCC Records, NA.

67. February 18, 1935 issue of "Mountain Eagle" is in PLSP Records; a February 1941 copy of "Co. 305" is in RFSP Records, and PGFSP has an October 1936 issue of "Bunker Hill Bunk."

68. Memo to Adjutant-General, August 14, 1934, "Value of Educational Programs in CCC Camps," Howe 70, FDRL.

69. "Bunker Hill Bunk" (camp newspaper of S-51), November 1936, PGFSP Records.

70. Howard Oxley, "Educational Activities in CCC Camps, March 1938," 14, 20, General Headquarters Letters, DS, CCC Records, NA.

71. "Minority Report to the Report of the Special Committee on Education in the CCC, January 1939," Entry File 21, CCC Records, NA.

72. Howard Oxley, "Educational Activities in CCC Camps, March 1938," General Headquarters Letters, DS, CCC Records, NA.

73. Howard Oxley, director of CCC camp education, claimed a rate of 87.7 percent in 1938 and 88.3 percent in 1940. *Annual Report, 1938*, Educational Division, CCC Records, NA; *Annual Report of the Director of CCC, 1940*, 37; Howard Oxley, "Educational Activities in CCC Camps, March 1938," General Headquarters Letters, DS, CCC Records, NA. Holland and Hill, *Youth in the CCC*, 106–7, 162.

74. "Minutes of the Committee on CCC Instruction, November 22, 1939," Educational Program, CCC Records, NA. A good example of these instruction and reference manuals for foremen and enrollees is Kylie et al., CCC *Forestry*, which contains much scientific and practical information. Joseph De Cenzo, who taught courses at SCS-5, reports that he effectively used Sears catalogues to demonstrate spelling and arithmetic lessons. Interview by author, June 26, 2004. Some 1936 and 1937 copies of "The Adviser" are in the Fort Necessity Records.

75. Johnson, "CCC and the Army," 230; Jonathan Mitchell, "Roosevelt's Tree Army, Part Two," *New Republic* 83 (June 12, 1935): 127–28; "The Civilian Conservation Corps: Recommendations of the American Youth Commission and the American Council on Education, December 1940," 15, Educational Division, CCC Records, NA.

76. A copy of the publication is in PLSP Records; "Sedition in the CCC," *New Republic*, 85 (February 12, 1936): 6.

77. Johnson, "CCC and the Army," 230.

78. Salmond, *Civilian Conservation Corps*, 162–63; *Annual Report of the Director of* CCC, *1938*, 73.

79. "Job Adjustment for the CCC: A Demonstration," PPF 226, FDRL. This Williamsport program was boasted about in "The Adviser," reporting on the Educational Advisory Conference for the Third Corps held at College Park, Maryland, on July 7 and 8, 1940; Educational Division, Inspection Report of S-80, November 25, 1941, CIR, CCC Records, NA.

80. *Happy Days*, April 20, 1935; Inspection Report on Camp S-95, July 12, 1935, CIR, CCC Records, NA.

81. Kurtz, Circular Letter #46, July 2, 1937, Circular Letter #11, November 23, 1937, DPA Records, PSA; Oxley's division prepared a booklet with thirty-nine pages of correspondence course offerings at seventy-six different institutions. "The Citizens [*sic*] Conservation Corps and the Penn State College," *School and Society* 40 (October 13, 1934): 485; "Correspondence Courses for the CCC," Educational Division, CCC Records, NA.

82. Lacy, *Soil Soldiers*, 149; Holland and Hill, *Youth and the* CCC, 151.

83. Holland and Hill, *Youth and the* CCC, 185–86. In the RFSP Records there is a certificate of enrollee Walter Hamil, who had completed a four-week course at the "School for Mess Stewards and Cooks" at New Cumberland.

84. *Annual Report of the Director of* CCC, *1938*, 26; Ralston, "Adult Education as a Welfare Measure," 282. Edwin Smith, who served in Camp S-155 near Wellsboro, Pennsylvania, as assistant educational adviser, was among the many for whom camp educational experiences provided springboards to later careers (communication to author, September 30, 2003). Walter Joyce, however, who served in the 1933–34 period at Camp S-91 near Watrous, did not find the classes useful and described the whole program as "lackadaisical" (communication to author, August 11, 2003). At Camp S-107, the CO and the superintendent cooperated in giving enrollee John Krull truck driving experience to help him to qualify for a promised job. Hetfield to Book, August 17, 1935, Camps S-107 Records, MSF Records.

85. Harper, *Administration of the Civilian Conservation Corps*, 99; *Happy Days*, November 3, 1934.

86. Holland and Hill, *Youth and the* CCC, 242.

87. Persons to Edward L. Russell (Pennsylvania DPA), November 22, 1939, Educational Division, CCC Records, NA; Persons to Fechner, May 10, 1939, RF, CCC Records, NA.

88. *Annual Report of the Director of* CCC, *1939*, 47. See Wecter, *Age of the Great Depression*, 213, on the decline in religious interest. Fechner also cooperated with the American Bible Society in distributing 265,700 Bibles to the camps.

89. *Annual Report of the Director of* ECW, *1933–35*, 2; *Annual Report of the Director of* CCC, *1939*, 43; *Civilian Conservation Corps Annual*, *1936*, Third Corps, District No. 1, 16.

90. *Civilian Conservation Corps Annual*, *1936*, Third Corps, District No. 1, 24; interview by author, August 11, 2003.

91. Alfred C. Oliver and Harold M. Dudley, *This New America: The Spirit of the* CCC (London: Longmans, Green, 1937), 120–21.

92. Hoyt, *We Can Take It*, 53.

93. Harper, *Administration of the Civilian Conservation Corps*, 45; *Happy Days*, April 29, 1939, 1.

94. Adjutant-General to Corps Commanders, November 16, 1933, RF, CCC Records, NA; Johnson, "CCC and the Army," 40.

95. Persons to Russell, September 26, 1940, CWSSA, NA; Persons, Circular Letter, September 27, 1940, Circular Letters, DS, CCC Records, NA.

96. Harper, *Administration of the Civilian Conservation Corps*, 45.

97. ACM, April 20, 1937, CCC Records, NA. The desertion rate for the first year was 8 percent. Paige, *Civilian Conservation Corps and the NPS*, chap. 3.

98. *Daily Worker* clipping, February 16, 1937, CWSSA, CCC Records, NA.

99. Persons to Arthur Howe, November 15, 1938, CWSSA, CCC Records, NA.

100. Howard Rowland, "Can the CCC Blaze a New Trail?" *Survey Graphic* 26 (June 1937): 322; McEntee sent the FERA reports to the president, OF 268, FDRL.

101. Holland and Hill, *Youth in the CCC*, 127.

102. "Accumulative Schedule of Discharges, December 31, 1941," Records Relating to the Proposed Merger of NYA and CCC, 1939–42, CCC Records, NA.

103. Kurtz to Persons, October 28, 1937, CWSSA, CCC Records, NA. Kurtz referred to a "study" he had done on this subject but gave no specifics.

104. Persons to Kurtz, October 1, 1940, CWSSA, CCC Records, NA; Kurtz, Circular Letter #79, February 21, 1941, Circular Letter #97, September 10, 1941, DPA Records, PSA.; "Fewer Youth Props," *Newsweek* 18 (November 10, 1941): 24; Discharge Reports, September 1941 to January 1942, Monthly Discharge Reports, DS, CCC Records, NA.

105. Salmond, *Civilian Conservation Corps*, 107–8, on incidents in 1937 and 1939.

106. Kenlan to McEntee, December 29, 1935, James Hagan to Third Corps Commander, December 2, 1935, CIR, SCS-7, CCC Records, NA. This camp was still being reported in poor condition in 1940, with a "protective association" operating in camp and intimidating enrollees. Interview with Robert Ward, August 26, 1903; CIR, S-130, October 8, 1934, McEntee to Charles Kenlan, January 23, 1936, CIR, S-120, CCC Records, NA.

CHAPTER 4

1. Most of the integrated CCC camps were in New England and usually had only token numbers of blacks. Holland and Hill, *Youth in the CCC*, 112; John A. Salmond, "The Civilian Conservation Corps and the Negro," *Journal of American History* 52 (June 1965): 82. After 1935, Director Fechner insisted on complete segregation of all camps except in states where there were too few blacks to form separate companies. Olen Cole Jr., *The African-American Experience in the Civilian Conservation Corps* (Gainesville: University of Florida Press, 1999), 48.

2. Arthur S. Link, *Woodrow Wilson and the Progressive Era, 1910–1917* (New York: Harper and Row, 1954), 64–66.

3. Raymond Wolters, "The New Deal and the Negro," in Braemen et al., *New Deal*, I, 205.

4. Guffey, *Seventy Years*, 170; Otis L. Graham Jr., *The New Deal: The Critical Issues* (Boston: Little, Brown, 1971), 45. Guffey was introduced to Vann by his sister Emma's manicurist. Halt, "Joseph F. Guffey," 120.

5. "Remarks of Senator Joseph Guffey at Negro Democratic Rally at Pittsburgh, October 25, 1940," "Address of Senator Joseph Guffey at a Negro Meeting in Pittsburgh, November 25, 1940," Guffey Papers, Washington and Jefferson College.

6. Salmond, *Civilian Conservation Corps*, 95, 101.

7. Fechner to Kurtz, October 23, 1937, CWSSA, CCC Records, NA; Fechner occasionally made the point that blacks preferred to be in segregated camps. See Fechner to Thomas L. Griffith, president, NAACP, Los Angeles, September 21, 1935, "African Americans in the CCC," http://newdeal.feri.org/aaccc04.htm. Kenneth E. Hendrickson, "The Civilian Conservation Corps in the Southwestern States," in Donald W. Whisehunt, ed., *The Depression in the Southwest* (Port Washington, N.Y.: Kennikat Press, 1980), 18.

8. The army was somewhat more flexible on running integrated camps than was Fechner. Johnson, "Army and the CCC," 173–77.

9. Luther C. Wandall, who entered the CCC in New York City in 1935, expressed the ambivalence of some African-Americans with the organization in a very articulate way. He concluded by writing that, despite the prejudices he encountered, "On the whole, I was gratified rather than disappointed with the CCC." Luther C. Wandall, "A Negro in the CCC," *Crisis* 42 (August 1935): 253. "Some Characteristics of CCC Enrollees," a booklet put out by the DPA in May 1939, pointed out the inadequate educational opportunities available to blacks. DS, CCC Records, NA.

10. Salmond, *Civilian Conservation Corps*, 89–91.

11. A study done by the FERA in 1933 showed blacks in the country to be twice as likely to be on relief as whites and half as likely to find jobs. Wolters, "New Deal and the Negro," in Braeman et al., *New Deal*, I, 170. Fechner reported on this study to Roosevelt and noted that, while 39.4 percent of enrollees who had left camps during the winter of 1934–35 had obtained jobs, the figure for blacks was only 23 percent. Fechner to FDR, September 7, 1935, OF 268, FDRL.

12. By June 19, 1933, the army reported 16,875 white enrollees and 1,696 black enrollees in Pennsylvania. General Paul Malone to Adjutant-General, GAF, A-G Records, NA.

13. Telegram from Haines to Fechner, June 9, 1933, Advisory Council Minutes, June 10, 1933, CCC Records, NA. The statistician for SERB in 1936 reported only 4 or 5 black families on relief in all of Adams County, where Gettysburg is. Only one local black boy in the county was considered eligible for the CCC at that time. Robert Prother to Kurtz, August 3, 1936, CWSSA, CCC Records, NA.

14. Kurtz to Persons, May 18, 1934, Persons to Kurtz, May 18, 1934, Biddle to Persons, June 12, 1934, Army Report, June 8, 1934, Persons to Biddle, June 15, 1934, Chester County ERB to Kurtz, July 17, 1934, Persons to Kurtz, August 28, 1934, CWSSA, CCC Records, NA.

15. Salmond, "Civil Conservation Corps and the Negro," 85; Salmond, *Civilian Conservation Corps*, 97–99.

16. ECW press release, April 20, 1935, OF 268, FDRL. There is a list of ten of these camps in a letter sent to FDR from Arthur P. Hayes, April 15, 1935, asking for the appointment of Colored officers. OF 268, FDRL. Snyder refers to twelve Colored camps in Pennsylvania in a memo to Persons, April 1, 1936, CWSSA, CCC Records, NA.

17. Kurtz to Snyder, April 15, 1937, Carl Turner to Kurtz, October 19, 1937, Pauline Lewis to Kurtz, October 18, 1937, CWSSA, CCC Records, NA; Kurtz, Circular Letter #30, December 20, 1938, PDFW Records, PSA.

18. Kurtz to Snyder, March 23, 1936, Kurtz to Persons, October 20, 1936, Snyder to Persons, April 1, 1936, Fechner to Persons, July 28, 1936, Kurtz to Snyder, August 10, 1936, CWSSA, CCC Records, NA.

19. Kurtz, Circular Letter #25, September 15, 1938, DPA Records, PSA; Snyder to Kurtz, August 19, 1938, Howard L. Russell to Joseph Givens of the Pittsburgh Urban League, March 21, 1939, Kurtz to Persons, November 27, 1940, CWSSA, CCC Records, NA.

20. These numbers were garnered from the various sources mentioned in the discussion of the number of camps in chapter 3. By 1940, blacks constituted about 10 percent of enrollees in the country. Paige, *CCC and the NPS*, chap. 3.

21. See correspondence concerning the assignment of twelve white leaders to Camp S-83 near Straight, Pennsylvania, May 15, 1933, CWSSA, CCC Records, NA. This argument that white communities would more readily accept black camps if they had white supervisory personnel became the standard CCC defense against appointing black personnel to such positions. Charles G. Gower, "The Struggle of Blacks for Leadership Positions in the CCC, 1933–1942," *Journal of Negro History* 61 (April 1976): 128, 130.

22. Malone to Adjutant-General, May 9, 1934, Duncan Major to Malone, May 17, 1934, GAF, A-G Records, NA.

23. Carl Murphy to FDR, March 6, 1935, Callan to Murphy, March 13, 1935, GAF, A-G Records,

NA; Report on MP-1 and MP-2, October 29, 1935, Records of Branch of Recreation Land Planning and State Cooperation, NPS Records, NA.

24. MacArthur to Howe, March 30, 1934, endorsing the appointment of Colored educational advisers for Colored camps, but opposing the appointment of Colored officers, Fechner to Howe, April 4, 1934, Howe to Fechner, April 7, 1934, Records of CCC Educational Program, CCC Records, NA. This disdainful reply of Howe is at odds with the usual portrayal of him as someone deeply opposed to racial discrimination. See Kenneth S. Davis, *FDR: The New Deal Years, 1933–1937, A History* (New York: Random House, 1986), 630; Gower, "Struggle of Blacks for Leadership Positions in the CCC," 128; Holland and Hill, *Youth in the CCC*, 112. The *Philadelphia Tribune* was complaining about discrimination in the appointment of educational advisers as early as March 15, 1934, 1.

25. R. R. Wright to Howe, June 5, 1934; Fechner to Wright, June 2 [*sic*], 1934, FDR OF 268, FDRL.

26. FDR to Early, May 8, 1935, Memo from E. M. Watson to Stephen J. Early, May 13, 1935, OF 268, FDRL. This vaunted policy of appointing the best officers to the black camps apparently was not applied to the second black camp in Pennsylvania, F-4 near Kane. The commander had to be relieved in January 1934 for laxity and intoxication and his successor allegedly referred to his enrollees as "n———s." Duncan Major Report to Fechner, April 4, 1934; news clip from the *Philadelphia Tribune,* March 8, 1934, GAF, A-G Records, NA; Kenlan to McEntee, June 21, 1934, CIR, CCC Records, NA.

27. Gower, "Struggle of Blacks for Leadership Positions in the CCC," 128–29; Cole, *African-American Experience in the Civilian Conservation Corps,* 16–17. Inspection report on MP-2, November 9, 1938, CIR, CCC Records, NA. Charles W. Johnson claims Roosevelt pushed to have at least one all black camp for the 1936 election. "CCC: The Role of the Army," 167.

28. McEntee to Fred Morell of Advisory Committee, May 16, 1938, Documents Relating to the Organization and Operation of the CCC, CCC Records, NA. Remote locations also meant that the educational opportunities were meager and confined to what could be offered in camp. Undated "Report on Colored Education in Pennsylvania Camps," probably 1937, State Procedural Records, DS, CCC Records, NA.

29. Fechner to Conrad Wirth, November 16, 1937, Records of Project Applications, NPS Records, NA. This controversy generated much correspondence. See Secretary of War George Tyner to Conrad Wirth, February 7, 1939; William H. Hastie, October 23, 1939, memo to Assistant Secretary of Interior; Paul E. Johnson to Harold Ickes, October 25, 1939, Records of Project Applications, CCC Camps, NPS Records, NA. The company was later transferred to S-78 at Keating.

30. There is extensive correspondence of both state and federal officials on this matter in Records of Project Applications, NPS Records, NA. See also correspondence between NPS and state officials in Bureau of Parks Correspondence, PDFW Records, PSA; *Happy Days,* October 8, 1938.

31. Theodore Frisbee to FDR, May 11, 1933; Malone to Frisbee, May 23, 1933; Malone to Captain F. R. Chamberlain, May 23, 1933, Chief of Police to Mayor T. P. Thompson, May 25, 1933, GAF, A-G Records, NA; O. M. Deibler of the Board of Fish Commissioners to Pinchot, May 15, 1933, GP 1560, PP, LC.

32. Biddle to Persons, August 3, 1934, State Procedural Records, DS, CCC Records, NA; H. K. Robertson, acting regional director, NPS, to Stanton Smith, liaison officer, Third Corps, September 22, 1939, Records of Project Applications, NPS Records, NA.

33. Salmond, *Civilian Conservation Corps,* 92; Lacy, *Soil Soldiers,* 76. Mention should also be made of the curious case of a William W. McAlister of Mifflintown who was discharged as a forester from Camp S-56 in 1934 and then spent much of the next year writing some two hundred letters to Fechner and the president, charging corruption and the covering-up of Negro

crimes in the town of Lewistown. His letters are long and ranting and difficult to follow. Clearly, CCC officials thought him a crank. CIR, Camp s-56, CCC Records, NA. The Pennsylvania State Archives has a small collection on video of CCC films, both silent and with sound, showing various aspects of camp life in Pennsylvania.

34. Guffey to McEntee, July 3, 1941; Adjutant-General to McEntee, July 22, 1941, GAF, A-G Records, NA.

35. Adjutant-General to Guffey, August 4, 1941, GAF, A-G Records, NA.

36. Guffey to Adjutant-General, August 20, 1941; army inspector's report, September 6, 1941, GAF, A-G Records, NA; inspection report, s-146, November 28, 1941, CIR, CCC Records, NA.

37. Johnson, "CCC: The Role of the Army," 165.

38. "Statement" of two boys from s-83 to local relief officials, July 9, 1935; Kurtz to Snyder, December 19, 1935, CWSSA.

39. Clipping from the *Philadelphia Record*, March 27, 1934, in inspection report, MP-2, CIR, CCC Records, NA.

40. ACM, January 8, 1937, CCC Records, NA.

41. Col. Duncan Major to Fechner, April 4, 1934, GAF, A-G Records, NA; Charles Kenlan to McEntee, June 21, 1934, CIR, CCC Records, NA. The CO, Captain John Mosely, was a southerner and the boys claimed he had called them "n——s." *Philadelphia Tribune* March 8, 1934, 1, 4; March 15, 1934, 1, 15; April 5, 1934, 1.

42. Inspection reports, s-119, October 17, 1939, and February 5, 1940, CIR, CCC Records, NA.

43. *Happy Days*, January 27, 1940, 5.

44. Inspection report, SP-13, November 28, 1938, CIR, CCC Records, NA.

45. "Company 321," http://members.aol.com/famjustin/Co321his.html. *Civilian Conservation Corps Annual, 1936*, Third Corps, District No. 1, 113, 121.

46. Johnson, "CCC: The Role of the Army," 151.

47. James R. McConaghie to Quartermaster, Third Corps, April 21, 1933, GAF, A-G Records, NA; superintendent report, May 15, 1934, Records of Branch of Recreation Land Planning and State Cooperation, NPS Records, NA.

48. *New York Times*, August 16, 1933, 19; Edward Robb Ellis, *A Nation in Torment: The Great American Depression, 1929–1939* (New York: Capricorn Books, 1970), 301.

49. Narrative report, October–December 1934, Camp MP-1, Gettysburg National Military Park, Records of Branch Recreational Land Planning and State Cooperation, NPS Records, NA.

50. "Narrative Report on ECW Work Done at Gettysburg, January 17, 1935," Records of Branch Recreational Land Planning and State Cooperation, NPS Records, NA. "Fences in the Gettysburg National Military Park," by Louis King, NPS junior historian, 1935, Records of Branch Recreational Land Planning and State Cooperation, NPS Records, NA; Edgar Brown, *What the Civilian Conservation Corps Is Doing for Colored Youth* (Washington, D.C.: GPO, 1941), http://newdeal.feri.org/aaccc/acccc03.htm.

51. Inspection reports, June 30, 1934, and July 31, 1936, CIR, CCC Records, NA.

52. J. Howard Diehl, camp superintendent, to McConaghie, April 24, 1935, Records of Branch Recreational Land Planning and State Cooperation, NPS Records, NA.

53. Conrad Wirth to John Butt (a Gettysburg lawyer), April 2, 1937; Agreement of Army and Superintendent of Gettysburg, April 20, 1937; Fechner to Wirth, November 16, 1937, Wirth to Fechner, November 26, 1937, Records of Projects Applications, CCC Camps, NPS Records, NA.

54. *Happy Days*, June 4, 1938, 1; inspection reports, MP-2, July 15, 1939, and February 2, 1942, CIR, CCC Records, NA.

55. Russell to Persons, February 19, 1941, CWSSA, CCC Records, NA; Kurtz, Circular Letter #93, June 20, 1941, PDFW, PSA.

CHAPTER 5

1. David Brody, "The New Deal and World War II," in Braeman et al., eds., *New Deal,* I, 270; Kennedy, *Freedom from Fear,* 783. Federal government spending jumped from a high of 5.9 percent GNP in the 1933–36 period to more than 33 percent of GNP during the war. Badger, *New Deal,* 111, 115.

2. Wecter, *Age of the Great Depression,* 316. Tom Watson, a leader of the People's Party, wrote of the Spanish-American War that "the blare of the bugle drowned out the voice of the Reformer." C. Vann Woodward, *Origins of the New South, 1877–1913* (Baton Rouge: Louisiana State University Press, 1951), 369.

3. David L. Porter actually writes of a "Third New Deal" in 1939 even after the conservative coalition had begun to form. *Congress and the Waning of the New Deal* (Port Washington, N.Y.: Kennikat Press, 1980), xi, xii.

4. Republicans made impressive gains in the first congressional elections held after Pearl Harbor in 1942, picking up 44 House seats and 7 in the Senate. James MacGregor Burns, *Roosevelt: The Soldier of Freedom, 1940–1945* (New York: Harcourt Brace Jovanovich, 1970), 280. For a discussion of these trends, see John Morton Blum, *V Was for Victory: Politics and American Culture During World War II* (San Diego: Harcourt Brace Jovanovich, 1976), 222–34.

5. *New York Times,* December 16, 1938, 26; Salmond, *Civilian Conservation Corps,* 195. Salmond has the best discussion and analysis of the last days of the CCC.

6. Summary Notes on Congressional Authorization of June 26, 1940, RF, CCC Records, NA.

7. Kurtz to Persons, June 26, 1940, CWSSA, CCC Records, NA.

8. Employers were now coming into the CCC camps to interview. In early 1941, Westinghouse sent recruiters to Camp S-54 at Richmond Furnace to interview twelve enrollees. "Co. 305," February 1941, RFSP Records.

9. Adjutant-General to Corps Commanders, December 10, 1941, informing them that seven companies of the Third Corps would be transferred to the Ninth Corps, RF, CCC Records, NA; Persons, Circular Letter, February 5, 1942, DS, CCC Records, NA; Kurtz, Circular Letter #102, February 11, 1942, DPA Records, PSA; *Annual Report of the Director of* CCC, *1942,* 4–5.

10. ACM, April 4 and May 8, 1942, CCC Records, NA.

11. Quarterly Selection Reports, March 1942, DS, CCC Records, NA; SSR, January 30, 1942, April 30, 1942, and May 31, 1942, CCC Records, NA. The last Pennsylvania camps were S-54, S-88, S-158, and AF-1.

12. *New York Times,* April 18, 1942, 22; *Annual Report of the Director of* CCC, *1942,* 4; CIR, SCS-12, April 15, 1942, S-88, April 8, 1942, S-51, December 31, 1941, CCC Records, NA; ACM, March 17, 1942, CCC Records, NA; Kurtz to Harold Dunn, CWSSA, n.d., probably mid-May, CCC Records, NA.

13. FDR to Congress, May 20, 1942, Documents Relating to the Organization and Operation of the CCC, CCC Records, NA; FDR to Harold D. Smith, director of the Bureau of the Budget, June 17, 1942, Nixon, *FDR and Conservation,* II, 557.

14. *Congressional Record,* 77th Cong., 2nd sess., June 26, 1942, 5601, 5602, 5604, 5612; June 30, 1942, 5789; July 2, 1942, 569; Salmond, *Civilian Conservation Corps,* 212–17; Blum, *V Was for Victory,* 235–36; Reiman, *New Deal and American Youth,* 178. Conrad Wirth of the NPS hoped for a smaller Corps with smaller camps and less emphasis on relief and academic education. "Civilian Conservation Corps Program of the United States Department of Interior, March 1933– June 30, 1943: A Report to Harold L. Ickes," January 1944, 2. (Copy in NPS Records, HFC.)

15. *Annual Report of the Director of* CCC, *1942,* 1. Robert Ermentrout comments on the end of the CCC: "There is no dignity in this type of demise." *Forgotten Men,* 75.

16. ACM, July 1, 1942, CCC Records, NA; Jonathan Daniels to McIntyre, December 8, 1942,

OF 268; Paul McNutt to Congressman Butler Hope, August 11, 1944, Records of the Liquidation Unit, CCC Records, NA. McNutt reported that McEntee was able to distribute $6.5 million of CCC equipment to the Boy Scouts and other private charitable groups over the next two years.

17. Melzer, *Coming of Age in the Great Depression*, 268; Camp ANF-3 at Kane was used for conscientious objectors, at least until 1944. Lewis Kosch of Selective Service to Stephens, November 24, 1944; a smaller side camp at Howard had also been used by the Selective Service for conscientious objectors. M. A. Stephens to A. J. Imirie, executive officer, Camp Operations, Selective Service System, January 22, 1947, Records of Liquidation Unit, CCC Records, NA; *New York Times*, February 17, 1943, 17.

18. Liquidation report on NP-2, Gettysburg, October 7, 1942, Records of Liquidation Unit, CCC Records, NA.

19. Chad Pysher, "The Crafting of a Treasure Chest: The Legacy of the Civilian Conservation Corps," www.allegheny-online.com/ccccorp.html, 5; "Camp Sideling Hill," http://members.aol.com/famjustin/Oregonroad.html; Buchanan State Forestry site, www.dcnr.state.pa.,us/forestry/stateforests. After rumors circulated in the Lewisburg area that the army was considering using Camp S-148 for POWS, a mysterious fire consumed the entire camp on the night of May 2, 1945. Shively, *Camps of Union County*, 77–78.

20. M. S. Reifsnyder, "A History of Camp Michaux," in PGFSP Records; Camp Michaux files of Ms. Carol Jones of PGFSP.

21. *Philadelphia Inquirer*, March 8, 1942, 1; Republican Senator James Davis of Pennsylvania called for an investigation by the Office of Price Administration. *Congressional Record*, 77th Cong., 2nd sess., March 12, 1942, 2313.

22. McEntee to Congressman Harry L. Haines (Democrat-Pennsylvania), March 13, 1942, in *Congressional Record*, 77th Cong., 2nd sess., appendix, March 16, 1942, A-1039, A-1040; Kenlan to McEntee, March 12, 1942, McEntee to J. Edgar Hoover, April 13, 1942, S-51 report, CIR, CCC Records, NA.

23. Kenlan to McEntee, March 16, 1942, S-71 report, CIR, CCC Records, NA; adjutant-general report, March 17, 1942, GAF, A-G Records, NA.

24. Transfer Department of S-86, January 5, 1943, Records of the Liquidation Unit, CCC Records, NA; memo to Third Corps, August 13, 1942, GAF, A-G Records, NA; memo, Stephens to Department of Interior, August 27, 1942, Stephens to Superintendent of Hopewell Village, May 6, 1946, Records of the Liquidation Unit, CCC Records, NA; Shively, CCC *Camps of Union County*, 65; liquidation report, NP-3, Stephens to Port Matilda Mining Co., May 27, 1943, Records of the Liquidation Unit, CCC Records, NA.

25. "Final Report of the Director of CCC, 1943," 27, 108; McEntee to McNutt, November 25, 1942, Records of Liquidation Unit, CCC Records, NA. McEntee later reported that all the remaining "S" camps in Pennsylvania were under the authority of the Department of Forests and Waters. McEntee to Advisory Council, December 4, 1942.

26. Eleanor Roosevelt, *This I Remember*, 162–63; John A. Salmond, "Aubrey Williams: Atypical New Dealer?" in Braeman et al., eds., *New Deal*, I, 239; Aubrey Williams, "A Crisis for Our Youth: A Task for the Nation," *New York Times Magazine*, January 19, 1936, 112–19.

27. There were forty-seven of these FERA camps for women in 1934. NYA used eleven of them for its programs for women in 1936. Reiman, *New Deal and American Youth*, 146.

28. The NYA set up some two hundred youth centers in the state, including forty Negro Centers. Isaac Crawford Sutton and Dixie Lee, "History of the National Youth Administration in Pennsylvania: 1935–1942." This study, a copy of which is in the Guffey Papers, is undated and seems to have been a NYA project itself.

29. Reiman, *New Deal and American Youth*, 180; McEntee address to Conference of State Selection Agencies, December 9, 1940, 26, Circular Letters, DS, CCC Records, NA; McEntee to

Marvin McIntyre, December 12, 1941, FDR OF 268, FDRL; Paul McNutt to FDR, March 17, 1942, referring to Roosevelt's request of October 24, 1941, asking McNutt to work on a merger plan. Records Relating to Proposed Merger of NYA and CCC, CCC Records, NA. A Gallup poll taken about this time showed only 38 percent in favor of the abolition of the NYA, compared to 54 percent who thought the CCC should be ended. *New York Times,* April 18, 1942, 22; memo of chief, Project Development Division, August 9, 1940, Records of Project Applications Section Concerning Abandoned CCC Camps, NPS Records, NA; June 1940 Report in Records Relating to Proposed Merger of NYA and CCC, CCC Records, NA. Technically, NYA was not part of WPA after 1939 when the president's reorganization put it in the Federal Security Agency with the CCC.

30. Lash, *Eleanor and Franklin,* 536. Lash cites an interesting exchange on this subject between the president and his wife, recorded by Fulton Oursler on p. 538. If the CCC was known as the president's fairest child, *Time* magazine referred to the NYA as Mrs. Roosevelt's "pet." "End of the CCC," *Time* 39 (June 15, 1942): 10.

31. Stuart to Howe, April 15, 1933, OF 1a Agriculture, FDRL. *Four Year Summary Report of the Department of Forests and Waters, 1933–38,* 24.

32. Fechner to Pinchot, May 5, 1933; Pinchot to Fechner, October 3, 1934, GP 2560, PP, LC.

33. Fechner to Earle, February 26, 1935, Earle to Fechner, March 11, 1935, Earle to Fechner, May 3, 1937, Fechner to Earle, December 19, 1938, Correspondence with Governors, CCC Records, NA.

34. Roosevelt to Governors, February 8, 1937, Nixon, *FDR and Conservation,* II, 586.

35. January 1943 Report on State Reimbursements; see also Guthrie memo, April 29, 1938, on the confusion caused by these demands for state reimbursements. Documents Relating to the Organization and Operation of the CCC, CCC Records, NA.

36. ACM, July 1, 1942, CCC Records, NA. The discharge certificate of thirty-six-year-old Charles Kerlin, who worked as a cook, is in the RFSP Records. The honorable discharge is dated July 31, 1942, and the reason given is "Convenience of the Government." "Final Report of the Director of CCC, 1943," 1; War Department to C. W. Bailey, August 24, 1942, RF, CCC Records, NA.

37. "Final Report of the Director of CCC, 1943," 103, 108.

38. The FERA study of former CCC men in 1934 showed that only 112 of the 30,000 men studied joined the armed forces. In 1935 the percentage was only a bit higher, at 0.7 percent. Johnson, "Army and the CCC," 152.

39. These "benefit letters" are in the Division of Planning and Public Relations, CCC Records, NA.

40. Kurtz, Circular Letter #38, May 8, 1939, Kurtz, Circular Letter #59, December 11, 1939, DPA Records, PSA.

41. Correspondence from 1934 and 1935 in OF 268, FDRL; unsigned letter, September 10, 1933, from S-117, Company #1361, General Correspondence, CCC Records, NA. Roosevelt also retained the admiration of former CCC men, even from self-styled lifelong Republicans as well; see communication of Leo Ruvolis to author, February 21, 2004.

42. Kurtz to Persons, August 28, 1935, CWSSA, CCC Records, NA.

43. Interview with Walter Joyce, August 11, 2003; interview with Robert Ward, August 26, 2003; communication of Edwin Smith to author, September 8, 2003. In the RFSP Records is a copy of the *Menu Manual,* published by the Third Corps in 1938, offering more than one hundred pages of advice on mess management, the ordering of food, and the preparing of balanced meals. Sample menus are included.

44. A condition of low morale at Camp SP-1 in 1935 was attributed to a new commander's alteration of recreational practices. Progress Reports of CCC Projects in Pennsylvania State and Local Parks, NPS Records, NA; CIR, September 22, 1937, CCC Records, NA.

45. CIR, S-125, December 7, 1940; S-120, 1934; S-57, July 26, 1939, CCC Records, NA; Ruth

Bradbury, executive director of Emergency Relief Board to Kurtz, March 27, 1934, complaining about the CO of a camp near Wellsboro, DPA Records, PSA; Report by Patrick King on S-139, PLSP Records.

46. Holland and Hill, *Youth and the CCC*, 111.

47. For example, see the extensive correspondence on Camps S-96 at Hillsgrove, October–November 1934, and S-90 at Cedar Run, February 1934, CWSSA, CCC Records, NA; June 18, 1939, findings of Patrick King at Camp S-139, PLSP Records; inspection of Camp S-128 in Sullivan County, December 18, 1934, wherein charges of a commander striking an enrollee with a flashlight were dismissed, CIR, CCC Records, NA.

48. Edmond Dochod communication to author, October 20, 2004; M. Chester Nolte, ed., *The Civilian Conservation Corps: The Way We Remember It, 1933–42* (Paducah, Ky.: Turner Publishing, 1990).

49. NACCCA *Journal*, February 4, 1981. CCC alumni were instrumental in getting the New Mexico Youth Conservation Corps established in 1992. Melzer, *Coming of Age in the Great Depression*, 277.

50. James Gabarino, *Lost Boys: Why Our Sons Turn Violent and How We Can Save Them* (New York: Free Press, 1999). "The Lost Boys," *New York Times*, September 29, 2003, op-ed.

51. The American Youth Commission study and critique of the CCC described the organization of the CCC: "It is an administrative miracle that so disjointed an organization has functioned as well as it has." "Recommendations of the American Youth Commission and the American Council of Education, December 1940," 20; Records of CCC Educational Division, CCC Records, NA.

52. See the report on the Socialist Party platform of 1936 in *New York Times*, May 27, 1936, 10.

53. In *Roosevelt*, 120, Burns shows the opposition to the draft in 1940 and 1941 coming from the conservative isolationists. Charles B. Rangel, "Restore the Draft," *New York Times*, December 31, 2003, op-ed. The war in Iraq, with its unevenly distributed sacrifices, has inspired other voices to call for some kind of national service for young people. See Jane Eisner, "To Make Us Stronger," *Philadelphia Inquirer*, May 30, 2004, C-1.

54. "Final Report of the Director of CCC, 1943," 27.

55. Fechner estimated the annual cost of an enrollee at $1,020 in 1936. *Happy Days*, January 4, 1936, 1. In 1938 he told Congress the cost was $1,140. General Headquarters Letters, March 15, 1938, DS, CCC Records, NA. Conrad Wirth of the NPS claimed the cost for each enrollee had soared to $1,400 near the end. Wirth, *Parks, Politics and the People*, 146.

56. A 1938 critique of the CCC pointed out that $671 a year was a high relief amount for direct relief. Marie Dresden and Francis Steegmuller, *America on Relief* (New York: Harcourt, Brace, 1938), 145; Salmond, *Civilian Conservation Corps*, 129.

57. "Role of the Department of Forests and Waters in CWA," PDFW *Service Letter*, March 8, 1934, PDFW Records, PSA The cost of these workers on 180 projects was $1.3 million, or about $200 apiece for the six-month duration of the program.

58. McEntee, among his postmortems, recommended that any future version of the Corps should provide training schools for camp commanders. "Final Report of the Director of CCC, 1943," 86.

59. *Annual Report of the Director of CCC, 1942*, 13.

60. So, for example, I was told by Barbara Davey-Triol, park manager at PLSP on September 23, 2003. She expanded her remarks in an e-mail on April 23, 2004, pointing out some of the different kinds of conservation work that are needed today, such as curtailing deer damage. W. C. Morton, park manager of the White Clay Creek Preserve, also thinks that an infusion of labor such as the CCC provided, would allow park officials to get to projects that have to be put off because of inadequate funding. Communication to author, August 17, 2003.

61. November 19, 1930, address, cited in Reiman, *New Deal and American Youth*, 24–25.

62. "Message from the President of the United States on Unemployment Relief, March 21, 1933," in Paige, CCC *and the* NPS, chap. 1.

63. Quoted by Wirth, *Parks, Politics and the People*, 87.

64. Harold L. Ickes, "Where Our Nation Is Heading," *New York Times Magazine* (May 27, 1934), in Carl Degler, ed., *The New Deal* (New York: Quadrangle Books, 1970), 207–19.

65. There are none in the useful collection of hundreds of CCC photographs by Stan Cohen, *The Tree Army: A Pictorial History of the Civilian Conservation Corps, 1933–1942* (Missoula, Mont.: Pictorial Histories Publishing), 1980.

66. Leighton and Hellman made this point in an early and perceptive critique of the CCC. See "'Half Slave, Half Free,'" 347–49.

67. At the end McEntee touted the CCC's role in providing training for 50,000 reserve officers and doing more for war preparations than any agency outside the army and navy. *Annual Report of the Director of* CCC, *1942*, 14–15.

68. "CCC Needs a Clearer Policy on Conservation," *American Forests* 44 (May 1938): 204.

69. Lash, *Eleanor and Franklin*, 537. Others were critical of the CCC's segregating young men into artificial communities. Howard Rowland, "Can the CCC Blaze a New Trail?" *Survey Graphic* 26 (June 1937): 321. These arguments raised issues that go back to Greek debates between Athenian and Spartan ideals.

Bibliography

MANUSCRIPT SOURCES

Michaux State Forestry Office, Fayetteville, Pa.
 One box of documents dealing with Camp s-107, Caledonia State Park
National Archives, College Park, Md.
 Records of the Fish and Wildlife Service, RG-22
 Civilian Conservation Corps Records, RG-35
 File Title and Box Lists Relating to the Civilian Conservation Corps—Finding Guide.
 Helm, Douglas, comp. *Preliminary Inventory of the Records of the* CCC. Washington,
  D.C.: National Archives Records and Services, 1980.
 Records of the National Park Service, RG-79
 Records of the Forestry Service, RG-95
 Records of the Soil Conservation Service, RG-114
 Records of the Adjutant-General's Office, RG-407
National Park Service Records, Harper's Ferry Center Library, W.Va.
 Series I, General
 Series II, States and Territories
 Series IV, Annual Reports
 Series IX, Alumni and History
Pennsylvania State Archives—Harrisburg, Pa.
 Department of Forests and Waters Records, RG-6
 Department of Public Assistance Records, RG-23
 William K. Sowers Collection, RG-363
Franklin D. Roosevelt Library, Hyde Park, N.Y.
 President's Personal File (PPF)
 President's Secretary's File (PSF)
 President's Official File (POF)
 President's Vertical File (PVF)
 Eleanor Roosevelt Pamphlet Collection
 Louis M. Howe Papers
 Democratic National Committee: Women's Division, General Correspondence
Washington and Jefferson College, Washington, Pa.
 Senator Joseph F. Guffey Papers

STATE PARK ARCHIVAL SOURCES

Black Moshannon State Park
 A small file of photographs and news clippings dealing with Camp s-71 and a few photographs of area camps in the main office
Cowan's Gap State Park
 A very extensive collection of photographs, news clippings, discharge and educational certificates, about twenty copies of the camp journal, and various printed and handwritten sources dealing with the activities of Camp s-54 and attractive display of ccc materials in the visitor center
Fort Necessity Battlefield Site
 Box of materials in library, including tapes of interviews with two men associated with Camp sp-12, one of whom was a lem, and dozens of photographs of the camp
 Ten folders of miscellaneous ccc materials, including camp newspapers of sp-12
Greenwood Furnace State Park
 A very extensive collection of photographs and miscellaneous items dealing with the activities of Camps s-59, s-60, s-61, s-62, s-64, and s-112; two audiotape interviews made in 1990 with two members of Camp s-62, Penn-Roosevelt: Walter Kaufman and Carl Huston
Hickory Run State Park
 Five file drawers of project requests for the Hickory Run Recreational Demonstration Area of the National Park Service, 1935–42
Pine Grove Furnace State Park
 Two folders of documents relating to ccc Camp s-51
Promised Land State Park
 Four trunks of artifacts, pictures, and publications relating to Camp s-139; two file drawers of documents relating to ccc Camp s-139
 A Civilian Conservation Corps museum
 Blacksmith shop with dozens of ccc tools
Raccoon Creek State Park
 Two folders of ccc materials, including camp newspapers and a history of Camps sp-6 and sp-16

INTERVIEWS

Adams, Lou. Penfield, Pa. Interview, June 26, 2004.
Adams, Louis M. Mansfield, Pa. Written questionnaire, September 1, 2003.
Bubernak, Steve. Myrtle Beach, S.C. Letter, May 5, 2004, and telephone, May 21, 2004.
De Cenzo, Joseph L. Clinton, Md. Interview, June 26, 2004.
Dochod, Edmond. Written questionnaire, April 20, 2004.
Frantz, Tom. Newville, Pa. Written questionnaire, September 20, 2003.
Joyce, Walter. Ambridge, Pa. Telephone, August 11, 2003.
Oravecz, Stanley. Portage, Pa. Telephone, May 29, 2004.
Ruvolis, Leo. Dover, Pa. Written questionnaire and audiotape, February 21, 2004.
Smith, Edwin E. Cayuta, N.Y. Written questionnaire, September 8, 2003.

Swarmer, Clair "Rusty." Gainesville, Fla. Written questionnaire, oral interview, June 26, 2004.

Ward, Robert B. Wellsboro, Pa. Telephone, August 26, 2003.

Wilson, Robert P. Madison, Ohio. Written questionnaire, April 20, 2004.

GOVERNMENT DOCUMENTS

Pennsylvania

Civilian Conservation Corps Annual, 1936. District No. 1, Third Corps Area, New Cumberland, Pa., State Library, Harrisburg.

Civilian Conservation Corps Annual, 1936. District No. 2, Third Corps Area, Pittsburgh, Pa., Promised Land State Park Files.

Civilian Conservation Corps: Fiftieth Anniversary, 1933–1983; June 4, 1983. Harrisburg: Department of Environmental Resources, 1983.

Forrey, William C. History of Pennsylvania's State Parks. Harrisburg: Department of Environmental Resources, 1984.

Four Year Summary Report of the Department of Forests and Waters, 1935–1938. Typed copy in RG-6, Pennsylvania State Archives.

United States Government

Annual Reports of the Director of Emergency Conservation Work, Washington, D.C.: Government Printing Office, for the years 1933–1937.

Annual Reports of the Director of the Civilian Conservation Corps, Washington, D.C.: Government Printing Office, for the years 1938–1942.

Congressional Record, 1933–42.

"Final Report of the Director of the Civilian Conservation Corps, 1943." Typescript, CCC Records, National Archives.

Paige, John C. The Civilian Conservation Corps and the National Park Service, 1933–1942: An Administrative History. www.cr.nps.gov/history/online_books/ccc/ccc1a.htm.

Statistical Abstract of the United States: 1933. Washington, D.C.: Government Printing Office, 1933.

United States Department of Commerce, Bureau of the Census. Fifteenth Census of the United States, 1930.

———. Sixteenth Census of the United States, 1940.

BOOKS AND DISSERTATIONS

Allen, Frederick Lewis. Since Yesterday: 1929–39. New York: Bantam Books, 1965 (1940).

Badger, Anthony. The New Deal: The Depression Years, 1933–1940. Chicago: Ivan R. Dee, 1989.

Bernstein, Irving. The Lean Years. Boston: Houghton Mifflin, 1961.

———. The Turbulent Years. Boston: Houghton Mifflin, 1970.

Blum, John Morton. V Was for Victory: Politics and American Culture During World War II. San Diego: Harcourt Brace Jovanovich, 1976.

Braeman, John, Robert H. Bremner, and David Brody, eds. The New Deal. 2 vols. Columbus: Ohio State University Press, 1975.

Brokaw, Tom. *The Greatest Generation.* New York: Random House, 1998.

Brown, Josephine Chapin. *Public Relief, 1929–1939.* New York: Henry Holt, 1940.

Burns, James MacGregor. *Roosevelt: The Soldier of Freedom, 1940–1945.* New York: Harcourt Brace Jovanovich, 1970.

Cochran, Thomas. *Pennsylvania: A Bicentennial History.* New York: W. W. Norton, 1978.

Cohen, Stan B. *The Tree Army: A Pictorial History of the* CCC, *1933–1942.* Missoula: Pictorial Histories Publishing, 1980.

Cole, Olen, Jr. *The African-American Experience in the Civilian Conservation Corps.* Gainesville: University of Florida Press, 1999.

Conkin, Paul K. *The New Deal.* New York: Thomas Y. Crowell, 1967.

Conti, Philip M. *The* CCC: *Salvaging Boys and Other Treasures.* Privately printed, 1998.

Conzen, Michael P., ed. *The Making of the American Landscape.* Boston: Unwin Hyman, 1990.

Coode, Thomas H., and John F. Bauman, eds. *People, Poverty, and Politics: Pennsylvania During the Great Depression.* Lewisburg: Bucknell University Press, 1981.

———. *In the Eye of the Great Depression: New Deal Reporters and the Agony of the American People.* DeKalb: Northern Illinois University Press, 1988.

Cordell, Glenn. *The Cowan's Gap* CCC *Camp of Fulton County, Pennsylvania.* McConnelsburg, Pa.: Fulton County Historical Society, 2004.

Cox, Thomas R., et al. *This Well-Wooded Land: Americans and Their Forests from Colonial Times to the Present.* Lincoln: University of Nebraska Press, 1985.

Cupper, Dan. *Our Priceless Heritage: Pennsylvania State Parks, 1893–1993.* Harrisburg: Bureau of State Parks, 1993.

Davis, Kenneth S. *FDR: The Beckoning of Destiny, 1882–1928: A History.* New York: G. P. Putnam's Sons, 1971.

———. *FDR: The New York Years, 1928–1933: A History.* New York: Random House, 1979.

———. *FDR: The New Deal Years, 1933–37: A History.* New York: Random House, 1986.

Davis, Maxine. *The Lost Generation: A Portrait of American Youth.* New York: Macmillan, 1936.

Dearborn, Ned H. *Once in a Lifetime: A Guide to the* CCC *Camp.* New York: Charles E. Merrill, 1936.

De Coster, Lester A. *The Legacy of Penn's Woods: A History of the Pennsylvania Bureau of Forestry.* Harrisburg: Commonwealth of Pennsylvania, 1995.

Degler, Carl, ed. *The New Deal.* New York: Quadrangle Books, 1970.

Dunaway, Wayland F. *A History of Pennsylvania,* 2nd ed. New York: Prentice-Hall, 1948.

Ellis, Edward Robb. *A Nation in Torment: The Great American Depression, 1929–1939.* New York: Capricorn Books, 1970.

Ermentrout, Robert Allen. *The Forgotten Men: The Civilian Conservation Corps.* Smithtown, N.Y.: Exposition Press, 1982.

Freidel, Frank. *Franklin D. Roosevelt: The Apprenticeship.* Boston: Little, Brown, 1952.

———. *Franklin D. Roosevelt: Launching the New Deal.* Boston: Little, Brown, 1973.

Graham, Otis L., Jr. *The New Deal: The Critical Issues.* Boston: Little, Brown, 1971.

Greeley, William S. *Forests and Men.* Garden City, N.Y.: Doubleday, 1951.

Guffey, Joseph F. *Seventy Years on the Red Fire-Wagon: From Tilden to Truman Through New Freedom and New Deal.* Privately printed, 1952.

Halt, Charles Eugene. "Joseph F. Guffey: New Deal Politician from Pennsylvania." Ph.D. diss., Syracuse University, 1965.

Harper, Charles P. *The Administration of the Civilian Conservation Corps*. Clarksburg, W.Va.: Clarksburg Publishing, 1937.

Hill, Frank Ernest. *The School in the Camps*. New York: American Association for Adult Education, 1935.

Holland, Kenneth, and Frank Ernest Hill, *Youth in the* CCC. Washington, D.C.: American Council on Education, 1942.

Hoyt, Ray. *We Can Take It: A Short Story of the* CCC. New York: American Book, 1935.

Huthmacher, J. Joseph. *Senator Robert E. Wagner and the Rise of Urban Liberalism*. New York: Atheneum, 1968.

Ickes, Harold L. *The Secret Diary of Harold L. Ickes: The First Thousand Days, 1933–1936*. New York: Simon and Schuster, 1953.

———. *The Secret Diary of Harold L. Ickes*, vol. 2, *The Inside Struggle, 1936–1939*. New York: Simon and Schuster, 1954.

———. *The Secret Diary of Harold L. Ickes*, vol. 3, *The Lowering Clouds, 1939–1941*. New York: Simon and Schuster, 1954.

Johnson, Charles W. "The Civilian Conservation Corps: The Role of the Army." Ph.D. diss., University of Michigan, 1968.

Keller, Richard C. *Pennsylvania's Little New Deal*. New York: Garland Publishing, 1982.

Kennedy, David M. *Freedom from Fear: The American People in Depression and War, 1939–1945*. New York: Oxford University Press, 1999.

Ketchum, Richard M. *The Borrowed Years, 1938–1941*. New York: Random House, 1989.

Kett, Joseph F. *Rites of Passage: Adolescence in America, 1790 to the Present*. New York: Basic Books, 1977.

Klein, Philip S., and Ari Hoogenboom. *A History of Pennsylvania*. New York: McGraw-Hill, 1973.

Kylie, H. R., G. H. Hieronymous, and A. G. Hill. CCC *Forestry*. Washington, D.C.: Government Printing Office, 1937.

Lacy, Leslie Alexander. *The Soil Soldiers: The Civilian Conservation Corps in the Great Depression*. Radnor, Pa..: Chilton Book, 1976.

Lane, Marie Dresden, and Francis Steegmuller. *America on Relief*. New York: Harcourt, Brace, 1938.

Lash, Joseph P. *Eleanor and Franklin*. New York: W. W. Norton, 1971.

Leonard, Jonathan Norton. *Three Years Down*. New York: Carrick and Evans, 1939.

Leuchtenburg, William. *Franklin D. Roosevelt and the New Deal*. New York: Harper and Row, 1963.

———. *The New Deal: A Documentary History*. New York: Harper and Row, 1968.

Link, Arthur S. *Woodrow Wilson and the Progressive Era, 1910–1917*. New York: Harper Torchbooks, 1954.

Lowitt, Richard, and Maurine Beasley, eds. *One-Third of a Nation: Lorena Hickock Reports on the Great Depression*. Urbana: University of Illinois Press, 1981.

McElvaine, Robert S. *Down and Out in the Great Depression: Letters from the Forgotten Men*. Chapel Hill: University of North Carolina Press, 1983.

———. *The Great Depression: America: 1929–41*. New York: Times Books, 1984.

McEntee, James J. *Now They Are Men: The Story of the* CCC. Washington, D.C.: National Home Library Foundation, 1940.

McGeary, M. Nelson. *Gifford Pinchot, Forester and Politician*. Princeton: Princeton University Press, 1960.

Melzer, Richard. *Coming of Age in the Great Depression: The Civilian Conservation Corps Experience in New Mexico, 1933–1942.* Las Cruces, N.M.: Yucca Tree Press, 2000.

Merrill, Perry H. *Roosevelt's Army: A Pictorial History of the* CCC. Montpelier, Vt.: Perry H. Merrill, 1981.

Miller, E. Willard, ed. *A Geography of Pennsylvania.* University Park: Pennsylvania State University Press, 1995,

Miller, Randall M., and William Pencak, eds. *Pennsylvania: A History of the Commonwealth.* University Park: Pennsylvania State University Press, 2002.

Minehan, Thomas. *Boy and Girl Tramps of America.* New York: Farrar and Rinehart, 1934.

Mitchell, Broadus. *Depression Decade.* New York: Holt, Rinehart and Winston, 1947.

Moley, Raymond. *After Seven Years.* New York: Harper and Brothers, 1939.

Murphy, Raymond E., and Marion Murphy. *Pennsylvania: A Regional Geography.* Harrisburg: Pennsylvania Book Service, 1937.

Nixon, Edgar B., ed. *Franklin D. Roosevelt and Conservation, 1911–1945.* 2 vols. Hyde Park, N.Y.: Franklin D. Roosevelt Library, 1957.

Nolte, M. Chester, ed. *The Civilian Conservation Corps: The Way We Remember It, 1933–42.* Paducah, Ky.: Turner Publishing, 1990.

Oliver, Alfred C., and Harold M. Dudley. *This New America: The Spirit of the* CCC. London: Longmans, Green, 1937.

Osborne, Peter. *High Point State Park and the Civilian Conservation Corps.* Charleston, S.C.: Arcadia Publishing, 2002.

———. *We Can Take It: The Roosevelt Tree Army at New Jersey's High Point State Park, 1933–1941.* Bloomington, Ind.: First Books Library, 2002.

Otis, Alison T., William D. Honey, Thomas C. Hogg, Kimberly K. Lakin. *The Forest Service and the Civilian Conservation Corps, 1933–42.* Washington, D.C.: U.S. Department of Agriculture, Forest Service, 1986.

Patterson, James T. *Congressional Conservatism and the New Deal: The Growth of the Conservative Coalition in Congress, 1933–1939.* Lexington: University of Kentucky Press, 1967.

———. *The New Deal and the States: Federalism in Transition.* Princeton: Princeton University Press, 1969.

Perkins, Frances. *The Roosevelt I Knew.* New York: Viking Press, 1947.

Pinchot, Gifford. *Breaking New Ground.* New York: Harcourt, Brace, 1947.

Pinkett, Harold. *Gifford Pinchot: Private and Public Forester.* Urbana: University of Illinois Press, 1970.

Potts, James E. "Civilian Conservation Corps, Bear Valley, 1933–36." Privately printed, 1979.

Pyne, Stephen J. *Fire in America: A Cultural History of Wildland and Rural Fire.* Seattle: University of Washington Press, 1982.

Ralston, Charles Frederick. "Adult Education as a Welfare Measure During the Great Depression: A Historical Case Study of the Educational Program of the CCC." Ph.D. diss., Pennsylvania State University, 2000.

Reiman, Richard. *The New Deal and American Youth: Ideas and Ideals in a Depression Decade.* Athens: University of Georgia Press, 1992.

Robinson, Edgar Eugene. *The Roosevelt Leadership, 1933–45.* Philadelphia: J. B. Lippincott, 1955.

Rollins, Albert B. *Roosevelt and Howe.* New York: Alfred A. Knopf, 1962.

Roosevelt, Eleanor. *This I Remember.* New York: Harper and Brothers, 1949.

Rosenman, Samuel I., ed. *The Public Papers and Addresses of Franklin D. Roosevelt*. 13 vols. New York: Russell and Russell, 1938–50.

Salmond, John. *The Civilian Conservation Corps, 1933–1942: A New Deal Case Study*. Durham: Duke University Press, 1967.

———. *Southern Rebel: The Life and Times of Aubrey Williams, 1890–1965*. Greensboro: University of North Carolina Press, 1983.

Schlesinger, Arthur M., Jr. *The Crisis of the Old Order*. Boston: Houghton Mifflin, 1957.

———. *The Coming of the New Deal*. Boston: Houghton Mifflin, 1958.

———. *The Age of Roosevelt: The Politics of Upheaval, 1935–36*. Boston: Houghton Mifflin, 1960.

Schwarz, Jordan A. *The Interregnum of Despair: Hoover, Congress and the Depression*. Urbana: University of Illinois Press, 1970.

Sherwood, Robert E. *Roosevelt and Hopkins: An Intimate History*. New York: Harper Brothers, 1948.

Shively, Tony. *The CCC Camps of Union County, 1933–1942: Life and Work in the Civilian Conservation Corps*. Lewisburg, Pa.: Union County Historical Society, 2002.

Stave, Bruce. *The Last Hurrah: Pittsburgh Machine Politics*. Pittsburgh: University of Pittsburgh Press, 1970.

Steen, Harold K. *The U.S. Forest Service: A History*. Seattle: University of Washington Press, 1976.

Steen, Harold K., ed. *The Conservation Diaries of Gifford Pinchot*. Durham, N.C.: Forest History Society, 2001.

Sternsher, Bernard, ed. *Hitting Home: The Great Depression in Town and Country*. Chicago: Quadrangle Books, 1970.

Sypolt, Larry N. *Fort Necessity: Civilian Conservation Corps, Camp SP-12*. Morgantown, W.Va.: privately printed, 1988.

Thorpe, R. R. *The Crown Jewel of Pennsylvania: The State Forest System*. Harrisburg: Commonwealth of Pennsylvania, Department of Conservation and Natural Resources, Bureau of Forestry, 1997.

Tugwell, Rexford G. *The Democratic Roosevelt*. Garden City: Doubleday, 1957.

———. *The Roosevelt I Knew*. Baltimore: Penguin Books, 1957.

———. *The Brains Trust*. New York: Viking Press, 1968.

———. *Roosevelt's Revolution: The First Year: A Personal Perspective*. New York: Macmillan, 1977.

Vare, William S. *My Forty Years in Politics*. Philadelphia: Roland Swain, 1933.

Watkins, T. H. *The Hungry Years: A Narrative History of the Great Depression*. New York: Henry Holt, 1999.

Wecter, Dixon. *The Age of the Great Depression, 1929–41*. New York: Macmillan, 1948.

Weigley, Russell F., *History of the United States Army*. Bloomington: University of Indiana Press, 1984.

Whisenhunt, Donald W. ed. *The Depression in the Southwest*. Port Washington, N.Y.: Kennikat Press, 1980.

Widner, Ralph R., ed. *Forests and Forestry in the American States*. N.p.: National Association of State Foresters, 1967.

Winter, Raymond B. *Halfway to Winter*. Privately printed, 1967.

Winters, Robert K. *Fifty Years of Forestry in the United States*. Washington, D.C.: Society of American Foresters, 1950.

Wirth, Conrad L. *Parks, Politics and the People.* Norman: University of Oklahoma Press, 1980.

Works Progress Administration, Writers' Program. *Pennsylvania: A Guide to the Keystone State.* New York: Oxford University Press, 1940.

ARTICLES

"Appraising the ccc." *American Forests* 44 (February 1938): 75.

Bremer, William W. "Along the American Way: The New Deal's Work Relief Programs for the Unemployed." *Journal of American History* 62 (December 1975): 636–72.

Bronner, Edwin B. "The New Deal Comes to Pennsylvania: The Gubernatorial Election of 1934." *Pennsylvania History* 27 (January 1960): 44–68.

Brown, Cecil B. "Roosevelt's Tree Army" (s-67 focus). *Pittsburgh Press,* August 26, 1935.

Captain X. "A Civilian Army in the Woods." *Harper's Magazine* 168 (March 1934): 487–97.

"The ccc in Our State Forests." pdfw *Service Letter* (January 18, 1934): 1.

"ccc Needs Clearer Policy on Conservation." *American Forests* 44 (May 1938): 224.

Chepetz, John D. "Biography of John D. Chepetz, ccc Man, Company 2323, Camp scs-5. Sligo." www.geocities.com/oralbio/chepetzjdbio.html.

"The Citizens Conservation Corps and the Pennsylvania State College." *School and Society* 40 (October 13, 1934): 485.

Clement, Priscilla Ferguson. "The wpa in Pennsylvania, 1935 to 1942." *Pennsylvania Magazine of History and Biography* 95 (April 1971): 244–60.

Clepper, Henry. "20,000 Men in Penn's Woods." *American Forests* 39 (September 1933): 406–7.

———. "The Birth of the ccc." *American Forests* 79 (March 1973): 8–11.

Collingwood, G. H. "Forestry Aids the Unemployed." *American Forests* 38 (October 1932): 550.

"Conservation: Poor Young Men." *Time* 33 (February 6, 1939): 10–12.

Cornebise, Alfred Emile. "Heralds in New Deal America: Camp Newspapers of the Civilian Conservation Corps." www.scripps.ohiou.edu/mediahistory/mhmjour2-1htm.

Cox, Thomas R. "Transition in the Woods: Log Drivers, Raftsmen, and the Emergence of Modern Lumbering in Pennsylvania." *Pennsylvania Magazine of History and Biography* 104 (April 1980): 345–64.

Curreri, Joe. "Legacy of the ccc." *Pennsylvania Magazine* 26 (March–April 2003): 34–40.

DuBay, Robert W. "The Civilian Conservation Corps: A Study in Opposition." *Southern Quarterly* 6 (1968): 341–58.

Durham, Arthur. "Pennsylvania and Unemployment Relief, 1929–1934." *Social Service Review* 8 (June 1934): 246–88.

"ecw Work in Forbes State Forest." pdfw *Service Letter* (September 13, 1934): 1.

"ecw Work in Penn's Woods." pdfw *Service Letter* (July 5, 1934): 1.

"Eight Years of ccc." *Newsweek* 17 (April 14, 1941): 23–24.

"Emergency Labor Camps in Pennsylvania." *Monthly Labor Review* 34 (June 1932): 1289–91.

"End of the ccc." *Time* 39 (June 15, 1942): 10.

"Fewer Youth Props." *Newsweek* 18 (November 10, 1941): 24.

"Forestry and the Depression." pdfw *Service Letter* (January 19, 1933): 1.

"Forestry as Relief to Unemployed Takes Limelight." *American Forests* (August 1932): 38, 468–69.

Garraty, John N. "The New Deal, National Socialism and the Great Depression." *American Historical Review* 78 (October 1973): 907–44.

Gorham, Eric. "The Ambiguous Practices of the CCC." *Social History* 17 (May 1992): 229–49.

Gower, Charles. "The Struggle of Blacks for Leadership Positions in the CCC, 1933–1942." *Journal of Negro History* 61 (April 1976): 123–35.

Guthrie, Major John. "The CCC and American Conservation." *Scientific Monthly* 57 (October 1943): 401–12.

Halgren, Mauritz A. "Mass Misery in Philadelphia." *The Nation* 134 (March 9, 1932): 275–77.

Hendrickson, Kenneth E., Jr. "The Civilian Conservation Corps in Pennsylvania." *Pennsylvania Magazine of History and Biography* 100 (January 1976): 66–96.

Hoover, Herbert, and Gifford Pinchot. "I Am Opposed to the Dole and The Case for Federal Relief." *Survey Graphic* 67 (January 1, 1932): 346–49, 390.

Hull, James Howard. "Our Permanent Conservation Corps." *Conservation* (May–June, 1940): 10–12.

"The Human Side of CC Camps." PDFW *Service Letter* (November 23, 1933): 1.

Jackson, Donald Dale. "They Were Poor, Hungry and They Built to Last." *Smithsonian* 25 (December 1990): 66–77.

"Jobs for Jobless in Penn's Woods." PDFW *Service Letter* (July 27, 1933): 1.

Johnson, Charles W. "The Army and the Civilian Conservation Corps, 1933–42." *Prologue* 4 (February 1, 1972): 139–56.

Kehl, James A., and Astorino, Samuel J. "A Bull Moose Response to the New Deal: Pennsylvania's Gifford Pinchot." *Pennsylvania Magazine of History and Biography* 88 (January 1964): 37–51.

Lanpher, H. C. "The Civilian Conservation Corps: Some Aspects of Its Social Programs for Unemployed Youth." *Social Service Review* 10 (December 1936): 623–36.

Leighton, George R., and Richard Hellman. "'Half Slave, Half Free': Unemployment, the Depression and American Young People." *Harper's Magazine* 171 (August 1935): 342–53.

McKinney, Guy D. "An Army in the Forests." *Natural History* 24 (February 1934): 141–50.

Mitchell, Jonathan. "Roosevelt's Tree Army, I and II." *New Republic* 83 (May 29, 1935, and June 12, 1935): 64–66 and 127–29.

"A Month's Work for Two Million Men." *American Forests* 39 (February 1933): 76.

Pope, James Gray. "The Western Pennsylvania Coal Strike of 1933, Part One: Lawmaking from Below and the Revival of the United Mine Workers." *Labor History* 44 (February 2003): 15–48.

———. "The Western Pennsylvania Coal Strike of 1933, Part Two: Lawmaking from Above and the Demise of Democracy in the United Mine Workers." *Labor History* 44 (May 2003): 235–64.

"Porcupine Damage in Northern Pennsylvania Forests." PDFW *Service Letter* (October 20, 1932): 1.

Porter, John A. "The Enchanted Forest." *Quartermaster Review* (March–April 1934): 1–10, www.qmmuseum.lee.army.mil/ccc_forest.htm.

"Relief Needs and Conditions in Pennsylvania, August, 1931: Report of Governor's Planning Committee on Unemployment Relief." *Social Service Review* 54 (December 1931): 596–628.

Richardson, Elmo R. "Was There Politics in the Civilian Conservation Corps?" *Forest History* 16 (July 1972): 13–21.

"Robert Y. Stuart, Forester." *American Forests* 39 (December 1933): 535.

"The Role of the Department of F & W in the CWA." PDFW *Service Letter* (March 8, 1934): 1.

Rowland, Howard. "Can the CCC Blaze a New Trail?" *Survey Graphic* 26 (June 1937): 321–35.

Salmond, John A. "The Civilian Conservation Corps and the Negro." *Journal of American History* 52 (June 1965): 75–88.

Schultz, Michael. "'Puny' Fire at Pepper Hill Claimed Lives of Seven CCCers." NACCCA *Journal* (June 2001): 1, 6–8.

"Sedition in the CCC." *New Republic* 85 (February 12. 1936): 6–7.

Sherraden, Michael W. "Administrative Lessons from the Civilian Conservation Corps (1933–42)," *Administration in Social Work* 9 (summer 1985): 85–97.

Silcox, Ferdinand. "Our Adventure in Conservation." *Atlantic* 160 (December 1937): 714–24.

Staley, Lewis. "Jobs for the Jobless in Penn's Woods." PDFW *Service Letter* (July 27, 1933): 1.

Stuart, R. Y. "That 250,000 Man Job." *American Forests* 39 (May 1933): 195–97.

Swing, Raymond Gram. "Take the Army Out of the CCC." *The Nation* 141 (October 23, 1935): 459–60.

"Unemployment: First Army of Idle Now in Camp." *Newsweek* 1 (April 15, 1933): 6.

Wandall, Luther C. "A Negro in the CCC." *Crisis* 42 (August 1935): 244–53.

Wirt, George H. "Joseph Trimble Rothrock: Father of Forestry in Pennsylvania." *American-German Review* 8 (February 1942): 5–8.

"With the Civilian Conservation Corps." *American Forests* 39 (July 1933): 302, 334.

NEWSPAPERS

Evening Bulletin (Philadelphia)
Happy Days
Harrisburg Telegraph
National Association of CCC *Alumni Journal*
New York Times
Philadelphia Inquirer
Philadelphia Tribune
Pittsburgh Post-Gazette
Pittsburgh Press
Public Ledger (Philadelphia)

Index